THE
Little Italy Cookbook

THE
Little Italy Cookbook

MARIA PACE
AND
LOUISE SCAINI-JOJIC

Warwick Publishing
Toronto Los Angeles

ISBN 1-895629-72-1

Published by:
Warwick Publishing Inc., 24 Mercer Street, Toronto, Ontario M5V 1H3
Warwick Publishing Inc., 1424 N. Highland Avenue, Los Angeles, CA 90027

Distributed by:
Firefly Books Ltd., 3680 Victoria Park Avenue, Willowdale, Ontario M2H 3K1

Design: Kimberley Davison and Diane Farenick
Editorial Services: Edward Ditore
Indexing and Proofreading: Melinda Tate
Photographs: Vincenzo Pietropaolo; Multicultural History Society of Ontario

Printed and bound in Canada

Second Printing, 1996

For my mother, Anna Grazia Pace (Guadagnoli)
who gave me free rein in the kitchen and
afforded so many opportunities to cook.
M.P.

and

To Micol
L.S-J.

Acknowledgements

There are many people who deserve thanks for their contributions to this book, in particular, all the people who took time out to speak to Louise and me and who contributed recipes. Their names are acknowledged in the titles of each recipe. Special thanks are due to others who helped in less visible ways and to those who volunteered extra time and energy to the project. Thanks goes to those who helped with testing recipes: to Paula Bambrick, Lynne Delfs, Elizabeth Giacometti, Milos Jojic and Jelica Panich. Many people were extremely generous with their time and information, helping us to connect with a larger community and giving history and background to the recipes: the Borgo Family, at Quality Cheese Ltd., Toronto; Joe Melara at King and Raphael Toronto Ltd.; the staff at the Jane Fruit Market; Domenic and Martha Muzzi at Watsonville Produce, CA; Tommaso Mauti at Prosciutto Jolly, Woodbridge; Sergio Santarossa; Paola Bagnatori at the Museo ItaloAmericano, San Francisco; and Leo Ayers at Jack Auer Produce, Virginia.

Many friends and family members lent their support, both moral and technical: Joanne and Randy Kerr provided their computer wizardry; Anne Roper and Doris Eisen gave editorial feedback; Madeleine Thompson offered insights and encouragement about writing as well as access to a fax machine; Vanni Pavero assisted with translation. Special thanks goes to Steve Jukic for generously sharing reference materials and technical information. He also provided many useful contacts.

I am forever indebted to Lorraine and Oliver Pace, my friends and mentors over many years, in particular for their long-standing support for my food ventures. Their passion and enthusiasm about food and wine has had a profound influence and been a constant source of inspiration. This book would not have happened without the vision and gentle persistance of Jim Williamson at Warwick Publishing. Louise and I are also extremely grateful to Nick Pitt at Warwick for his patience, tolerance and his competence in dealing with an unwieldy manuscript. To any others who have helped and supported but whose names are not mentioned, we would like to extend our heartfelt appreciation.

CONTENTS

INTRODUCTION

an Italian ... in the service of the late Cardinal Caraffe as maitre d'hotel... gave me a lecture on the science of eating with a magisterial seriousness and countenance, as if he were speaking of some great point of Theology. He listed the different appetites ... the organization of sauces, first in general, then particularizing the quality of the ingredients and their effects; the different salads, according to their season, those which should be reheated and those which should be eaten cold, the way to decorate and embellish them to make them more pleasing to view. .. and all this puffed up with rich, magnificent words, like the ones used in dealing with the government of an Empire.

From Montaigne's Essays "On the Vanity of Words."

For years I have been talking to Italians on both sides of the Atlantic about food, collecting ideas for menus, drawing out hints about methods and ingredients, sometimes getting written recipes. Next to eating it, talking about food is one of my favorite pastimes and it seems to be a national trait among Italians and those of Italian descent. Evidence of this characteristic is documented as far back as the early Renaissance as the quotation from Montaigne's essay demonstrates.

from Italian communities in North America - favorite family recipes, but not just the traditional ones handed down from one generation to the other. It was also to include what and how people of Italian descent are eating now.

The occasion to talk to more people about food and to discover what Italians were really eating at home was irresistible. Added to that was the opportunity to organize what I had already collected over the years. Once the collecting got underway, the enthusiastic responses of the individuals and the great pride they felt in being invited to share their cooking secrets convinced me even more that the idea was worthwhile.

When the idea of writing an Italian cookbook was presented, my first thought was, what could possibly be written that hadn't already been done elsewhere - and extremely well, I might add - by writers and cooks like Marcella Hazan, Giuliano Bugialli, Lorenza di Medici, Umberto Menghi, Biba Caggiano and Nick Malgieri to name a few. Their works provide detailed information about how to prepare just about any kind of Italian food. Could there be anything new to add? But the focus of this book, according to the vision of the publisher, Jim Williamson, was to be recipes collected

This collection of recipes does not claim to present the definitive way to prepare Italian food. It is, instead, a testament to the adaptability of Italian cooking and the resourcefulness of individuals who were faced with adjusting to new circumstances. The importance of good ingredients balanced against the need for practicality is a theme that recurred during the conversations with the many contributors. It was exhilarating to discover how the passion for good food has been kept alive by several generations of Italians living in North America.

The term "Little Italy" needs some definition in order to clarify the broad parameters of this collection of recipes. To do this, it is necessary to delve briefly into the history of Italian immigration to North America.

"LITTLE ITALY" - WHY AND WHERE?

When it's a bad year, there is no money and no wine...so we eat polenta and drink water. We don't die because that is sufficient to keep alive. The shops in the town give us credit. This is how we run into debt, and are forced to go to America...

Robert Harney,
The Italian Experience in the United States

There were two huge waves of emigration out of Italy; one in the period just before and after World War I, and another in the 1950's and 60's. Between 1901 and 1910 over 2 million Italians arrived in the U.S. while less than 60,000 came to Canada. But in the 1950's and 60's, Canada's active recruitment of "bulk labor" offered many Italians a door to North America and economic advancement. They came in droves, sometimes as whole villages and effectively "built the infrastructure of an expanding economy." By 1961, there were 450,000 people of Italian descent in southern Ontario.

Before the era of mass migration, Italians who came to North America - chiefly the United States - were merchants, political exiles, musicians, painters, and fruit vendors. One famous migrant worker was Giuseppe Garibaldi (the Italian revolutionary leader) who worked as a candle maker on Bleecker Street. It was mainly Italian men who came as migrant workers on temporary sojourns. They moved wherever there was heavy, manual work often returning to Italy when the work ended. Those who stayed formed small "colonie" or settlements.

Once whole families started to come over during the period between 1900 and 1910, the pattern shifted from migration to immigration and permanent settlement. As cities developed and grew, they provided greater opportunities for work building trolley lines, subway systems and sewers. With the greater numbers, Italian communities with a stronger neighborhood "ambiente" developed.

The largest and oldest community of Italians was in New York City on the Lower East Side. The population reached its peak in 1910 - there were 544,449 persons of Italian birth or parentage in New York City. Little Italy was a rather pejorative term. The area around Mulberry Street and Five Points was the biggest receiving area and both were slums. Five Points used to be a garbage dump and was an area of vice and crime previously inhabited by German and Irish immigrants. People came as part of a group and settled in blocks forming societies and clubs that were regionally based. This eventually broke down, and the "campanalismo" or regional rivalry gave way to "umbrella"

organizations like the United Italian Societies. Life on the streets was lively with festas and processions happening regularly. Despite the unfavorable conditions, the district provided a familiar ambiance where those newly arrived could bridge the gap between the old-world culture and the new. As the city developed, new opportunities for settlement elsewhere appeared. By the 1930's, there was only half the number of Italians as there was in 1910.

The pattern of settlement in Toronto was similar. Once work shifted from temporary labor in mines and on the railroad to stable work in cities, women and families were brought over and small communities developed. Usually these areas grew where the jobs were - around ports, railway stations, construction sites and factories. The later immigrants in the 1950's and 60's naturally went to large cities where there were already established kinship ties. Sometimes whole villages moved en masse. First came people from the Friuli-Veneto region, then from regions in the south: Molise, Calabria, Abruzzo, Sicily, Campania, Apulia, Lazio. Some from Umbria. Most were "contadini" or farm workers and came as unskilled or semi-skilled laborers. They started off

in the old Italian neighborhoods where there were already "paesani" from the early wave of immigration. As they attained a greater degree of economic comfort and security, they moved up the economic ladder and went off to new developments and sub-divisions. Again, they moved en masse. The old designation, "Little Italy," cannot be applied to these new, comfortable neighborhoods where the homes are spacious, have double garages, finished basements with a cantina and enough land for a vegetable garden.

...with more than 400,000 residents claiming an Italian heritage, Toronto today ranks behind only New York City, Sao Paolo and Buenos Aires as the city with the largest Italian population outside of Italy. Moreover... the 160,000 Italian-born immigrants in Toronto match their counterparts in number in those other cities.

from Such Hardworking People: Italian immigrants in Post war Toronto. *Franca Iacovetta. McGill-Queens University Press. 1992*

To reach the broader Italian community in the 1990's, it is necessary to go outside the boundaries of the old districts that acted as the receiving areas. There may still be a notable Italian presence, and even a revival of the Italian "ambiente" in the old Little Italy of the 1950's and 60's (as is the case in Toronto's Little Italy around Grace, Clinton and College Streets). But now, the areas with the greatest concentration of Italians are districts outside the downtown core, like Downsview and Woodbridge in Toronto, or St. Leonard in Montreal.

As economic conditions improved in Italy, immigration declined. Those who left for North America after the 1970's tended to be of a different class. Merchants, tradesmen and professionals hoping to set up businesses or advance their careers brought with them a different brand of Italian culture not rooted in rural, peasant traditions. In addition to these "modern" Italians, the steady traffic back and forth to Italy of the now prosperous and thriving 1st, 2nd and 3rd generation Italians forged new links. Exposure to new products and to contemporary and regional cooking has made an impact on how Italians living in North America eat. The recipes in this collection reflect these various influences on the Italian table.

COLLECTING THE RECIPES

After the initial outreach into the Italian communities, it became apparent that the work of collecting recipes from as broad an arena as possible would require assistance. Louise Scaini-Jojic was invited to help with this as well as with the testing and revision of recipes. This enabled us to contact a wider range of people. Those who contributed recipes are from many parts of Italy and represent several generations of immigrants from the different stages of immigration. The primary sources were family, friends and acquaintances - especially anyone who had acquired a reputation for a particular dish. Recipes also came from people who work in the food business - merchants, importers, manufacturers, growers, cooks, caterers. We deliberately excluded recipes from chefs in Italian restaurants as that would have taken us out of the realm of home cooking and required a second volume. In some cases the recipes were given to us in written form, but for the most part, they were collected through interviews. Notes were taken and tapes transcribed, then the recipes were tested and, occasionally, developed.

Both Louise and I observed some interesting details during the process of collecting that revealed a fundamental characteristic about the way Italians approach cooking. Very frequently, a first response from a prospective contributor was, "Yes, but I don't measure anything. Do you want a sweets recipe?" It seems that when it comes to written recipes, they are virtually non-existent except in the case of sweets where ingredients need to be weighed. The reluctance to be pinned down to exact measures and procedures comes from the fact that cooking depends on the ingredients. For example, if the tomatoes you are using in a sauce make it too dense, you simply add water. There is no need to specify the amount and in many instances, people neglect to mention it at all when explaining a recipe. This is not a deliberate oversight, but it makes an assumption about using common sense in cooking.

This does not apply for baked goods. Many people prefer to write down the quantities and weigh them, but even here there is plenty of latitude. Often when, people use words like a cup and a glass they mean the tea cup with the broken handle which only measures 6 ounces or the small, chipped wine glass which is only four. Or they might say one big spoon meaning a heaping soup spoon or a big handful meaning their hand, of course. Another favorite expression - which also appears frequently in Italian recipe books - is "quanto basta." It means as much as needed. This is difficult to determine if you have never seen the process or tasted the end result. "A piacere" simply means to taste, so a subjective response and lots of sampling are called for.

Yet another general response to the invitation to submit a recipe was, "I'll have to show you because it's not possible to explain it. You have to watch" - as was the case for the Cjalcons recipe on page (p. 60) and the recipes for Torrone and Gubana. In these instances, the processes are rather intricate and words do not describe as efficiently as direct experience. Among Italians, sharing a recipe often means going to someone's house and making the new dish along with the person. This was the case when Lorraine had to go and watch her friend Nancy make the almond candy (Croccante p. 239) before she got the hang of it. For novices, making the recipe with someone who has done it before is highly recommended - especially for certain types of recipes

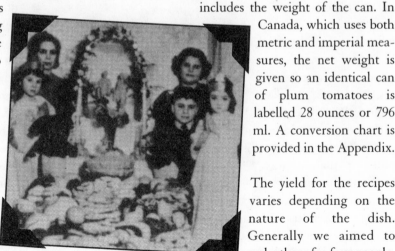

in the book, particularly the ones involving complex or unusual procedures that are described in anecdotal form.

NOTES ABOUT THE RECIPES

Strict adherence to the proportions indicated are not absolutely required, especially for many of the savory dishes. A small amount more or less of a particular spice, herb or liquid will not change a dish dramatically. Another thing to note is that salt, oil and water may be listed only once in a recipe, but often these are added several times during the cooking. When it comes to making doughs, it is generally a good idea to hold back some flour and add it gradually at the end. Oil is used in larger quantities than many North Americans are accustomed to. If you are inclined to cut back on this fat, remember that there will be some loss in flavor and the dish may not taste "Italian."

The weights are given in U.S. imperial measure with a few minor exceptions. It is important to note that there are differences between the weight of cans in the U.S. and in Canada. A 32 ounce can of plum tomatoes in the U.S. includes the weight of the can. In Canada, which uses both metric and imperial measures, the net weight is given so an identical can of plum tomatoes is labelled 28 ounces or 796 ml. A conversion chart is provided in the Appendix.

The yield for the recipes varies depending on the nature of the dish. Generally we aimed to make them for four people. In some cases, a larger serving size is more appropriate, such as when preparing dishes for a buffet. How much a person will eat is also relative - depending on what else is being eaten and whether it's as a main course or appetizer. In principle, a one-pound package of pasta can yield five to six servings, but it might only feed two with a little left over if they happen to be big eaters and it's the only course. Sometimes recipes are given for larger numbers as it is more practical to do this and have leftovers or freeze the rest. In each instance, it is necessary for the reader to make the decision about whether to make the full recipe, or cut it down.

ABOUT COOKING AND INGREDIENTS

All the recipes were tested on regular electric ranges and ovens. There can be as much as a 25 or 50 degree difference between what the temperature on an oven thermometer registers and what the dial on your range indicates. For best results when baking, use an oven thermometer. Leave plenty of space for the heat to circulate, and rotate the pan if there are hot spots at the back or sides of the oven. Once you are familiar with how your oven works, it's best to follow your instincts and use the temperatures and cooking times in the recipes as a general guide. Following are some notes on ingredients and Italian expressions:

EGGS: unless otherwise stated, all eggs called for in the recipes are large size.

OIL: many Italians use several oils, not just olive oil. Where the contributor insisted, we specified the type - for example, olive oil, extra virgin olive oil, and corn oil. If no particular type is specified, use whatever vegetable oil you like. Sunflower and canola oil are the most commonly used for light cooking, frying and combining with olive oil.

FLOUR: Unless otherwise stated, the flour used is all-purpose, bleached. Although there are significant differences in the all purpose flour used in Canada, the United States and Italy, for the recipes in the book, the differences are not appreciable enough to cause concern. All the recipes were tested with all-purpose Canadian flour which is from hard wheat. The higher gluten content from hard wheat tends to make dough with more elasticity. American flour labeled all-purpose is generally from a blend of hard and soft wheat and is especially good for cakes, and pastries. For the bread, pizza and pasta all'uovo recipes, unbleached, all-purpose flour is recommended.

FOREIGN WORDS: Italian words (including some dialect words) are used throughout the book and are sometimes translated in the text. A list of all the foreign words is explained in the Glossary at the end.

IMPORTED INGREDIENTS: Certain imported ingredients may not be readily available if you do not live in a large urban center or one with a significant Italian population. Refer to the Glossary for a possible substitute.

Antipasti/Starters

The Antipasto Table

A huge table laden with local specialties: olives, artichoke frittata, roasted peppers, caponata, seafood salad, marinated mushrooms, cold cuts and cheeses greeted us as we ventured down the steps to the terrace overlooking the beach next to the ruins at Selinunte, Sicily. It was March and very warm but the terrace was still closed in with glass to keep the cool sea breezes at bay. Only one other table was occupied. It appeared to be our waiter and the owner of the establishment with two serious looking men in suits. We wondered what would happen to all that wonderful food on the antipasto table and hoped the rest of the extended family would appear as there seemed to be no other visitors to this ancient site at this time of year.

A lavishly arranged buffet table with a variety of savory dishes is a common feature of many Italian restaurants. At home, antipasto tends to be simpler. For a special small dinner, it may consist of only one dish like a caprese salad or prosciutto with melon. For larger parties and special holidays when lots of guests are invited, an antipasto buffet with several selections is convenient. Because most antipasto dishes are served at room temperature or cold, it can all be made ahead and laid out well before the guests arrive. The antipasto keeps everyone busy eating while the pasta and other courses are being prepared.

The simplest, most traditional antipasto is a plate of salume (cold cuts) with a few olives, some celery or fennel and crusty bread. Can a person eat any more after that, you might ask. Sometimes not. At his very first Italian wedding banquet, my British brother-in-law made the mistake of politely finishing everything on the plate put before him. He was full after the antipasto course but valiantly carried on until the end suffering through the torment of a bloated gut with a stiff upper lip. He did not realize that at banquets of this kind, most of the courses were there to make a good impression but not necessarily to be eaten.

Antipasto selections can include cooked, marinated vegetables, meats and fish; fried foods, salads, grilled breads and pizza are common. They can be very simple, like wrapping prosciutto around lightly steamed asparagus spears, or labor intensive like the seafood salad.

MUSEO ITALOAMERICANO - SAN FRANCISCO
The choices for antipasto are wide ranging. To get an idea of some of the possibilities, Annette De Nunzio, caterer at The Museo ItaloAmericano in San Francisco sent us a copy of the menu presented at the Antipasto Buffet on May 4, 1996. It is their annual fund-raising event for the CIAO - the Children's Italian Art Outreach program.

The Museo ItaloAmericano is a non-profit organization based in San Francisco. Its mission is "to research, collect, and display works of Italian and Italian-American artists and to promote educational programs for the appreciation of Italian art and culture, thereby preserving the heritage of Italian-Americans for future generations. It offers classes in Italian, lectures on Italian art and culture, workshops for teachers and conferences on subjects like Italian-American women.

A permanent collection of paintings, sculptures, photographs and works on paper is housed in a National Landmark Building in Fort Mason Center which has been the home of the Museo since 1985.

MENU

Arancini (Sicilia) - Rice balls
Baccala mantecato (Trentino) - Creamed salt cod
Caponata (Sicilia) -Eggplant stewed with olives and tomato
Cipolle ripiene (Emilia romagna) - Stuffed onions
Cozze in salsa verde (Puglia) - [Mussels in green sauce]
Crostini con fegatini (Emilia Romagna) - Toasts with chicken livers
Crostini di polenta con funghi (Veneto) - Polenta toasts with mushrooms
Frittatine (Liguria) - Little omelettes
Insalata di arance, finocchio e acciughe (Sicilia) - Orange, fennel and anchovy salad
Insalata di asparagi (Friuli) - Asparagus salad
Insalata di calamari (Veneto) - Squid salad
Insalata russa (Toscana) - Russian salad
Involtini di melanzane (Sicilia) - Eggplant rolls
Mandorlata di peperoni (Basilicata) - Peppers with almonds
Mozzarella con pomodori secchi (Lombardia) - Mozzarella with sundried tomatoes
Peperoncini piccanti al tonno (Calabria) - Hot peppers with tuna
Peperoni ripieni (Campania) - Stuffed peppers
Prosciutto e grissini - Prosciutto with breadsticks
Rotolo di pollo ripieno (Abruzzi) - Stuffed chicken rolls
Rotolo di vitello (Toscana) - Veal roll
Verdure marinate (Piemonte) - Marinated Greens
Zucchini ripiene (Liguria) - Stuffed Zucchini
Biscotti - Cookies
Ciao Bella Gelato - Ice cream
Cucidati - Sicilian fig cookies
Salame al cioccolato - Chocolate salami

Bruschetta (Basic Recipe)

TOASTED GARLIC BREAD

½ loaf round, crusty Italian bread (4 long slices)

2 cloves fresh garlic, unpeeled and cut in half

⅓ cup good quality olive oil

Salt and freshly milled black pepper to taste

O ne November in Italy, I watched my cousin Anita Spadaforo deftly move a few hot coals under a metal frame in the big fireplace in her kitchen. In moments, the thick slices of crusty bread became golden brown. They were quickly coated with a few spoons of oil mixed with garlic and anchovies, sprinkled with some black pepper and brought directly to the table. We had the bruschetta while it was at its best, still hot, crunchy outside and soft inside. Anita said she likes to vary the basic bruschetta occasionally with the addition of anchovy or pureed olives. She rarely puts tomato on it as the bread might get soggy. In North America, this plain version of bruschetta is rarely found in restaurants, perhaps because they want to impress clients with something more. Tomato goes on, even cheese, onions and olives! Whatever your preference for topping, be sure to make bruschetta at the last moment so the bread does not become soggy. A handy trick is to mix the oil, garlic and salt and allow this to sit before brushing it on the freshly grilled bread.

Cut bread into four long, ¾-inch thick slices. Place over hot coals, (or on a barbecue or under a hot broiler) and toast both sides till lightly colored. This takes only moments.

While still hot, rub one side of each slice with the cut side of garlic, brush generously with olive oil and season with salt and pepper. Cut into half and serve immediately.

Makes 8 pieces

VARIATION

For a stronger garlic flavor, do not rub garlic on toasted bread, instead add 2 cloves finely minced raw garlic to the tomato mixture.

Bruschetta con Pomodoro e Basilico

GRILLED GARLIC BREAD WITH FRESH TOMATO AND BASIL

Peeling tomatoes is optional if the skins are tender. Remove stems and seeds from tomatoes and chop into small dice. Marinate the tomatoes briefly in 2 - 3 tablespoons of the oil, the basil and a little salt.

Grill bread as for basic bruschetta recipe. After bread has been brushed with oil, spoon some of the tomato/herb mixture over each slice. Season with more salt and freshly milled pepper. Cut each slice into half. Serve immediately before the bread gets soggy.

Makes 8 pieces

5 to 6 very ripe large tomatoes

5 to 6 fresh basil leaves, torn into little bits

½ cup good quality olive oil

½ loaf round, crusty Italian bread (4 long slices)

2 cloves fresh garlic, unpeeled, cut in half

salt and freshly milled pepper to taste

Insalata di Mare

MARINATED SEAFOOD SALAD

Whenever Louise Scaini prepares an assorted antipasto, this standard fish salad is included. It can be served in a bowl or on a platter over a bed of lettuce. It's refreshing because it's served cold but is also quite a rich salad. The key to producing the maximum flavor, according to Louise, is to saute the fish and shellfish separately, seasoning each batch as it is cooked.

Shell, de-vein and wash the shrimp. If the monkfish is not already filleted, remove the skin, and bone the tough membrane around the flesh. Cut into one-inch cubes. Wash the scallops. Slice the "crab" sticks into one-inch pieces. Drain and rinse the clams. Combine the olive oil and corn oil. In a medium-sized skillet, heat 1 or 2 tablespoons of the mixed oil with some of the garlic, a little wine, parsley, salt and pepper. Before the garlic colors, add the shrimp and cook for two minutes, shaking the pan. When the shrimp turns pink, remove them with a slotted spoon and place in a bowl large enough to hold all the fish. Keep the

1 pound medium shrimp

1 pound monkfish

1 pound bay scallops

8 sea-legs (imitation crab meat)*

1 cup canned baby clams, drained

⅓ cup corn oil

⅓ cup olive oil

2 cloves garlic, minced

⅓ cup white wine

⅓ cup parsley, finely chopped

Salt and pepper to taste

1 cup fresh mushrooms, cleaned and trimmed

1 ½ cups pickled vegetables (giardiniera), finely chopped

3 tablespoons small capers

2 celery stalks, finely diced

1 lemon, juiced

2 to 3 tablespoons white vinegar

Salt and pepper to taste

Lemon wedges and fresh parsley sprigs for garnish

*Imitation crab meat, sometimes known as sea-legs, is generally made of reconstituted, seasoned pollock and is sold fresh or frozen. It comes in chunks or in uniform logs that can used for making Sushi. If fresh crab meat is easily available and affordable it is preferable to use instead of the sea-legs.

seasoned cooking liquid in the skillet. Repeat the same procedure for each fish, adding a little more oil and seasonings each time, if needed. The monkfish will take 5 to 7 minutes; the scallops 2 to 3 minutes. The crabmeat and clams only need one minute to absorb the seasonings in the pan. Let all the fish and seafood cool.

Cook the whole mushrooms in a small pot of boiling water for about 5 minutes. Drain, cool and slice finely. Combine mushrooms with the pickled vegetables, capers, celery, and add to the cooled fish. Dress with the lemon juice, vinegar and any remaining garlic, parsley and oil. Mix well.

Refrigerate for a few hours to allow the flavors to soak in. Taste before serving. Add a little more oil and lemon if needed. When ready to serve, place on a platter and garnish with lemon wedges and sprigs of fresh parsley.

Makes 10 to 12 servings

Insalata Caprese

TOMATO AND BOCCONCINI SALAD

6 firm, ripe tomatoes

½ pound mozzarella di buffala (5 to 6 balls approximately)

6 tablespoons extra virgin olive oil

Salt and pepper to taste

1 clove garlic, slivered

5 fresh basil leaves, torn into small bits

Some years ago, I asked my brother, Oliver, to find out as much as he could about the plum tomatoes known as San Marzano, seeing as he was going to be in Campania, a major tomato-growing area of Italy. He and his travelling buddy, Mickey, were sitting on one of the most beautiful terraces in Ravello, a charming town overlooking the Amalfi coast. Having climbed the steep steps up to the Albergo Villa D'Amore in the sweltering heat of August, they were amply rewarded with the simple yet delicious lunch. A salad of perfect tomatoes with soft, fresh mozzarella marinated in olive oil and herbs was the first course. Oliver took this opportunity to make enquiries. "Excuse me, Signora," he asked of the owner/cook who also brought the food to the table. "This salad is wonderful. The tomatoes are so good. Are they San Marzano tomatoes?" he questioned, hoping to draw out more information. "Nossignore," she emphatically replied, "sono Ravellese" (they are from Ravello). She must have thought they were strange to think she would go to San Marzano, a town many kilometers away to buy tomatoes when the local ones were the best.

Whether they are beefsteak type, plum, or golden varieties, for a caprese salad, it is important to use tomatoes only when they are in season, freshly picked, ripe and juicy yet firm. The imported mozzarella di buffala can be replaced with regular bocconcini cheese but do not try to make this with ordinary mozzarella.

Wash tomatoes and cut into ¼-inch horizontal slices, discarding the stem slice. Cut bocconcini into ¼-inch slices. Arrange alternating slices of tomato and cheese on a serving plate. (You'll need approximately 4 slices of each per person). Dress with extra virgin olive oil, salt, pepper, garlic and fresh basil. Allow to stand at room temperature for at least 30 minutes before serving. Serve as an antipasto or starter to a summer meal accompanied by crusty bread to mop up the juicy sauce.

Makes 4 servings

TIP

Marinate the bocconcini separately for 1 hour in some of the oil, salt, pepper and garlic before assembling with the tomatoes. Pour the marinade over everything and finish by adding the remaining dressing ingredients.

Insalata di Riso

RICE SALAD

The use of wurstel (like our wieners) points to the Austrian influence in some of the traditional dishes of northern Italy. In North America, wieners were found to be the closest substitute for wurstel. It is absolutely essential to have them in, according to Mrs. Dametto. If wurstel is not available and regular wieners do not appeal to you, use extra-cooked ham. Prepare the salad the night before so the flavors have a chance to mellow and soak into the rice. The rice should be tender but firm, not mushy. If you prefer olive oil, make sure it is light, extra virgin oil, or use half olive and half corn oil. Rice salad is a great summer dish for barbecue parties and picnics.

3 cups Arborio rice

3 lemons

½ cup corn oil (or half olive, half corn oil)

2 tablespoons capers

½ cup black olives, pitted and slivered

⅓ cup green olives, pitted and slivered

1 cup boiled mushrooms, thinly sliced

½ pound cooked ham in 1 thick slice, cubed

3 wurstel sausages (or wieners), cubed

Salt and pepper to taste

Lemon wedges for garnish

Sprigs of parsley

Cook the rice in 3 to 4 quarts boiling, salted water for about 13 to 15 minutes. Briefly rinse under cold water and drain well. While the rice is still warm, dress it with some oil and the juice of one lemon. Set aside for 10 minutes.

Add capers and olives and mix well. Stir in the mushrooms, cooked ham and wurstel. Season with salt and pepper, a little more oil and the juice of another lemon. Mix well. Refrigerate for a few hours or overnight. Before serving add the rest of the oil and the juice of one lemon. Check seasoning, adding more salt and pepper if needed. Serve garnished with lemon wedges and sprigs of parsley.

Makes 12 servings

Insalata Russa

RUSSIAN SALAD

¾ pound whole chicken breast

1 cup carrots

1 cup potatoes, boiled and finely diced

2 egg yolks

Salt and pepper to taste

1 to 2 tablespoons lemon juice or white wine vinegar

Dry or Dijon mustard to taste

1 ½ cup oil

1 cup canned tiny peas

¾ pound prosciutto cotto or cooked ham, finely chopped

2 cups baby dill pickles, finely diced

3 eggs, hard boiled, finely chopped

The first time Louise returned to Italy as an adult, she was astounded by the amount of mayonnaise that appeared in some salads. Zia Anute was the housekeeper/cook for an industrialist in Torino, and she had to learn to make sauces with mayonnaise and dishes set in gelatin on big platters.

Mayonnaise is not part of the repertoire of southern Italy. Those who have been exposed to North American culture long enough have no trouble using it. Some refuse to set a fork near anything with a gloppy white sauce. This salad has lots of mayonnaise so prepare it only for those who love it.

Boil the chicken breast and the carrots in salted water for about 45 minutes. Remove the chicken and carrots from the pan and allow to cool. Skin and bone the chicken breast. Dice the chicken and carrots.

Beat together yolks, salt and pepper, 1 tablespoon lemon juice and mustard. Add oil by drops, beating constantly. As mixture thickens, oil can be added more quickly. When all the oil has been added, taste the mayonnaise and adjust seasoning adding more salt and pepper and lemon juice.

1 ½ cups oil

Parsley sprigs and radish rosettes for decoration

In a large bowl, combine the diced chicken, carrots, potatoes, peas, prosciutto cotto, pickles and the eggs. Mix with a wooden spoon. Stir in the oil, mayonnaise and mix well. Place in a serving bowl. Decorate with sprigs of parsley and radish rosettes.

Serves 10

Panzanella

BREAD AND TOMATO SALAD

No one spoke about panzanella with as much relish as Luciano Guadagnoli. In the little mountain village where Luciano grew up and returned each summer during his retirement, card playing in the piazza was a serious, all day pastime. One day I offered to make him a lunch of pasta and meat but he declined. "I'll just fix a little panzanella salad for me and Ma. It's so good for my stomach and it's easy for Ma to chew," he said smacking his lips in anticipation. His mother, Maria Agostina, was 91 at the time and refused to wear false teeth, yet ate everything with a good appetite. Luciano left soon after, very contentedly, to meet his buddies in good time for another session of "scopa," cigars and espresso in the piazza.

Soak the stale bread in some cold water until it softens. Squeeze out excess water and place the slices on a platter. Season with a little olive oil and salt. Wash the tomatoes and basil leaves. Slice the tomatoes and lay them over the bread. Scatter the basil leaves and onions over top. Season again with salt and pepper, olive oil and a splash of vinegar. Allow to sit a few minutes for the oil and tomato juice to seep into the bread.

Makes 4 servings

4 thick slices country style bread, several days old

5 ripe tomatoes

6 fresh basil leaves, torn into small pieces

4 tablespoons chopped red onion (optional)

Salt and pepper to taste

½ cup olive oil

Splash of wine vinegar (optional)

NOTE

It is essential to use a dense, substantial bread that is several days old. The bread should be able to stand up to the soaking and become soft but not mushy. Usually the bread and tomatoes are broken up into pieces and tossed together in a bowl to form a more homogeneous mixture. It is a matter of preference whether you want the bread in whole slices or not.

Caponata

EGGPLANT APPETIZER

2 pounds large purple eggplant

Salt as needed

½ to ⅔ cup olive oil

2 cups celery, chopped

¼ cup onion, chopped

⅓ cup white wine vinegar

2 tablespoons sugar

3 cups Italian canned plum tomatoes, drained and chopped

1 small can (5 ½ ounces) tomato paste, or to taste (optional)

20 large green salad olives, sliced

2 tablespoons capers

Freshly ground pepper to taste

NOTE

Different brands of canned plum tomatoes vary in consistency. Some are very firm and watery and need to be thickened with some tomato paste. Others are softer and darker in color and are in a thick tomato juice. These may not need any tomato paste to achieve the desired denseness. The need for tomato paste will depend on personal preference and the type of canned tomatoes you use.

Regina Casciato loves to go to the Farmer's Market near the Ferry Building in San Francisco on Saturday morning to watch chefs do demonstrations and, of course, see what organic produce is available. Regina grew up in the predominantly Italian Bay Ridge neighborhood in Brooklyn and her husband's parents are from Calabria and Abruzzo so she is in her element preparing Italian dishes. Caponata can be made year round. It is usually served room temperature as part of an antipasto and eaten with crusty bread. Use the regular large purple eggplants.

Peel the eggplant and cut into 1½-inch cubes. Salt generously and place in a colander for 30 minutes for the excess water to drain.

Heat ¼ cup of the oil in a Dutch oven pot. Add the celery and cook for about 10 minutes. Add the onions and continue to cook until they are transparent.

In a separate skillet, heat some of the remaining oil. Dry the eggplant and saute at high heat for about 12 minutes or until soft and lightly colored. Cook in batches, adding more oil to the skillet. Combine the cooked eggplant with the celery/onion mixture in the Dutch oven. Add the vinegar, sugar, tomatoes and optional tomato paste. Season with salt and pepper to taste and simmer for about 15 minutes. Add the sliced olives and capers during the last 2 minutes of cooking. Taste and adjust seasoning. Allow to cool and refrigerate until ready to use. Serve cold, or room temperature along with some crusty bread as part of an antipasto.

Makes 6 to 7 cups

Carpaccio

MARINATED BEEF FILLET

"Tell me," I have often enquired of the first-generation Italians who came from small towns or had rural backgrounds, "do you ever eat raw, marinated beef slices?" The usual response is a wincing grimace, at times a definite "are you nuts" kind of expression. Carpaccio is definitely not part of the repertoire of "la cucina casalinga." Its origins are aristocratic and its popularity in elegant restaurants comes from the penchant for copying the tastes of the nobility. La Contessa Amaglia Mocenigo, the wife of the last Doge of Venice, had the eccentric habit of eating raw meat. It was served to her simply with fresh lemon juice. She eventually tired of this and started to have it with a sauce made with mayonnaise and Worcestershire. When Harry's Bar began serving carpaccio much later, it was accompanied by a sauce called Marie-Robert made with ketchup, mayonnaise and Worcestershire. Today, it is served with the simple, original dressing: extra virgin olive oil, salt, pepper and slivers of Parmigiano-Reggiano. The lemon comes wrapped in cheesecloth, on the side. A variation of carpaccio, for those who prefer to abstain from raw meat, can be made with the air dried, cured beef sausage called Bresaola.

Pound the beef slices carefully between two sheets of sturdy plastic wrap. Flatten with a rolling pin until uniform in thickness.

Carefully place the beef slices in the centre of a serving platter. Drizzle the olive oil over the beef, season with salt and pepper and let stand for 20 minutes. Just before serving, scatter shavings of Parmigiano over beef. Arrange arugola leaves around the platter.

Serve with slices of crusty bread and small pots of one or more of the following: Artichoke Puree (p. 256); Salsa Piccante (p. 257); or Dijon mustard.

Makes 4 servings

8 slices beef fillet, cut very thinly (8 ounces)

½ cup cold-pressed, extra virgin olive oil

Salt and freshly milled black pepper to taste

¼ cup Parmigiano cheese shavings

8 to 10 arugola leaves for garnish

Slices of crusty bread, cut ½ inch thick

TIP

If you are cutting the beef yourself, it helps to put it in the freezer until it is almost but not quite frozen before slicing thinly. Use only the choicest beef fillet that has had the fat trimmed away completely.

Peperoni Arrostiti

ROASTED PEPPERS

3 large red bell peppers

2 cloves fresh garlic, sliced

¼ teaspoon salt (or to taste)

4 tablespoons good quality olive oil

1 tablespoon fresh parsley, chopped

1 teaspoon chives, chopped (optional)

Every summer when bushels of brilliant red peppers appear on the sidewalks in front of grocery stores, this recipe is what most Italians have in mind.

Preheat broiler to 475 degrees. If using a gas barbecue, set it to medium and preheat. Wash and dry whole peppers. Place on a foil-lined baking sheet under the broiler. (If roasting on a barbecue, set peppers directly on grill). As the skin blackens, turn peppers until they have darkened all around. Place in a bowl, cover with a cloth to trap the steam and loosen the skin. When cool enough to handle, remove the stems and seeds and slide off all the skin. It should come off easily if the peppers have been roasted thoroughly.

Slice the peppers into strips. Place in a clean bowl and dress with garlic, salt, oil, and fresh herbs. Allow to stand at room temperature for at least 1 hour before serving. Serve with crusty bread or plain focaccia.

Makes 4 to 5 servings

How to Keep Roasted Peppers

To put up a batch of roasted peppers for the winter, all you need is a good outdoor barbecue, plastic freezer bags and many hands. Once the peppers are roasted and allowed to cool, they can be put into freezer bags whole with the skin and seeds. This takes less time initially but it means you'll have the job of skinning the peppers and removing the seeds after they have been thawed. The skins slide off easily but this method also takes a little more space. The other way to keep them is to cut the roasted peppers in half, remove the skin and seeds and place the large pieces in freezer bags (approximately 8 to a bag), removing as much air as you can from the bag before sealing it. You'll save some freezer space and it's very handy when you need a quick appetizer for company. One bushel makes about 16 small freezer bags.

Involtini di Peperoni

ROASTED STUFFED PEPPER ROLLS

These are a great summer antipasto and would be a good addition to a cold buffet. A wire basket is handy for blanching peppers in boiling vinegar-water. It is important to use large bell peppers that are at least 4 inches high so there is enough length to form a roll. Either red or yellow bell peppers will do as long as they are thick and meaty. Grilling the peppers in halves after removing the seeds, helps them to maintain the firmer texture which is necessary for filling and rolling up.

Cut the peppers in half lengthwise, remove the stem, seeds and the inside pulp. Wash thoroughly if they are sandy, otherwise, wipe them clean. Roast the pepper halves on a grill (skin side down), or under the broiler, until the skin turns brown completely. Place in a bowl and cover with a towel. When cool, peel off the skins. Bring to a boil water, vinegar and salt. Plunge the roasted, skinned peppers into the boiling liquid for 2 minutes. Drain and dry on paper towels.

Mix together the lemon juice, oil, some parsley and garlic for the marinade. Lay the peppers flat in a glass or ceramic dish. Pour on the marinade ingredients and season with pepper. Cover and refrigerate for about 1 hour.

Make the filling by combining the olives, anchovies and capers, and chop finely. Mix in the mustard and oil.

Remove the peppers from the marinade. Spread ½ teaspoon of the filling over the inside of each piece of pepper. Roll up and secure with a toothpick. Fill the other pieces and return the filled pepper rolls to the dish with the marinade. Dress with a little more oil and fresh parsley. Keep covered in the refrigerator until 30 minutes before serving. Remove the toothpicks. Serve as part of a cold, assorted antipasto plate.

Makes 8 rolls

4 large red or yellow bell peppers

3 cups water

1 cup white vinegar

1 teaspoon salt

Juice of 1 lemon

⅓ cup olive oil

2 tablespoons parsley, finely chopped

1 clove garlic, minced

Pepper to taste

⅓ cup green olives, pitted

6 fillets of anchovies

2 tablespoons capers

1 teaspoon Dijon mustard

2 tablespoons corn oil

DRESSING:

2 tablespoons olive oil

1 tablespoon finely chopped, fresh parsley

Funghi Ripieni

STUFFED MUSHROOM CAPS

45 large white mushrooms

1 cup Spanish onions, finely chopped

3 tablespoons oil

⅓ cup parsley, finely chopped

1 teaspoon capers, finely chopped

3 ounces cooked ham, finely chopped

½ cup grated Parmigiano

2 eggs

½ cup bread crumbs

Salt and pepper

These appetizers can be served hot or room temperature. In fact, they taste better the second day when reheated in a toaster oven. When removing the stems from the mushrooms, be extra careful to snap them off gently. Handpick the mushrooms so they are all the same size. Mrs. Iolanda Dametto does not use garlic in the filling and they taste wonderful anyway.

Wash mushrooms one by one, removing the stem gently. Drain caps on a paper towel. Chop the stems. Cook the onion in heated oil and add the stems. Simmer for about 10 minutes and allow to cool.

In a bowl, combine the parsley, capers, cooked ham, onion/mushroom mixture, Parmigiano, eggs and bread crumbs. Season with salt and pepper and mix well.

Fill each mushroom, pressing the filling well into the caps and mound the top slightly. Place the filled mushrooms on a greased cookie sheet and bake for about 20 to 25 minutes in a preheated 350 degree oven. Set under broiler for about 1 minute to brown the tops. Serve hot or room temperature.

Makes 32 caps

Bigne al Parmigiano

PARMESAN CHEESE PUFFS

1 cup water

½ teaspoon salt

½ cup unsalted butter (¼ pound)

When a very light first course is called for, a clear, strong broth with a simple garnish is a good solution. Dress up the broth with some spinach leaves and float a few of these puffs on top. Add cooked noodles or chunks of meat for a more substantial soup. The sensation of eating cheese-wrapped air is utterly delightful. As kids, we most often had them at big wedding banquets and an on special occasions like when Uncle Frank came to visit from Colorado. His youngest sister, Erminia Brucculeri, happened to find some in a store and bought several packages. They were such a novelty, floating in the soup. The kids fought over them and tried to make them sink in the soup until we were properly chastised. Commercial puffs were most often served at big parties but homemade ones are tastier and chemical free and quite easy to prepare. The recipe below makes quite a lot. Make the full batch and divide the paste in half. Put half the amount of cheese in one portion and make the other portion into larger shapes to make dessert cream puffs. Larger cheese puffs can also be stuffed with savory fillings and served as hors d'oeuvres.

1 cup all purpose flour, sifted

4 to 5 eggs

6 to 8 tablespoons grated Parmigiano cheese

Piping bag with a ¼ inch tip

Pre-heat the oven to 400 degrees. Line two baking sheets with parchment paper. In a heavy saucepan, heat water, salt and butter. As soon as it comes to a boil, remove from heat and add the flour all at once. Stir vigorously with a wooden spoon. Return to the heat and cook, stirring continuously for about 5 minutes or until the mixture comes away from the sides of the pan.

Allow to cool slightly. Off the heat, beat in 4 eggs, one at a time, beating vigorously after each egg is added. Set aside about 1 tablespoon of the last egg for glazing. Add only as much of the remaining egg as is needed to make a thick, shiny, paste-like dough that barely falls from a spoon. Stir in the grated Parmigiano.

Transfer the mixture to a piping bag fitted with a ¼ inch tip. Pipe small mounds about the size of a cherry onto the prepared baking sheet. Flatten the pointed tops with a moistened finger and smooth a small amount of the reserved beaten egg on the tops. Bake in a 400 degree for 10 minutes. Lower the temperature to 350 and bake another 5 minutes until golden. Remove from oven, allow to cool completely before storing. Keep in a dry place. If they get a little limp from humidity, reheat in a 350 degree oven for a few minutes to make them crisp. Serve them separately in a bowl as an accompaniment to a broth or float several of them in each soup bowl just before it goes to the table.

SHAPING TIPS

Do not overfill the pastry bag. Keep the bag perpendicular as you squeeze out the paste, then release the pressure and tip the bag straight up briskly. A pointed tip will form. This can be flattened by pressing it down with a wet finger.

Makes 2 full trays (about 120 small puffs).

Arancini di Riso

RICE CROQUETTES

1 ⅔ cups Arborio rice (or short-grain, Italian)

1 pound ricotta cheese

4 eggs

¼ cup grated Parmigiano

1 tablespoon finely chopped parsley (optional)

Salt to taste

½ cup of mozzarella cheese, grated (optional)

1 ½ cups breadcrumbs

3 cups corn oil, for frying

This recipe for rice balls, unlike the Sicilian version, has cheese mixed throughout the rice and also used as a filling. Elizabeth Giacometti prefers to cook a fresh batch of rice instead of using leftover risotto. The mixture is very sticky but this can be alleviated by chilling and by putting some breadcrumbs in your hands when shaping the balls. Arancini are generally served as a snack but can also be appetizers or starchy accompaniments to meat or fish.

Boil the rice in lightly salted water for about 12 to 15 minutes. Drain and allow to cool. Allow excess liquid to drain from the ricotta and if lumpy, pass through a sieve. Combine the ricotta with the rice. Add the egg, Parmigiano, parsley and season with salt.

Shape into golf ball-sized portions. Insert ½ teaspoon mozzarella into the center of each ball. Roll the filled rice balls in 3 beaten eggs and coat with breadcrumbs.

In a deep skillet or deep fryer, cook the Arancini in hot oil until they are golden brown all over. Remove with a slotted spoon and drain on paper towels. Serve warm or cold. They can be kept warm in the oven or made ahead and reheated.

Makes 36 croquettes

Tortellini Fritti

FRIED TORTELLINI

With a busy career in the travel industry, Tia doesn't have a lot of time to prepare things from scratch. She came up with this fast and easy appetizer on her own to serve when entertaining. Ravioli as well as tortellini can be used but only those filled with meat - the cheese filled ones don't work. Tia likes to dip them in Mexican style salsa but a tomato and meat sauce makes a good dipping medium as well. They can also be dipped in plain sour cream in which case a little chili pepper can be added to the crumb mixture.

Bring to a boil 2 quarts lightly salted water. Cook the tortellini for about 2 to 3 minutes. Drain well, rinse under cool water and allow to cool slightly. Combine the bread crumbs and cornflake crumbs, salt and pepper to taste. Dip the tortellini in the lightly beaten egg. Coat in the crumb mixture, pressing well to coat them completely.

Heat oil in a deep fryer (or put 1 inch of oil in a deep skillet). Fry the breaded tortellini, in batches, until golden brown and cooked through. Remove with a slotted spoon and drain on paper towels. Keep warm until the remaining tortellini are fried. Serve hot with the dipping sauce.

Makes 60 pieces

1 package (½ pound) meat filled tortellini (frozen or vacuum packed)

2 eggs, lightly beaten

¼ cup bread crumbs

¼ cup corn flakes, finely crushed

Salt and pepper to taste

½ teaspoon chili flakes (optional)

Oil for deep frying

2 cups dipping sauce

Soups

About Brodo (Broth)

Brodo forms the basis of many recipes - particularly soups and risotto - so it's a good idea to always have some on hand in the freezer. There are two ways of obtaining a good brodo. One is the cold water method which is very much like a classic recipe for stock (see Brodo di Carne p. 22). The other is a by-product of a bollito (boiled meat, see p. 110), in which case the meat goes into boiling, vegetable-seasoned water.

Like a good stock, brodo takes a long time to prepare but does not require a lot of attention except for the first half hour or so. It's best to make it a day ahead since that makes it easier to remove all the fat which congeals at the top after it has been chilled. In the cold water method, a great deal of residue bubbles to the surface. The temperature should immediately be lowered as soon as the water comes to a boil and the froth skimmed off. Much less frothy matter is given off in the hot water (bollito) method, but skimming it off is equally important.

Brodo keeps well for 3 to 4 days in the refrigerator but it should be boiled before using if a longer time has elapsed. Do not store a finished brodo with the meat or cooking vegetables as they cause it to spoil rapidly. Freeze it in 1 or 2 cup containers for when you need small amounts in sauces.

"Il Dado" - The Bouillon Cube

There is no substitute for the flavor of a good brodo, but when necessity prevails, the judicious use of the bouillon cube - "il dado" - can produce satisfactory results. The Italian cook is generally adaptable. He or she will make the most of what is on hand and, in the absence of a good stock, will improvise with a few boiled vegetables and "il dado." In fact, bouillon cubes are ubiquitous in Italian recipe collections and have become a staple in the pantry.

When there are many other good ingredients to support the dish, a bouillon cube can be used not as a substitute but as an enhancement to flavor. Purists may not agree, but almost every Italian household keeps chicken and beef bouillon cubes on hand. Some people even add them to a well-flavored broth like an additional spice! The key is to use them not as the foundation for flavor but as a boost when time does not permit making a good brodo. A quick soup enhanced by bouillon cubes takes minutes to prepare. Try boiling some onion, carrot and celery with a bouillon cube and adding tiny noodles, and lightly beaten egg and Parmigiano. Vary this and instead of egg and cheese, add leftover tomato sauce, half a can of beans and a some chopped spinach and you'll have a satisfying supper with a piece of toasted bread. These have become my favorites for cold winter nights after a long day's work when there is no time to shop and I crave a warm, nourishing meal.

Brodo di Pollo

CHICKEN BROTH

One rainy day at the cottage, I made some homemade noodles to put in some chicken broth with beaten egg and cheese. Papa looked at it and said in his acerbic way, "Am I breast-feeding children?" (He had been expecting pasta not soup.) According to old Italian folklore, chicken soup was the best thing to help lactating mothers produce milk. As a result, it was customary for relatives and friends to visit the mother and new-born with a chicken in hand.

A good, strong broth needs a long, slow simmer. For this, a tough old bird is required. Most Italian butcher shops sell large, old boiling fowls complete with feet and partially formed eggs inside. They are usually sold split in half lengthwise as one whole bird can weigh 6 pounds or more. The feet can be added, as they are in traditional Jewish-style chicken broths, to give a stronger chicken flavor and a deeper yellow colour. Make the broth the day ahead so it can be degreased easily.

Discard excess fat from chicken and rinse well. Place in a large stock pot with the cold water and slowly bring to a boil. Skim the froth as it rises to the surface. When the meat stops giving off a lot of froth, add the vegetables, parsley stems, bay leaves and salt. Simmer, uncovered, for about 3 hours, removing any more residue that may float to the surface. The water should be barely moving as it simmers.

3 pound boiling chicken

5 quarts cold water

1 large carrot, peeled and cut in half

1 onion, peeled

1 stalk celery including the top

4 to 5 parsley stems

2 bay leaves

1 tablespoon salt

When the broth is well-flavored and the chicken quite tender, remove the chicken carcass. Discard the skin and bones and save the meat for use in fillings for pasta or sandwiches.

Strain the broth through a fine mesh sieve. Discard all the vegetables. Pour the broth into a tall container and chill overnight or until the fat congeals at the top. Remove the layer of solidified fat. Keep in the refrigerator for 4 to 5 days. Reboil before using if it is kept longer. Use for soups, risotto or to add to sauces.

Makes about 4 quarts

Brodo di Carne

BEEF AND CHICKEN BROTH

2 pounds beef shoulder

1 ½ pounds boiling fowl
(half a chicken)

4 to 5 quarts cold water

2 stalks celery, cut in half

2 carrots, peeled and cut in half

1 onion, whole

1 clove garlic, whole

1 parsley root, peeled and cut in half

1 bay leaf

2 tablespoons salt

SERVING SUGGESTION

Reheat broth until boiling. Beat 1 egg with 2 tablespoons of grated Parmigiano and stir into the boiling broth. Garnish each bowl with fresh chopped parsley and a handful of Parmesan Cheese Puffs (p. 14).

This is a medium broth, the strong beef flavor being balanced by the milder taste of poultry. It's delicious just on its own in a mug. Mr. Gino Scaini, who is 81, makes this broth once a week in the winter and most often has it just with bread sticks crumbled in. For this reason he always salts the broth as it cooks. If using a salted broth in other recipes remember that the saltiness increases as a liquid cooks down, so the amount of salt indicated in those recipes will need to be adjusted accordingly.

Wash and remove any excess fat from the beef and chicken. Fill a large stock pot with cold water, add the beef and chicken and bring to a boil. Lower the heat and carefully remove the residue that floats to the top. Continue to simmer until the liquid is fairly clear. Add the vegetables and seasonings. Simmer at a low heat, uncovered, for about 3 ½ hours. The liquid should just barely boil.

Remove the meat (save it for other recipes). Strain the broth through a dampened cloth or fine wire mesh sieve. Discard the vegetables. Refrigerate the broth overnight or until the fat has solidified on top. Remove and discard the fat. The brodo can be kept refrigerated or frozen. It may gel somewhat when it is cold. To use, reheat broth till it comes to a boil.

Makes 3 ½ quarts

Brodo di Pesce

FISH BROTH

Fish broth is quick to make and can be kept frozen for up to 2 or 3 months. Salting the broth is customary. If, however, the stock is going to be reduced considerably, it is better to under-salt or omit it, adding salt to taste in the finished dish.

In a soup pot, cook the onion, carrot and celery in the oil. Season with salt and pepper. When the vegetables have softened, add the wine, bay leaf and the optional tomato paste dissolved in half a cup of water. Simmer for 2 minutes. Add the fish pieces and bones and cover with cold water. Bring to a boil, lower heat and simmer for about 25 minutes. Skim any froth that rises. Do not boil longer or the broth becomes bitter. Strain through a fine mesh sieve. Discard the vegetables and bones. Store in the refrigerator until needed. The broth can be frozen in small containers for use in sauces, risotto and soups.

Makes 2 to 3 quarts

1 small onion, chopped

1 small carrot, chopped

1 stalk celery, chopped

2 tablespoons oil

Salt and pepper to taste

½ cup white wine

1 bay leaf

1 heaping tablespoon tomato paste (optional)

3 pounds fish bones and heads

Brodo con Passatelli

BROTH WITH PARMESAN DUMPLINGS

"This is what my children were brought up on when they were very young. It's my grandmother's recipe from Le Marche," stated Anna Amello-Busca. The recipe goes back even further to the early Renaissance (mid 1400's). Maestro Martino da Como in his *Libro de Arte Coquinaria* has several versions of "zanzarella" which are dumplings made of eggs, bread crumbs and cheese and cooked in a broth with saffron.

Bring broth to a boil. In a large bowl, combine the bread crumbs, cheeses, lemon zest, nutmeg and season with salt and pepper. Mix well. Add the beaten eggs and mix together with your fingers until well combined. It will be sticky. Pass this

2 quarts of chicken broth

3 cups bread crumbs

1 cup Parmigiano and Pecorino Romano, grated

1 lemon, zest only

Nutmeg, freshly grated (to taste)

4 eggs, beaten

Salt and pepper

mixture through a food mill fitted with the disc with the large holes directly into the boiling broth. Turn the heat off and let stand for a few minutes before serving.

Makes 6 servings

Brodo di Pollo con Spinaci e Riso

CHICKEN BROTH WITH SPINACH AND RICE

3-4 quarts chicken broth

2 cups spinach, boiled and chopped

¾ cup Arborio rice

2 eggs, beaten

⅓ cup mixed Parmigiano and Asiago cheese, grated

To the Vatri-Thomas family of Algonac, Michigan, this is known as "Nonna's soup." Louise remembers her mother made it frequently the same way her own mother had done. Before she married, Louise didn't cook a lot so she was glad to borrow from her mother's repertoire of recipes something that was quite simple to make. She changed it slightly when the kids came, adding some egg to make it more nutritious.

Bring the broth to a boil, add the spinach and the rice and cook for 13 to 15 minutes until the rice is cooked. Beat the eggs with the Parmigiano and Asiago and add to the soup pot at the very end, stirring vigorously. Serve immediately.

Makes 8 servings

Brodo di Cardi e Polpettine

CHICKEN BROTH WITH CARDOONS AND MINIATURE MEATBALLS

3 quarts chicken broth

½ portion meatball mixture for tiny meatballs (p. 115)

1 cardoon stalk

1 celery stalk

Freddie loves his mother-in-law's cooking, especially this soup which he said we had to include in this collection. Dina Esposito usually makes it at Christmas or Easter since that is when cardoons are available. If you can't find them in your local market, you can substitute more celery and fennel.

Wash, trim and dice the cardoon and celery stalks. Remove the top portion of the fennel, cut into quarters and dice. Boil the cardoon, celery and fennel in salted water for about half an hour. When tender, drain and set aside.

Make the tiny meatballs as per instructions. Heat the broth, add the vegetables and cook for about 20 minutes. Add the cooked tiny meatballs. Beat the eggs with the Parmigiano. Add to the boiling broth, stirring vigorously. Season with salt and pepper. Serve immediately.

Makes 6 to 8 servings

1 cup fennel, diced

3 eggs

½ cup Parmigiano, grated

Salt and pepper

ABOUT CARDOONS

This uncommon, celery-like vegetable is part of the artichoke family. However, only the thick, long stalks are eaten, not the flowering part. They are grown in California and shipped all over North America, wherever Italian communities exist. The are available generally from November to April. Like artichokes, they have some inedible parts - namely the tough, outer stalks and the long strings which should be removed before they are cooked. They also discolor, like artichokes do, as soon as they are cut. It is standard practice to pre-cook them first "in bianco" which means in a solution of water, flour and lemon. The proportions are: 1 quart water, 1 ounce flour, the juice of one lemon and a piece of butter.

Minestrone

It is impossible and unnecessary to be precise when describing the way to make minestrone. Every cook has a different version of this soup which, translated literally, means "big soup." And, indeed, the soup tends to grow to enormous proportions as the ingredients are added. A big soup pot is essential. Most Italian cooks never make it the same way twice. It is, therefore, a recipe in which you can be very creative. Nancy Vetere always adds cabbage and beans which she cooks the day before. Half this mixture is pureed and added at the end so it thickens the soup without scorching the bottom of the pot. Canned beans can be used instead of dried. Chickpeas (or garbanzo beans) are

½ pound dried white beans, (great northern or kidney)

½ savoy cabbage (or regular white cabbage)

4 tablespoons oil

2 large onions, chopped

6 carrots, sliced thickly

2 stalks celery, chopped

2 large potatoes, cut into large chunks

3 cloves garlic, chopped

3 quarts meat broth

2 cups cooked chick peas (1 tin), drained and rinsed

3 cups tomato sauce or canned tomatoes, pureed

Salt and pepper to taste

½ cup rice

1 cup dried, short soup noodles (ditali, tubetti, etc.)

1 zucchini, sliced

5 ounces fresh spinach, washed and chopped

1 tablespoon chopped, fresh parsley (or dried parsley)

1 cup grated Parmigiano

1 tablespoon butter

TIP

Have lots of broth or vegetable cooking water on hand to add to the soup as it thickens and grows.

always nice. Her version of the soup has tomato in it. Since Nancy's kids don't like pieces of tomato floating in their soup, she uses leftover sauce or tomato paste. Most times, she adds spinach or other leafy greens and sometimes peas, green beans or yellow wax beans. If she has time, she boils up beef bones for a broth, otherwise chicken and beef bouillon cubes season the cooking liquid, in addition to the cabbage and bean cooking water. Since it makes a huge quantity, invite a lot of people over and have plenty of crusty bread on hand.

One day before, cook the dried beans in 3 quarts of salted water. Simmer them gently, partially covered, until they are tender. (Great northern beans take 1 hour 45 minutes.) Cut the cabbage into chunks and cook in about 3 quarts boiling, salted water until it is tender (about 25 - 30 minutes). In a blender, puree half the cooked beans and half the cabbage. Set the puree aside. Save the remaining cooked beans and cabbage and the cooking liquid.

In a very large soup pot, heat oil and add the chopped onion, the carrots, celery, potatoes and the garlic. Stir and cook for about 10 minutes. Add the broth and bring to a boil. Simmer another 10 minutes or until the vegetables have softened but are not completely tender.

Chop the reserved, cooked cabbage and add to the pot along with its cooking liquid. Add the remaining cooked white beans including any cooking liquid, and the drained, rinsed chickpeas. Mix in the tomato sauce and season with salt and pepper to taste. When the mixture comes to a boil again, add the rice and simmer for about 15 minutes until rice is tender.

Add the noodles and the zucchini. If the minestrone is too dense, add more broth or water. Continue to simmer, stirring, occasionally just until the noodles are tender. Add the spinach and the reserved pureed cabbage and bean mixture to thicken. Do not boil the soup after this point or the puree will burn. Cook at low heat, stirring, just until the spinach wilts. Just before serving, stir in some parsley and a few spoons of Parmigiano. Float a piece of butter on top (optional). Serve with crusty bread with the remaining Parmigiano at the table.

Makes 10 to 12 servings

Minestra di Pollo con Riso

CHICKEN AND RICE SOUP

My father, Venanzio Pace, keeps a well-stocked pantry but his refrigerator always looks empty. This is because when Papa shops for meat or produce, he is extremely conscious of not buying more than he can consume in order not to waste anything. Yet he always manages to pull things out of a seemingly empty refrigerator whenever we drop in. It could be a few pieces of breaded chicken breast with some cooked rapini. Or perhaps it's leftover chicken and rice soup. He says you can make this soup in different ways, white or with tomato, with chick peas instead of noodles or just the rice. Here is one version of what he does.

Cut off the legs and thighs of the chicken and set aside for another use. Cut off the wings and neck. Remove the skin from the breast and detach the white meat from the bone. Cut it into fillets, wrap in plastic wrap and freeze in small portions. Pull off the skin from the back and neck and discard along with any excess fat. Combine the wings, neck, and back in a large pot. Cover with cold water, add salt and bring to a boil.

As the water comes to a boil, remove the froth that floats to the top. Lower heat and skim the froth as it rises. Add the chopped onion and potatoes. Simmer for about 40 minutes or until the chicken meat is tender. Take out the chicken, separate the meat from the bone. Return the meat to the pot and discard the bones. If the broth has cooked down too much at this point, add 2 or 3 cups more water with 1 bouillon cube and bring to a boil. Taste and add more salt and some pepper.

Add the rice, simmer for about 10 minutes. Add the optional egg noodles and cook until tender. Stir in any chopped, leftover cooked greens. Serve with plenty of grated Parmigiano.

Makes 4 servings

"COOKING FOR ONE"

The trick to having varied, balanced meals for a person living on his or her own is to have a definite plan for what you buy. My

1 large chicken or capon (about 5 pounds)

3 quarts cold water

2 teaspoons salt (or to taste)

1 onion, chopped

2 large potatoes, peeled and cut into large chunks

1 bouillon cube (if needed)

Pepper to taste

¼ cup rice

1 cup broad egg noodles (optional)

½ cup cooked greens, chopped (spinach, escarole)

father does this with chicken. Since a whole chicken is too much for him to have at once, he divides it up for various uses. He cuts off the legs and thighs and roasts them with potatoes. The breast is boned, cut into fillets and frozen for breaded chicken cutlets. The bones, back, neck and wings are boiled and transformed into a dense chicken and rice soup. He is very proud of the fact that one chicken provides him with meals for a week!

Minestra di "Taccozzelle" e Fagioli

CORNMEAL PASTA AND BEAN SOUP

TO MAKE CORNMEAL PASTA FOR TACOZZE

1 cup quick-cooking cornmeal

2 cups all-purpose flour

½ teaspoon salt

1 egg

¾ cup warm water

FOR THE MINESTRA:

3 cups pureed canned plum tomatoes

3 tablespoons oil

1 small onion, chopped

1 clove garlic, chopped

1 teaspoon dried herbs: basil, parsley, oregano

1 teaspoon salt

This was one of Sabina Masci's favorite meals when she was a kid. Her mother, Maria Spacca, used to cook everything from scratch, since that was how people ate when the family emigrated from Italy in 1912. Except for some things like olive oil, dried long spaghetti and olives in barrels, the Italians who came in the early years of this century did not find the imported ingredients that are available today. They used to get relatives to bring over the aged, hard cheeses for grating over pasta. Mrs. Spacca even made her own fresh cheeses once a year when they were able to go to the local Agricultural Fair at the Exhibition Grounds to get the unpasteurized milk to make scamorza and ricotta. They would always put up tomatoes and even make their own tomato paste, setting it on the veranda facing the west to get the maximum sun. They cured their own pork to make sausages, salami and prosciutto and preserved vegetables in season. Generally, they managed to maintain a diet very similar to what they had in Italy using fresh local products.

There were times when Mrs. Spacca, who cooked for boarders as well as her family, had to improvise and use whatever was on hand. In Italy, the thick pasta squares known as tacozze used to be made with whatever flour was available, often from very coarse grains with a little bran in them. And since eggs were scarce, the dough was mixed mostly with water. Here, Maria Spacca mixed regular flour and cornmeal, probably because it was available. I have found no other source that calls for adding cornmeal to a pasta dough so I believe it must have been her own creation. Whenever we had tacozze in my house, next door, my mother made them with regular pasta dough cut into large squares and usually served "asciutta," meaning with tomato sauce, not a broth.

I was skeptical at first but, when I tried following the instructions, to my surprise, the dough was fairly easy to shape, knead and roll. It is much coarser than pasta all'uovo and, of course, you can substitute regular pasta dough or even buy thick sheets of commercial fresh semolina pasta and cut it into squares. Dough made with regular cornmeal takes a long time to cook so it is best to use the quick-cooking variety. The noodles taste even better in the thick soup the next day. There is no need for meat as a second course as the combination of wheat, corn, beans and cheese supplies ample proteins.

The dough should not be rolled too thinly. The little squares have a pleasant stodginess which is very hearty and rustic. The starchiness from the cornmeal and the beans makes the soup very thick, dense and quite filling – a good choice for a cold winter evening.

Combine the cornmeal, flour and salt in a large bowl. Beat together the egg and warm water, adding enough water to make 1 cup. Pour the liquid into the flour mixture gradually, using a fork to mix it together. Shape it into dough. Place on a flat surface and knead until the dough is fairly smooth and pliable. (It will feel coarse due to the cornmeal.) The dough will not be elastic, so it can be rolled right away with a rolling pin. A pasta machine can also be used.

Roll the dough into a large circle about $\frac{1}{16}$ inch thick. Keep lifting and turning over the circle of dough as you roll to keep it from sticking. When it is the desired thinness, let it rest, uncovered, on the board to dry slightly. Turn it to dry the other side. If making pasta squares for "pasta asciutta" (pasta with tomato sauce), cut the dough into large 2-inch squares. For minestra, cut the dough into smaller squares, about $\frac{1}{2}$ inch. Cook as you would pasta all'uovo but for a much longer time. (Depending on the thickness, it can take up to 20 minutes.)

2 cups white beans, cooked (if using canned, drain and rinse them)

2 ½ quarts chicken broth

¾ cup cooked lettuce leaves, drained and chopped

½ cup grated Pecorino Romano

Freshly milled black pepper to taste

TIP

Cooking the outer leaves of romaine lettuce is a great way to use up less-than-perfect greens that you might otherwise throw out. Cook the leaves, drain them and squeeze them dry. Store in plastic bags in the freezer to have on hand for soups like this one. Other types of lettuce leaves can be used, too, as can escarole and curly endive.

Saute the onion in the oil in large pot until soft. Add the garlic, simmer for a minute or two but do not let it brown. Add the pureed tomatoes. Season with the herbs, using mainly basil and parsley and only a pinch of oregano. Add the salt and simmer for about 15 minutes.

Add the cooked white beans to the tomato base and cook just until heated through.

In a separate pot, bring to a boil the broth. Add the pasta squares and cook, stirring occasionally, for about 15 to 20 minutes or until the pasta loses its doughy taste.

Combine the cooked pasta, including the cooking broth with the tomato sauce and beans. Simmer everything together at a very low heat for another 10 minutes to allow the pasta to soften even more. Add the chopped greens and allow them to heat through. If the soup is very dense, add a little more water or broth. Taste and adjust the seasoning if necessary. Serve with lots of grated Romano cheese and some freshly milled pepper. This soup tastes even better the next day. You will need to add more liquid when reheating it.

Substitutions: Homemade pasta or tacozze can be substituted with regular dried pasta of the chunky variety such as ditali or tubetti. Cook commercial pasta in the broth until it is almost tender, then finish the cooking in the tomato base.

Makes 6 to 8 servings.

Nancy's "Jungle Soup"

Stracciatella means little rags and is a classic soup in which raw egg is beaten with grated Parmesan cheese and parsley then stirred into boiling broth. This creates little ragged bits much like Chinese egg drop soup. The addition of tiny noodles and occasionally meatballs is an optional feature. Nancy's thicker version includes the works and is a meal in itself as well as a treat for the eye. She called it jungle soup for her kids when they were younger because it looks a bit like a dense jungle with its contrasting textures, shapes and colors swimming in a flavorful broth.

Reheat meat broth that has been chilled and degreased. Trim all fat from chicken and cut into small chunks. Make half a portion of regular meatballs, shape into 30 to 40 tiny balls about ½ inch in diameter. Fry in a little hot oil. When cooked through, drain on paper towels and set aside.

When broth comes to a boil, taste for salt, add soup noodles and cook until tender. Add the chicken meat and meatballs. With a fork, beat together eggs and 2 heaping tablespoons Parmigiano. Bring soup just to a boil and stir in egg mixture using a fork. It will form ragged strands. Add chopped escarole, stirring it to break up the clumps. Serve immediately so noodles do not become overcooked. Garnish with some fresh, chopped parsley and serve with extra cheese at the table.

Makes 6 to 8 servings

3 quarts light meat broth

Salt to taste

1 ½ cups boiled chicken, cut into small chunks

½ portion meatball recipe (see p. 115)

Oil for frying

1 cup dried tiny soup noodles (quadrettini or acine di pepe)

2 small eggs

2 heaping tablespoons grated Parmigiano cheese

1 cup cooked escarole, squeezed dry and chopped finely

2 tablespoons chopped, fresh parsley for garnish

Grated Parmigiano to serve at the table

Zuppa di Verdura

PUREED VEGETABLE SOUP

3 tablespoons oil

2 tablespoons butter

1 small onion, finely chopped

1 clove garlic, minced

1 cup green beans, chopped

2 celery stalks, diced

2 medium carrots, diced

3 medium leeks, washed and diced (white part only)

3 medium potatoes, diced

4 peeled tomatoes, seeded and chopped

2 cups of shredded cabbage

6 cups light meat broth

3 cups thick, short, soup pasta (e.g., ditali)

⅓ cup Parmigiana

Salt and pepper to taste

This is a very thick soup, but, unlike minestrone, this vegetable soup is not chunky. A "zuppa" usually refers to a dense soup which is ladled over slices of country bread (pane casareccia). Sometimes, pancetta was added to give it a stronger flavor. In Luciana Mian's home in Italy, it was traditional to add some cut up old bread and cubed fresh cheese instead of rice or pasta. Use a thick, ridged soup noodle like ditali, as the more delicate ones get lost and become soggy. This soup is great the next day and can also be frozen (without the noodles).

In a large soup pot, heat the oil and butter, then add the onion, garlic, green beans and celery. Season with salt and pepper, and cook for about 10 minutes. Add the carrots, leeks, potatoes, tomatoes and shredded cabbage, season again and cook, stirring continuously, over medium heat until all the vegetables are transparent and glazed (about 10 to 15 minutes).

Add enough water to cover vegetables and simmer for 45 minutes or until they are completely cooked. Puree the vegetables and liquid through a foodmill and return to the stock pot. Add the broth, reheat and taste for salt and pepper.

Just before serving, bring to a boil 3 to 4 quarts salted water and cook the pasta until tender. Drain and add to the vegetable soup. Stir in the Parmigiano just before serving.

Makes 10 to 12 servings

Zuppa di Patate e Porri

POTATO AND LEEK SOUP

Although this soup can be made any time of the year, traditionally it was made in the summer when leeks were readily available in the garden. Make sure to wash the leeks thoroughly to rid them of all sand. For a tastier soup, prepare it the day before but don't add the rice. To make a thinner soup, add only half the potatoes. Carla Rossi often omits the cream, and uses low-fat milk to cut down on the richness.

Boil the peeled potatoes in lightly salted water until tender, drain and add to the hot chicken broth. In a skillet, saute the leek and parsley in the butter for about 10 to 15 minutes. If the leeks start to brown, add a little hot broth. Season with salt and pepper.

Add the leek to the broth and simmer for 30 minutes. Taste and adjust the seasoning. Add the rice and cook for about 12 to 15 minutes. Remove the pot from the stove and stir in the optional cream and the Parmigiano. Serve immediately.

Makes 8 servings

8 small potatoes, peeled

8 cups hot chicken broth

2 cups finely chopped leek, white portion only

2 tablespoons finely chopped parsley

3 tablespoons butter

½ cup Arborio rice

½ cup 10% table cream (optional)

⅓ cup grated Parmigiano cheese

Salt and pepper to taste

Risotto and Polenta

Risotto Bianco

BASIC RISOTTO

1 medium onion, chopped

2 tablespoons oil

4 tablespoons butter

1 pound Italian rice (Arborio,

Carnaroli or Vialone nano)

1 ½ quarts meat broth (p. 22),
boiling hot

Salt to taste

3 to 4 tablespoons grated Parmigiano
cheese

Risotto is more a method than a specific recipe. There are various ways to achieve the creamy texture that binds each tender kernel of rice. Some cooks are adamant about adding the broth very gradually and stirring attentively. Others are more casual and insist that there is no appreciable difference if you leave it alone for longer and add more broth at the beginning. Then there are the expedient but necessary shortcuts that large commercial kitchens must employ to make huge quantities of risotto for banquets. Whether you hover over it, boil it all at once or partially cook it and finish it later, your risotto will turn out as long as one follows certain basic precepts.

1. Use good quality rice that is more resistant to cooking than regular, par-boiled rice. There are several varieties of short-grain Italian rice but a few are especially good for risotto. In addition to the more commonly found "Arborio," there is also "Vialone nano" and "Carnaroli" which both have a high starch content. The cooking times will vary slightly depending on the plumpness and length of the rice kernel. Generally, risotto will take from 15 to 18 minutes unless you are dealing with very large quantities.

2. Use a good broth as a base for your risotto. Keep the broth at just below boiling point when adding it to the rice.

3. To maintain the consistency of the flavoring vegetables, you can cook them separately, then add them to the basic risotto when it is two-thirds cooked.

4. Allow the rice to sit a few minutes once it has reached the desired degree of tenderness (this is a personal judgment and varies from almost crunchy to very soft - but never mushy). Beating in some butter at the end, a process known as "mantecare," helps give a creamy consistency. (Though, I confess to omitting this step regularly and no one has complained.)

5. Serve the risotto as soon as it is ready. Leftover risotto can be made into rice balls. It tastes fine but it loses all the pleasant characteristics of its creamy consistency the day after it is made.

A basic risotto recipe follows. It can be varied in innumerable ways with the addition of other vegetables, meat, fish, seafood and seasonings. The particular risotto recipes from individual cooks reflect the diversity in personal approaches and experiences to this dish.

Cook the onion in the oil and 1 tablespoon of butter until it softens. Add the rice, stir well to coat it thoroughly. Cook for about 2 minutes or until it starts to crackle.

Add the broth gradually to the rice, stir. As the rice cooks and absorbs the broth, add more. Taste and add salt if desired. Continue to add broth in this way for about 15 to 18 minutes or until the rice is tender (or al dente, if you prefer) and a little bit of liquid is left forming a creamy sauce. Take the pot off the heat and vigorously stir in the remaining butter and the Parmigiano. Serve immediately with extra cheese at the table and the pepper mill.

Makes 4 large servings

Risotto alla Milanese

RISOTTO MILANESE STYLE

In a university night-school course on conversational Italian, our very erudite and stylish professor, born and bred in Milan, explained the definitive way of preparing this classic dish. There were not to be any compromises either! It seemed toying with the authentic flavors was not in her style. "One can't make it here," she pronounced, as you can't get "guanciale" or marrow easily, if at all. Pancetta was not, in her opinion, an acceptable substitute. Beef or veal marrow can be found in some butcher shops, but guanciale (or pork cheeks) are very hard to track down. I haven't given up the quest, but in the meantime, this version is perfectly delightful,

4 to 5 cups light meat broth (p. 22)

Salt to taste

5 tablespoons butter

2 tablespoons oil

3 tablespoons diced sweet pancetta

2 heaping tablespoons chopped shallot or onion

2 cups Arborio rice

½ cup dry white wine

¼ teaspoon chopped saffron threads
(or 2 packages powdered)

2 tablespoons fresh parsley, finely
chopped

½ cup freshly grated Parmigiano

Freshly milled black pepper

though it may not measure up to the Milanese professor's memories. This risotto is typically served with Ossobuco (p. 114) and generally put on the same plate - not as a separate, first course.

Bring the broth to a boil and keep it at a low heat on a back burner. Season with salt to taste.

In a deep, heavy-bottomed pan, heat 2 tablespoons of the butter with all the oil and cook the pancetta until it starts to color and releases much of the fat. Add the shallot and cook, stirring, until it becomes translucent. Add the rice, stir and cook for about 2 minutes. Add the wine and 1 cup of hot broth to the rice, stir occasionally and cook at very low heat until most of the liquid is absorbed. Continue to add broth in small amounts, stirring regularly. Taste and add salt and pepper if needed. (Remember that pancetta is quite salty.)

After about 10 minutes, add the saffron which has been dissolved in a small amount of the broth. Stir it in. Cook in this manner for another 5 minutes or until the rice becomes tender and the broth has been absorbed. Stir in the parsley, remaining butter and Parmesan. Serve immediately with freshly milled pepper and extra grated cheese on the side for those who like lots of cheese.

Makes 4 to 6 servings

ABOUT SAFFRON

Since ancient time, saffron has been valued for its flavor and the golden hue it can impart to food and clothes. It provided a cheaper alternative to real gold leaf which was used during the Renaissance to decorate foods. Saffron is made from the yellow stigmas of crocus flowers. Saffron threads packaged in small vials are more costly than the powdered saffron in thin packets that most Italians use. The threads have a stronger flavor, but considering the difference in cost, powdered saffron is more than adequate for most recipes. The expense is due to the vast number of crocus flowers needed to produce a single grain. To make an ounce of saffron requires 4320 flowers. It is no wonder that this spice was so highly valued that during the Renaissance, the penalties for adulterating saffron were extreme. In 1450 Nurnberg, a man was buried alive along with his fake supplies for selling adulterated saffron - but this is going too far! Be wary of any large, inexpensive packages of orange/gold powder labeled saffron. They are not the real thing.

Risotto al Funghi Porcini

RISOTTO WITH WILD MUSHROOMS

Mushroom hunting is a favorite pastime among many Italians. For hunters and fishermen, an excursion into a wooded area would not be complete without searching out edible funghi. You must know what you are doing, though, as the poisonous ones look deceptively enticing. The local gourmet fruit and vegetable market is as far as I have ever dared go for exotic mushrooms. These days there are many kinds to choose from. Oyster and Portobello appear regularly next to the common button mushrooms in most supermarkets. Shiitake and Chanterelles can be found in specialty grocery shops. Use whichever you prefer and can afford.

Soak the dried mushrooms in hot water for 20 minutes or until quite soft. Remove the mushrooms from the soaking liquid, rinse, chop and set aside. Save the soaking liquid, pass it through a sieve lined with a coffee filter or wet cloth to remove any sand.

In a large skillet, heat the butter, add the sliced mushrooms and cook at high heat, stirring. Season with a little salt to taste. When the mushrooms release their juice and start to brown, add the chopped Porcini. Continue to cook until the mushrooms are well colored, remove from heat and reserve for later.

Prepare the risotto as for the basic risotto recipe above but with less onion. After the rice has been sauteed and the first ladles of broth have been stirred in, add the mushroom soaking liquid. Season with salt to taste. Continue to cook, adding broth gradually and stirring until the rice is almost tender (12 to 14 minutes depending on the type of rice). Add the optional peas and cook until heated through. Add the chopped porcini and the fresh, sauteed mushrooms. Stir to combine well. Take the pot off the heat and beat in the butter and Parmigiano. Serve immediately with extra Parmigiano and the pepper mill.

2 packages dried Porcini mushrooms (.35 oz. each)

1 cup hot water

2 tablespoons butter

¼ pound fresh mushrooms, washed, dried and sliced

2 tablespoons onion, chopped

2 tablespoons oil

1 pound Italian rice (Carnaroli or Vialone nano type)

1 ½ quarts meat broth (p. 22), boiling hot

1 ½ cups frozen peas (optional)

3 to 4 tablespoons grated Parmigiano cheese

2 tablespoons butter

Salt and pepper

NOTE

For a more intense mushroom flavor, use 2 to 3 packages of Porcini soaked in 2 cups of water. It increases the cost of the dish but also deepens the flavor.

Risotto al Frutti di Mare

SEAFOOD RISOTTO

6 cups fish broth (p. 23)

¼ cup olive oil

½ small onion, finely chopped

2 cloves garlic, minced

¼ teaspoon fennel seeds, crushed

2 cups Italian rice (Arborio, Vialone nano or Carnaroli)

½ cup dry white wine

1 can (5 ounces) clams

¼ teaspoon saffron threads (or 2 packages powdered)

12 mussels (optional garnish)

1 halibut fillet (about ¾ pound), cut into small chunks

½ pound bay scallops

¾ pound medium shrimp, peeled and de-veined

Salt and pepper to taste

2 tablespoons butter

3 tablespoons fresh parsley, finely chopped

Normally, risotto is served as the starchy component of an Italian meal and is eaten, like pasta, as a single course. This risotto is so laden with rich seafood, it can be a meal on its own with a simple mixed greens salad before or after. It also makes an elegant starter course to an elaborate meal, in which case it should be served in very small portions. The optional garnish of black mussels is a striking contrast to the golden hue of the saffron-tinted rice. Though fish broth is called for in the recipe, a light meat broth can be used as there is sufficient fish and seafood to impart plenty of taste. It is very important to time the cooking of the fish carefully, starting with the longest-cooking and bigger pieces. Shrimp are done as soon as they turn pink and if overcooked will become hard and dry very quickly.

Heat the broth until it is barely simmering and keep it on a back burner. Season with salt if necessary. In a separate heavy saucepan cook the onion in the oil at medium heat for 3 minutes, stirring occasionally. Add the garlic, and fennel and cook 1 minute. Add the rice and cook, stirring, about 2 minutes. Add the wine and stir until it is absorbed. Drain the clams and reserve them. Add the clam juice to the rice.

Dissolve the saffron in a small amount of hot broth. Stir this into the rice. Add enough hot broth to cover the rice. Cook, uncovered, at medium heat, stirring regularly for about 10 to12 minutes. As the broth is absorbed, continue adding about 1 cup at a time.

If using the mussels as garnish, boil them in a separate pan with some of the broth. As soon as they open, remove the mussels and set them aside. Strain the cooking broth through a sieve lined with a damp paper towel to remove any sand. Add the mussel broth to the rice.

When the rice is nearly tender and most of the broth has been absorbed, start adding the fish – first the halibut, then the scallops, shrimp and reserved clams. Cook only about 2 minutes. When the fish and seafood are cooked, stir in the butter and parsley. Taste and adjust seasoning if needed.

Makes 6 to 8 servings

Risotto con Radicchio al Vino Rosso

RISOTTO WITH RADICCHIO AND RED WINE

The slightly bitter flavor of radicchio and the strong presence of wine makes this risotto appeal more to adults than children. Gianni Ceschia likes to cook the vegetables separately from the rice then add them later. This preserves the colors and textures of the vegetable. For convenience, it can be made in one pot as explained below or, if texture is less of a consideration, the rice can be added to the lightly cooked vegetables. The cooking time will vary depending on whether or not you like the rice slightly "al dente" (with some bite to it) which seems to be generally preferred by people from the Friuli and Veneto regions.

Bring the broth to a boil in a pan and keep it at a low heat on a back burner.

In a deep, heavy-bottomed pot, heat 2 tablespoons of the butter and half the oil, add the carrot and the onion and season with salt and pepper. Cook for a few minutes, then add the radicchio, season again and cook just until it wilts. Remove vegetables from pan and set aside.

Add the remaining oil and 2 more tablespoons of butter to the pan, set at medium heat. Add the rice and saute for about 3 to 4 minutes, stirring. When the rice becomes translucent, add enough of the hot broth to cover the rice. If broth is unsalted, add some salt to taste. Stir regularly and continue to cook at a very low boil, adding ladles of hot broth as it is absorbed by the rice. After about 10 minutes, add the vegetables mixture and the red wine and continue cooking. The risotto is done when the rice is tender and there is not an excess of broth - only enough creamy liquid to hold the grains together.

Stir in the Parmigiano and the remaining butter. Taste and adjust seasoning. Let the risotto sit for a few minutes. Transfer the risotto to a serving dish or individual plates. Sprinkle on some parsley and serve immediately with extra grated Parmigiano at the table.

Makes 4 to 6 servings

5-6 cups medium meat broth (see p. 22)

¼ pound butter

4 tablespoons olive oil

1 carrot, peeled and finely chopped

½ onion, finely chopped

salt and pepper to taste

½ head radicchio, washed and chopped

2 cups Arborio rice (Carnavoli, or Vialone nano)

½ cup red wine

½ cup Parmigiano cheese, grated

⅓ cup of chopped parsley

Polenta

Arlecchino used to dream of it. In one of Goldoni's comedies there is the definitive recipe that Rosaura promises to make for Arlecchino showing that the method has not at all changed from the 1700's until today – flour as yellow as gold dropped into boiling water and stirred, tracing circles and lines with a big "batocio" (stick), shaping it in big spoonfuls on the plate before dressing it with fresh, yellow, delicate butter and a big, yellow hunk of well grated cheese. Polenta was and still is a symbol of the cooking of the Veneto region. It is eaten with almost everything. In a poem dedicated to polenta written in 1787 by a Venetian doctor, we learn what goes well with polenta: "coi fongheti, col porcelo, coi oseleti, cole tenche, coi bisati, co le anguele" (mushrooms, pork, little birds, tench, eels). He also tells us that polenta was sold on the streets of Venice for one cent a slice which he would buy but eat surreptitiously, under his cloak, lest he damage the dignity of his position as a "dottore" (doctor). Polenta is eaten in all manner of ways – instead of bread, as a meal in itself, for breakfast like porridge with milk and sugar, grilled, fried and baked. It fills you up without adding lots of fat (except what goes in the sauces) and is easily digested.

Polenta is not exclusive to the northern regions of Friuli Venezia-Giulia. In the small mountain village my mother came from, nestled against one of the highest ranges of the Abruzzi mountains, corn grew very well. Polenta was a regular winter meal though it was never eaten as frequently as it was in the north. Typical of the south, they always dressed it with tomato and meat sauce and ate it alone as it was very filling. Because it was considered a poor person's meal, it was not often served to guests. So when my father went courting, after bicycling the 10 kilometers up the mountain to meet my mother, the women immediately threw out all the beautiful polenta they had been preparing and quickly started pulling out prosciutto and sausages and preparing pasta - the fare offered to preferred guests. He was very disappointed when he realized he had missed one of their inimitable polenta suppers.

Perhaps it was because of the way it was eaten that it was not deemed worthy for guests. The ordinary method of serving polenta in the Abruzzo and other regions of the south was very much a communal, family affair. The cooked polenta was poured onto a huge wooden board that covered almost the whole table. It was spread out and dressed with a rich tomato sauce and grated Pecorino cheese. Everyone sat around and dug in with a fork. As each person carved out mouthfuls of deliciously firm cornmeal, the board started looking like an ancient map with the land eroding dramatically. It was great fun playing geography in this way but definitely not something you did for a prospective fiancee.

If you don't plan to serve polenta peasant-style on a big wooden board, you can spread it out on low platters or mound it in layers in a deep pasta bowl the way my cousin did one January when I was visiting the old family home in the mountains. We had to borrow a special copper pot with a bottom that fit snugly into one of the circles on the wood-burning stove. This design was very practical as it allowed you to stir with both arms since the pot was anchored so securely. After 45 minutes of shared stirring, we ended up with masses of dense, creamy polenta that firmed up beautifully.

These days, many Italian grocery stores carry a quick-cooking variety of cornmeal which produces a tolerable result. For this type, you would omit the potato and cook it for about 10 to 15 minutes following package directions. It is worth noting, however, that the instructions for the proportions on the package are not always accurate or consistent, in my experience, so use your discretion. Add the cornmeal slowly, holding some back if it seems too dense and dry. Below are basic recipes for polenta - the northern and southern versions, plain, grilled and baked along with different dressings. There are also instructions for making small batches in the microwave.

Basic Polenta - Northern Style

12 cups water

2 tablespoons salt

3 ½ cups cornmeal

1 tablespoon butter or oil (optional)

The method Elizabeth Giacometti uses to make polenta these days is less labor intensive. She does not stand over it, stirring constantly, as she finds a vigorous stir once every ten minutes is quite sufficient. A common way to slice the polenta after it had set was with a piece of string. This method still works very well.

Bring water to a boil in a large pot, add the salt, and gradually add the cornmeal using a whisk. Add the (optional) butter or oil. Stir well, cover the pot and cook for an hour, stirring every 10 minutes. Wet a china or glass bowl with water and pour the cornmeal into the bowl. (The water prevents the polenta from sticking.) Let it sit for 5 minutes then invert onto a wooden board or a large platter. Serve immediately with the desired accompaniment.

Makes 6 to 8 servings

Grilled Polenta

Make the regular cornmeal as described above. Leave it in the bowl and allow it to cool completely. Slice the cold polenta into 1-inch thick pieces and place on an oiled cookie sheet. Place under the broiler set at 500 degrees for 10 minutes on each side or until golden in color. Makes 6 to 8 servings.

Microwave Polenta

To make polenta in the microwave you must have a heat-resistant, non-stick casserole with a vented lid. The type I use is made of polycarbonate plastic and comes in a 2 or 3 quart size. The microwave method is useful only when you want to make small portions of polenta as a garnish for meat or fish. The result is quite satisfactory, and it is particularly appealing since it does not involve lots of heavy stirring. This polenta can be chilled, cut into small slices and grilled or fried as a garnish, or it can be the main course for two servings.

Dissolve salt and oil in water. Slowly stir in cornmeal so there are no lumps. Microwave at high for 10 minutes, stopping twice to stir with a wooden spoon. After 10 minutes, allow the polenta to sit in the turned off microwave for 4 to 5 minutes. Stir well to remove any lumps. The mixture should resemble a slightly grainy cornmeal pudding at this stage.

Return to microwave and cook another 8 to 10 minutes, stirring periodically. Polenta is ready when the mixture is thick and comes away from the sides of the container when stirred.

Pour onto a flat plate to form a smooth, even layer about ¾ inch thick. Smooth the top with wet fingers. Allow to sit a few minutes before serving. Or, chill completely and cut into slices to be fried or broiled with grated cheese.

Makes 3 ½ cups

3 cups cold water

1 teaspoon salt

2 teaspoons oil or butter

¼ cup coarse cornmeal

Polenta Abruzzese

BASIC POLENTA - ABRUZZO STYLE

4 quarts water

1 small potato, peeled and thinly sliced

1 pound coarse cornmeal

2 teaspoons salt

The only difference in this style of polenta is the addition of the potato. It is, of course, optional in other basic polenta recipes but Zia Agostina insisted that a potato makes the mixture smoother and creamier. She had been making polenta this way for over 80 years so we followed her advice which we found was always a wise thing to do.

In a deep, heavy pot, bring the water to boil with the potato and salt; cook until the potato becomes soft. It will eventually disintegrate entirely. Slowly add handfuls of cornmeal to the boiling water; the water should never stop boiling. Stir and add all but 2 to 3 handfuls of the polenta. Adjust heat so the polenta boils but not too vigorously. Beware of big spatters. Cook, stirring continuously for about 20 minutes. Add the remaining cornmeal and keep cooking and stirring for another 20 - 25 minutes. The polenta will become more and more difficult to stir and eventually it will come away from the sides of the pot. It is ready when it can hold its shape if some of it is dropped from a spoon. Let the polenta sit for 5 minutes before pouring it out and dressing it.

Makes 6 to 8 servings

TIP

Use a heavy-bottomed Dutch oven pot to cook the polenta in order to prevent burning. Long-cooked polenta always forms a crust at the bottom of the pot. This peels off easily if the pot is soaked in cold water.

Polenta con Salsiccia

POLENTA WITH SAUSAGE

1 cup olive oil

3 cloves fresh garlic, sliced

1 pound Italian sausages, sweet or hot

4 to 5 sage leaves, torn

When visiting with Maria Incoronata Guadgnoli in Italy one Christmas, my cousin and I decided to undertake making a batch of polenta on the wood-burning stove. We borrowed the right copper pot, pulled out the huge wooden spoon and rolled up our sleeves in readiness as everyone was to take turns at stirring. As a change of pace from the customary tomato and meat sauce dressing typical of the South, we made a simple oil sauce seasoned with garlic and fresh pork sausage. It happened to be sausage-making time and we had been trying out various ones from different local butchers. If you don't have good Italian pork sausages, use ground pork seasoned with herbs and spices. The key to getting the maximum flavor is to simmer the oil and meat together very slowly. Just before we started cooking the polenta, Maria Incoronata put some smashed garlic cloves and oil in a skillet on the coolest part of the wood-burning stove. After a long while she added the meat and moved the pan back and forth between the hot and cool parts of the stove until the polenta was finished. The flavors had a long time to infuse into the oil and make it "saporito" (flavorful).

Heat olive oil and garlic together very slowly but do not let the garlic color. Split the sausages lengthwise and remove the casing. Break the sausage meat into small pieces and add to the pan. Cook at very low heat, stirring frequently to break up the pieces of meat. When the meat is completely cooked, add the sage leaves and set the pan aside in a warm place and cover. Let it sit until the polenta is ready.

Make the Basic Polenta - Abruzzo style. When it is finished cooking and has rested, warm a deep pasta bowl. Reheat the sausage and oil mixture. Assemble the polenta in layers in the bowl. Start with a layer of polenta. Spread some of the oil and sausage over top and sprinkle on some of the grated Parmigiano. Alternate layers of polenta, sausage and cheese. End with a layer of polenta and cheese only. Bring the big bowl to the table and serve with the remaining grated cheese and freshly milled black pepper.

Makes 6 substantial servings.

1 cup freshly grated Parmigiano

Basic Polenta - Abruzzo style, made with 1 pound cornmeal

TIP

To help make it easier to spread polenta, you can dip the spoon in some of the oil from the sausage mixture. Wet hands are the best way to pat down polenta when it is served in one large flat layer.

Polenta ai Quattro Formaggi

POLENTA LAYERED WITH FOUR CHEESES

Unsalted butter for greasing

6 cups water

2 cups milk

1 tablespoon salt

2 cups regular cornmeal

½ pound fontina cheese, cubed

½ pound gorgonzola cheese, cubed

½ pound Bel Paese cheese, cubed

¼ pound Parmigiano, freshly grated

2 to 3 tablespoons butter

Freshly ground pepper

Special Equipment: dome-lidded, 3-quart clay baker

TIP

Do not allow the polenta to sit when it is first cooked since it will become too firm and you will not be able to pour it. You can assemble the polenta and cheeses the night before and bake it next day.

This polenta dish is unique since it is baked, rather than stirred endlessly on the stovetop. Arrigo Rossi created this dish for a New Year's Eve celebration. Later it was served at a function promoting Valtelina wines at the Italian Trade Commission and got rave reviews. Other types of casserole dishes don't work as well as the unglazed, domed clay bakers because the cheeses do not melt in the same way. The container should be very damp when it is greased.

Soak a clay baker in hot water for 30 minutes. After soaking, grease the bottom and sides of clay baker with the butter.

In a saucepan, bring water, milk and salt to a boil. Gradually stir in the cornmeal. Continue stirring over low heat for about 10 minutes. Pour a layer of soft polenta in the bottom of the clay baker and cover with half the fontina, gorgonzola and Bel Paese. Dot with some butter and a few tablespoons of Parmigiano. Repeat making a total of three layers of polenta and two layers of cheese. The top layer should have only butter, Parmigiano and pepper.

Cover and bake in a 375 degree oven for 35 minutes. Remove the lid and bake for another 10 minutes. Let rest for about 5 minutes and serve in the baker.

Makes 8 servings

Polenta al Mascarpone con Spezzatino di Vitello

POLENTA WITH MASCARPONE AND STEWED VEAL

Maria Teresa Del Giudice came from the beautiful little mountain village of Pescacostanza which known for its magnificent lace work. She brought with her all the culinary traditions and continues to pursue them creating new dishes like this one out of her imagination and, of course, years of cooking experience. Both in Brooklyn where she settled for many years, and now in Staten Island, where 60% of the residents have an Italian background, Maria Teresa's accomplished cooking is widely known.

The novel way this polenta is made was a result of sheer expediency. Not being able to stand over the pot and stir for an hour, Maria Teresa applied her ingenuity and passed on this easy and hassle-free way to prepare an old classic. She often serves this creamy polenta with sauteed, seasoned greens such as rapini, swiss chard, or dandelion, or makes a one-dish meal of it with some veal spezzatino as described below.

In a heavy-bottomed pot, combine water, cornmeal and salt and stir well. Set over medium heat, uncovered. When it starts to boil, lower the heat, cover the pot and simmer for about 45 minutes. Stir the pot with a wooden spoon every 10 minutes or so during the cooking. When it has thickened and become dense, turn off the heat.

Add the Mascarpone, Parmigiano and some pepper. With an electric hand mixer, beat the polenta at high speed to incorporate the cheeses.

In a heavy-bottomed pot with a good lid, combine the meat, olive oil, butter, herbs and salt and pepper to taste. Cover tightly and simmer very slowly. The meat will give off a lot of water thus creating enough steam to cook it. If it starts to dry out during the cooking, add a little water. Simmer about 45 to 60 minutes or until tender. Just before serving, pour over the freshly squeezed lemon juice.

Makes 4 servings

8 cups cold water

2 cups coarse cornmeal

1 tablespoon butter

Salt to taste

½ cup Mascarpone cheese

3 to 4 tablespoons grated Parmigiano

Freshly ground pepper to taste

VEAL SPEZZATINO:

1 ½ pounds boneless veal shank (from pale, milk-fed veal)

1 tablespoon olive oil

½ tablespoon butter

1 sprig fresh rosemary

2 to 3 sage leaves

Salt and pepper to taste

1 lemon, juice only

Pasta and Sauces

Many Italians say they are not happy unless they have a meal of pasta at least 2 or 3 times a week - or more. Of course, the variety of shapes and textures of noodles and the multitude of sauces that can go on it make it possible to have a different pasta almost every day of the year. The fact is, though, that many families have a few favorite types of pasta and sauces and tend to stick to them, occasionally adding a new one to the repertoire. The type of sauce will vary according to the season and the menu planned.

How to match the sauce to the type of noodle is the most commonly asked question of novices to pasta cookery. There are a few guidelines that can help sort through the maze of choices. Traditionally, the flavored oil-type dressing is used mostly on long, thin dried pasta like spaghetti, spaghettini or linguine, though it will also suit short, thin pasta with a smooth texture - the "lisce" as opposed to the thicker ridged "rigate" types (e.g., Penne Lisce vs. Penne Rigate). Homemade egg pasta is very porous and will absorb too much oil. Thicker noodles, either long and hollow (Perciatelli) or short and ridged (Rigatoni), require more liquid to soak into the crevices, so tomato sauces or modified oil sauces with some tomato or cream are a better match. These thicker, sturdier noodles are also best for baked pasta (al forno).

The amount of sauce is another issue worth considering. Generally pasta is not served swimming in sauce. Because it is usually eaten as a first course and the meat or fish and vegetables as a second plate after the pasta, the chopped elements that go into the sauce should be sparse and not dominate the pasta. It is, after all, pasta you are eating, not the fish, or vegetable or meat. That does not mean that the pasta should be dry. In a dish of perfectly prepared pasta, each strand or piece of noodle should be slightly coated with sauce or dressing. A frequent error made by those not accustomed to using a lot of oil is to not put in enough.

In almost all dressings that are oil based, an important step that is often not referred to by cooks is the addition of pasta cooking water. The starchy, salted water is saved and added when the dressing and pasta are combined. This is because cooked noodles continue to cook after they are drained and will continue to absorb the liquid in the sauce or dressing. Even in tomato sauces, pasta should be dressed with sauce, allowed to sit a short while (over very, very low heat) in order for the sauce to be absorbed. Sometimes, an extra ladle or two of tomato sauce must be added before it goes to the table. When making any pasta that goes into the oven, always add a little extra sauce, or dilute your sauce with some water.

Pasta all'Uovo

BASIC EGG DOUGH FOR PASTA

4 cups unbleached, all-purpose flour

4 eggs

¼ to ½ cup water

Salt to taste (optional)

Some pasta makers insist that pasta all'uovo (egg noodles) should be made with eggs and flour and no water. Those who grew up in other regions of Italy during economic hard times sometimes added a little water to make the dough go further. There are no rigid rules about making homemade noodles apart from the essential fact that the dough must be kneaded vigorously to give it a good texture. Electric machines that spew out inadequately worked dough will create noodles lacking in body. Hand-cranked pasta machines are a convenient compromise and allow even novices to become adept very quickly. Once familiar with the proper consistency, some people find mixing the dough in a food processor and finishing it by hand a useful trick. There are even motorized pasta rolling machines for those who want to produce large quantities and find turning the crank by hand tedious.

Pasta was my favorite food as a kid - homemade pasta all'uovo in particular since we had it only on special occasions or when Ma was in the mood. After watching my mother do it so often, it looked fairly easy to me, so I nagged my mother into letting me try.

I was nine years old when I made my first attempt under her watchful eye. It was hard to keep all the eggs inside the well of flour on the big wooden board. I knew if I made a big mess, Ma wouldn't be too happy about letting me try it again, so I worked as fast as could to keep the egg from sliding outside the flour barrier. It was like making a sand fort at the beach but I felt like the juggler I had seen on the Ed Sullivan show who managed to keep 10 plates twirling on the top of poles all at one time. One false move and crash. My hands could barely go around the ball of dough made with 6 eggs. I threw my whole body into the kneading, trying to impress my mother with my mastery. "See Ma, I can do it." The rolling of the dough was another matter requiring more skill and coordination than strength. We used a very long rolling pin - a 24-inch plain dowel with no handles. The dough, once kneaded was flattened and wrapped around the wooden dowel. It was pushed and stretched into shape, turned and floured so it wouldn't stick. The big round disc - the diameter of the rolling pin - was folded in half then quartered and cut into long thin ribbons. I adored these coarse textured, slightly chewy noodles which was the chief motivation for my determination to learn how to make them. Now we could have them all the time, I thought, not just on special occasions. From my nine-year-old perspective, my first effort at making pasta was a big success, but I believe my mother must have intervened considerably to make sure that supper that night would not be ruined.

When we eventually got a pasta rolling machine, it made the whole process easier but, somehow, less special. The memory of those hand-rolled, hand-cut, grainy tagliatelle lingers. To achieve a similar texture with a hand-cranked pasta machine, it is necessary to roll the dough to a thicker setting (#5 on most machines). Flour the strips, allow them to dry until they are leathery but still malleable, then cut them by hand into uneven ribbons.

Place all the flour on a large wooden board. Make a large well in the center. Break the eggs into the well, add ¼ cup water and salt. Beat with a fork, gradually incorporating all the flour into the well. Continue working in this manner until a dough is formed. Scrape the board well, removing any unused flour and sticky bits of dough or add a little more water and knead this in. Discard this or sift it and use the excess flour for dusting the pasta later. Knead the ball of dough on a clean, lightly floured surface for about 5 minutes or until it is smooth and satiny.

Allow dough to rest, covered in plastic, for 30 minutes.
If using a hand-cranked pasta machine, cut off a quarter of the dough, keeping the rest covered. Flatten this small piece of dough and put it through the rollers of the pasta machine at the widest setting - usually 1 is the widest and 6 or 7 the thinnest. Fold the strip in half, press it together, and put it through again, folded end first. Repeat this folding and rolling at the widest setting until the strip of dough becomes smooth, free of ridges,

and feels like satin. Ideally, it should be about 3 inches wide.

To thin the dough strips, adjust the machine to the next narrower setting, roll the strip of dough through without folding it. Continue to roll band of the dough once through each subsequently narrower setting, without folding. Dust it lightly with flour before proceeding to the next setting only if it appears to be sticky. When it is at the desired thinness, lay the now elongated, widened band of dough on a lightly floured wooden board. Allow it to dry, turning it once, before cutting into long noodles. It should be dry enough that it will separate when cut, but it must still be malleable.

To make fettuccine or tagliatelle, the dough strips should be rolled to the thinnest setting. Cut the bands of dough by hand into 12-inch lengths. Starting with the cut end, put the band through the wider of the two cutting dies on the pasta machine. Lay cut pasta on a lightly floured surface until ready to cook. Proceed with the remaining dough in this manner. Cut pasta will keep, covered with a towel, for 1 hour. It starts to get brittle and hard if left longer and may stick if it is bunched together for too long.

To make stuffed pasta (like ravioli or tortellini), do not dry the dough strips. Fill the rolled out dough immediately while it is still moist enough to form a seal when the edges are pressed together.

Always count on making 1 egg's worth of pasta per person for long noodles. Only half as much dough is needed for filled pasta like tortellini and ravioli. The dough can be made ahead, covered in plastic and kept in the refrigerator up to one day before rolling and shaping. Knead the refrigerated dough on a lightly floured board before shaping.

To keep cut noodles, they can be allowed to dry completely. Since dried pasta is very fragile and brittle, it should be packed carefully in cardboard boxes (empty cereal boxes work well) and stored in a dry cupboard. Dried pasta will take longer to cook than fresh. It keeps indefinitely but is best if eaten within a couple of months.

To dry egg noodles, allow the bands of dough to dry as much as possible before cutting, but not to the point of being brittle. As each band is cut, carefully arrange the strands over thin wooden dowels (for example, broomstick handles or wooden clothes drying rack). Make sure the strands are separated. Allow them to dry to the point that they keep their bent shape, but before they become completely hard. Lift them from the dowel and place carefully on a wooden board or on brown paper to finish drying completely. Store in rigid cardboard containers.

Variations to the basic pasta recipe abound. Some exclude egg altogether in the dough. Recently, herbs and vegetables have become fashionable additions. As for the shapes, each region has developed its own peculiar methods for forming a basic dough using very simple or unusual tools and given the dough an interesting name. Whether it be a knitting needle for making "filatelle" (fusili) or a specially built guitar-like instrument called a "Chitarra" for making Maccherone alla Chitarra, or just fingers and thumbs (for orecchiette, cavatelli, pici, and strangozzi - these demonstrate the ingenuity of "la cucina casalinga" (home-style cooking). Often the dough for these rustic pasta shapes is made only with flour and water. Occasionally a small amount of egg goes in and often the flour used was of a coarser grain and from very hard wheat. Whatever the wheat used - even the soft wheat used in many North American brands - most flour will produce an acceptable dough as long as it is worked correctly and there is sufficient gluten in the flour used.

Pasta Integrale di Grano Duro

WHOLE GRAIN PASTA FROM DURUM WHEAT

One fall in Italy, I watched my cousin Anita pass brownish-beige sheets of dough through the fine cutters of her pasta machine. Ever conscious about her husband's diet and cholesterol intake, Anita told me that this pasta was much healthier and lighter as it was made without egg. She dressed it with a meatless vegetable sauce, tinged with a little tomato. The consistency is not as resilient as regular pasta all'uovo. To avoid breaking, the noodles should not be rolled to the thinnest set-

1 cup whole grain durum flour

1 ½ cup regular white flour (plus additional for dusting)

1 cup semolina

Salt to taste (optional)

1 ¼ cups warm water

ting, but cut into the wider setting (for tagliatelle) and not made excessively long (8 to 9 inches is sufficient).

Combine the flours and salt in a large bowl. Make a well in the center and start adding some warm water, mixing the flour gradually into the well with a fork. Continue to mix in water and flour until the mixture starts to form an irregular ball. Using your hands, incorporate any flour remaining in the bowl into the moist ball of dough. Set on a board, lightly dusted with regular flour and knead until the dough is smooth (about 10 minutes). Add flour only if the dough is excessively sticky. Cover with plastic and allow to rest 15 minutes before rolling and shaping.

Working with one piece of dough at a time and keeping the rest covered, flatten the dough and pass it through the pasta machine in the same manner for making regular pasta all'uovo. Roll the dough to the #5 setting on the pasta machine (or about two notches less than the thinnest setting on your machine). Allow the strips of dough to dry slightly before cutting.

Makes 4 servings.

Pasta alla Chitarra

1 ½ cup semolina flour

2 cups all purpose hard flour

2 eggs

¾ cup lukewarm water

A chitarra is a stringed instrument, resembling a harp, that is used to cut sheets of pasta into long noodles. A specialty of the Abruzzi region, it is made with a dough of hard flour and water with very little egg. When a thick sheet of dough is pressed against the wire strands, it forms a square noodle that is as thick as it is wide. These sturdy noodles are usually served with tomato sauce. Since it is unlikely you will find a chitarra unless you go to the market in Sulmona, the noodles can be cut by hand or with a pasta machine.

Combine the two flours. Beat together the eggs and water. Make a dough as for pasta all'uovo. Knead well, using only all-purpose flour for dusting the board. Cover and allow to rest.

Using a pasta machine, shape and roll the dough to the next to last setting on the machine (#5). It should be about ⅛ inch thick. Lay bands of dough on a wooden board or on brown paper to dry. Turn to dry both sides. When the pasta sheets have dried to a leathery texture, but are not brittle, flour well and stack two or three together. Cut with a pizza wheel cutter or a long, sharp knife. The strands should be as thin as they are thick. Separate the cut strands and dust lightly with flour.

If using the cutting attachment on a pasta machine, do not allow the dough to dry excessively before cutting. It should be quite malleable or it will not go through the cutters. Flour both sides well and cut with the thinner of the two dies. Flour the cut noodles and fluff them to separate the strands. Cook in the same way as pasta all'uovo.

Makes 4 servings.

NOTE

Some pasta machines are available with an additional cutting die that makes narrow but fatter noodles. It is called the die for spaghetti, but it actually creates squarish noodles, just like a chitarra does.

Pasta di Spinaci

SPINACH PASTA

Wash the spinach well and cook it until tender. Drain and allow to cool. Squeeze out the excess water with your hands. Chop the spinach very, very finely if you want a grainy, green color to the dough. Or, pass the spinach through a food mill for a darker green color. (A food processor or blender can also be used to puree the cooked spinach.)

Beat the eggs and pureed spinach together just until combined. Add salt to taste. Form the dough as for regular pasta all'uovo, adding a little more flour because of the extra moisture from the spinach.

Roll to the thinnest setting and cut into ¼ inch wide noodles (tagliatelle). Serve with Gorgonzola Sauce (p. 108) or Fresh Plum Tomato Sauce with Basil (p. 99).

Makes 6 servings

1 bunch spinach (or 10-ounce package)

4 eggs

4 to 5 cups flour

Salt

Pasta di Peperone Rosso (Red Pepper Pasta)

Roast and peel 1 pound of red peppers. Season with salt but no oil. Puree the peppers in a blender or pass through a food mill. Add 1 cup of the pureed peppers to the eggs before blending them with the flour and follow the recipe for Pasta all' Uovo.

Pasta per Orecchiette

"LITTLE EARS" PASTA

1 cup semolina flour

1 ½ cups all-purpose flour

¼ teaspoon salt

*1 cup warm water
(or more, as needed)*

1 tablespoon oil

This pasta shape is a specialty of Apulia and was not a familiar pasta to those who lived outside the region until recently. Many first- and second- generation Italians of Pugliese origin have told me they associate this pasta with memories of "Nonna" sitting at a table, flicking little morsels of dough at lightening speed. It takes some practice to do it quickly - but several hands make short work of it. Commercial, dried orecchiette are available but they don't have the same chewy texture of the homemade dough. If making these ahead, drying is not a good solution as they would take so long to cook. Freeze them on floured trays, as you would gnocchi then store in plastic freezer bags.

In a large bowl, combine all the semolina with 1 cup of regular flour and the salt. Stir in the warm water and oil. Mix vigorously with a fork, then use your hands to form the mixture into a ball of dough. The dough will feel coarse and grainy at this stage. The bowl should be quite clean as this is not a sticky dough.

Place the dough on a wooden board or counter that has been lightly dusted with all-purpose flour. Knead vigorously, adding the remaining all-purpose flour until it becomes a smooth , rather stiff ball of dough and loses its grainy texture (about 5 to 7 minutes). Allow the dough to rest covered in plastic for 30 minutes.

To shape orecchiette, remove dough from plastic and knead for a few moments with floured hands to get rid of any moisture that may have formed. Cut off small pieces of dough, keeping the rest covered as you work. Roll into a coil and cut into thin disks about the size of a thumbnail. Flour your hands well and press each disk into a cupped palm to form something resembling a little ear. The edges should be slightly thicker than the centre. Place in one layer on a floured tray. When all have been shaped, cover with a cloth till ready to cook.

These take longer to cook than regular pasta all' uova. Boil in 4 quarts of salted water for about 8 to 10 minutes or until they lose their floury texture. Most eggless pasta has a pleasantly gummy and chewy texture. Drain well and dress with sauce and grated cheese.

Traditionally, this pasta is dressed with greens and oil (see Orecchiette con Cime di Rape p. 81)

Makes 4 servings

Cavatelli di Ricotta

CAVATELLI WITH RICOTTA

1 pound ricotta cheese

1 cup water

1 egg

1 tablespoon salt

6 ½ cups flour

This is an unusual dough for cavatelli, which normally are made with flour and water. But adding ricotta is typical of the way they were done in the area around Campo Basso when Angelina Mastropietro was a child. It is a much softer, more tender dough. Making hand-shaped pasta may seem like a lot of work, but it gets easier after the first few and they can be made ahead and kept frozen. For special occasions, there's nothing like pulling several bags of these out of the freezer to have with a rich tomato sauce.

In a large bowl, beat together the ricotta cheese, water, egg and salt. Add the flour gradually, stirring it in until a dough starts to form. Place on a floured surface and knead in more flour – up to 5 ½ cups, saving the rest for shaping. The dough will feel very pliable but not too sticky. Let the dough rest, covered in plastic for one hour.

Roll out the dough with a rolling pin or press it down with your hands to form a large disc about ½ inch thick. Cut the dough into strips about the same width. Then cut these into 1-inch lengths. Flour the dough and your hands very well. Using a plastic dough scraper, make an indentation along the middle of the small strip, then roll it away pressing down as you drag it against the board. It should form a shape something like a tiny cigar with a seam down the middle. Shape all the dough in this manner. Place on a floured tray, in one layer and freeze. Once frozen, place in plastic freezer bags until ready to cook.

If cooked the same day they are made, cover the shaped cavatelli with a towel and cook them within 2 hours of when they were made in boiling, salted water for about 5 minutes. Frozen ones should not be thawed first and will take up to 10 minutes to cook. Drain and dress immediately with sauce.

Makes 6 to 8 servings

Cjalcons (Agnolotti Carnici)

FILLED PASTA WITH SMOKED RICOTTA

6 potatoes, peeled

1 onion, chopped

3 tablespoons oil

1 cup cooked spinach, squeezed dry and chopped

⅓ cup finely chopped parsley

7 ounces fresh ricotta or smoked ricotta

1 slice white bread, chopped

1 lemon, zest only

1 tablespoon mint and parsley

The sweet and savory combination of flavors in this dish may strike many as unusual but it goes back a long way. In the days when using spices, especially cloves, was a status symbol it was a tradition to make cjalcons on St. Jacob's Day in August. Adriano DeCillia's mother made them on special occasions but it's a lot of work so she would say to her son, "I'll make cjalcons only if you help me." As a result, Adriano has become an expert, perfecting the recipe over many years. There are several variations of this recipe which originates in the Carnia region, specifically the Valle Del But. Two indispensable ingredients which give it the distinctive flavor are mint and smoked ricotta (known in Friulano dialect as "scuete"). If you have a smoker, you can make your own smoked ricotta as Adriano does. There is very little demand for it commercially so local Italian cheesemakers make it only upon request. Adriano insists the taste is not the same without it, but, if it is impossible to find, he suggests using extra smoked bacon or more Parmigiano as a substitute.

Boil the potatoes and puree them through a ricer. Set aside half the puree for the dough. Cook the onion in some oil for about 5 minutes. In a bowl, combine the spinach and the next ten ingrediens for the filling. Mix well. Add some water if the mixture is too dry or more bread if it is too moist.

Place flour on a work surface, make a well in the centre and add eggs, warm water and salt. Work together to form a soft dough. Knead lightly and let it rest. Roll out the dough into a thin sheet ⅛ inch thick. Cut into disks 4 inches in diameter. Place one tablespoon of filling on each cjalcon. Brush some egg around the rim of the disc and press the edges together to seal. Fold the dough to make a half moon.

Boil about 3 to 4 quarts salted water. Add cjalcons to the boiling water; when they float to the surface, cook for three minutes, drain. Melt the butter, add whole sage leaves and toss with the cjalcons. Top with Parmigiano.

Makes 6 servings

3 tablespoons cocoa

¼ cup raisins

Pinch of cinnamon

Salt and pepper

1 tablespoon sugar

3 cups flour

2 tablespoons warm water

2 eggs

Salt

½ cup butter, melted

5 sage leaves

1 cup Parmigiano

RAVIOLI

Whenever we had ravioli, it was usually for a special occasion, like the time uncle Frank came to visit us all the way from Colorado. He hadn't seen my mother and aunts since he left the village to work in the mines in Aguilar, Colo. in the 1920's. He returned to the village every three years for months at a time, but then went back to where the money was. In the 1930's and during the Second World War, the visits stopped. Eventually, his sisters also emigrated, and since they were living on the same continent, just across the border in Canada, a visit was arranged. After a 27-year absence, the long-awaited reunion was an emotional and exciting event. The children looked forward with great anticipation to meeting our legendary American uncle who had, by this time, become a very prosperous and highly regarded Justice of the Peace in his community. He did not disappoint. There were about 15 family members at the train station to meet him. He arrived sporting a Panama hat, pale linen suit and two-tone shoes. He spotted a lovely young lady in a flowered nylon dress and thought how nice she looked. Being accustomed to doing things the American way, he promptly found a taxi and made his way to the house. No one in the welcoming party had recognized him. The sisters had grown and he didn't recognize them either or their mates. When the reunion finally occurred - though not as anticipated - the children were entranced. To us, he seemed larger than life with his suave demeanor and sophisticated American ways.

The two times he came, we prepared special meals for each day he was with us - and not making the obligatory round of visits to other relatives and "paesani." By the time of his second visit, I had already been introduced to making pasta all'uovo at the ripe age of 9. Naturally I was part of the team that got into mass producing ravioli for what seemed liked hordes of people in our tiny house. The assembly line took up all the space. Pasta sheets were laid out everywhere so there was no room to turn or set things down. But soon, this visit also came to an end and his weighty presence vanished along with the faint scent of tobacco that usually hung around him, and our days and meals went back to normal.

Ravioli di Spinaci e Ricotta

SPINACH AND RICOTTA RAVIOLI

It is most practical to make ravioli well ahead of time and freeze them. This recipe can easily be increased as long as there are plenty of hands to help. If you make a large amount, you will need to make double batches of sauce.

Drain the cooked spinach well and chop finely before measuring it. Combine all the filling ingredients and mix well. Make the dough, shape and fill following the instructions for making ravioli (p. 65).

Once the ravioli are shaped, set on floured trays, laying each one down without overlapping. Cover with towels until ready to cook or freeze. Once frozen, store in plastic freezer bags. Do not thaw them before cooking.

To cook, bring to a boil 2 large pots each with 4 to 5 quarts of water and 1 tablespoon salt. When the water is at a rolling boil, add one or two tablespoon of oil then the ravioli. Stir gently with a wooden spoon and keep pushing down the ravioli if they float above the water. Boil until the dough loses its raw texture, tasting a corner of a piece to check the consistency. (It can take from 6 to 7 minutes for freshly made and up to 10 to 12 minutes for frozen.)

When done, drain or lift out carefully into a colander. Pour a layer of sauce in a shallow pasta bowl, place the ravioli in the bowl and cover with more sauce. Turn the ravioli gently to coat them completely with the sauce. Sprinkle lots of grated cheese over top. Serve with the remaining cheese at the table.

Makes 6 to 8 servings

1 cup cooked spinach, densely packed

1 cup ricotta cheese

1 cup grated Parmigiano cheese

25 to 30 rasps freshly grated nutmeg or to taste

Salt and pepper to taste

Basic Pasta all'Uovo made with 4 eggs plus ½ cup water

8 to 10 cups Tomato Sauce with Meat p. 103 or Tomato and Sausage Sauce p. 104

½ cup grated Parmigiano or Romano cheese

Ravioli di Patate Dolci con Salvia

SWEET POTATO RAVIOLI WITH SAGE

1 cup sweet potato, cooked and mashed

5 tablespoons grated Parmigiano or grana-type cheese

4 to 5 tablespoons 18% table cream

Salt and pepper to taste

Several gratings of fresh nutmeg

2 eggs

2-3 tablespoons warm water

2 cups flour

½ cup butter

8 small, fresh sage leaves

3 slices prosciutto (3 - 4 ounces), chopped

5 to 6 tablespoons grated Parmigiano or grana-type cheese

This was first tasted in a trattoria near Bologna. In Italy it's made with a type of pumpkin called "zucca" but, according to Marcella Hazan, the Italian cooking guru who introduced me to this trattoria, our sweet potatoes are a good substitute. Mrs. Hazan did not present this recipe in the week-long cooking program I attended, but the following is my re-creation of those flavors. At the trattoria they were served with a tomato sauce but I prefer them coated with Sage Butter, lightly spiced with cooked bits of prosciutto.

Mix all the first 5 filling ingredients well and set aside, covered.

Make Pasta with the eggs, water and flour, roll out and fill as per instructions for making Ravioli (see p. 65).

Bring to a boil 3 quarts water and 1 tablespoon salt. Add the ravioli carefully to the boiling liquid. Stir and keep pushing them down into the water as they will float if air was trapped in the filling. Cook for about 10 to 12 minutes or till tender. To test, cut a small corner of the dough and taste. Drain or lift out carefully with a large, slotted spoon, place in a warmed, shallow pasta platter, and coat with the Sage Butter Dressing. Turn the ravioli very gently so they are completely coated with the butter. Serve in individual, warmed pasta plates (about 7 per serving) with lots of grated Parmesan sprinkled on top. Makes about 30 ravioli (4 servings).

Makes 4 servings

TO MAKE THE SAGE BUTTER DRESSING:

Slowly melt butter in a saucepan along with sage leaves torn into small pieces. If the butter is unsalted, add some salt to taste. Do not allow the butter to get so hot that it fries the sage. Add the chopped prosciutto and cook for 1 minute or just until it gets heated through.

HOW TO SHAPE AND FILL RAVIOLI

Make the pasta and allow it to rest, covered in plastic, for 20 minutes. Roll out into long sheets about 4 inches wide, rolling only one sheet at a time keeping the rest of the dough covered in plastic. Lay the sheet on a lightly floured surface and cut it lengthwise in half. Place 1 teaspoon of filling along one half at approximately 2-inch intervals. Work quickly so the dough does not dry out. Lay the other half over the filling, (unfloured surface down), and press gently in between and around the filling to form a good seal.

Using a ridged wheel cutter, trim lengthwise along both edges, then cut across to form ravioli about 2 x 2 ½ inches. Place on a floured tray and cover with a cloth until ready to cook.

These can be made up to 2 hours ahead but be sure the trays are well-floured as a moist filling can make the dough soggy and cause it to stick and break. Ravioli can also be frozen. Lay each one flat on a floured tray and freeze, uncovered. Once frozen, store in plastic bags. To cook, do not thaw before boiling and allow more time for cooking.

Rigatoni con Cavolfiore al Forno

BAKED RIGATONI WITH CAULIFLOWER

Frank De Francesco got this recipe from a Roman friend, Stefano Cirillo, a talented cameraman as well as an excellent cook. He has even produced his own cookbook with such exotic items as cooked nettles!

Frank's baked pasta has no such ominous-sounding ingredients. He has altered the original recipe slightly, as people often do. Some times he adds tarragon to the bechamel and he never bothers to boil the cauliflower first. This is a great dish for company since there is no last-minute fussing in the kitchen.

Heat oil in a large skillet, add minced garlic and cook. Just before the garlic turns brown, add the cauliflower and rosemary. Season with salt and pepper to taste. Cook for about 5 minutes, stirring

3 tablespoons oil

2 to 3 cloves garlic, finely chopped

½ cauliflower, trimmed and chopped into slices

1 tablespoon fresh rosemary, chopped

Salt and black pepper to taste

½ cup white wine

1 small chicken bouillon cube

Pasta and Sauces 65

1 pound dried rigatoni

2 cups bechamel sauce (see p. 104)

1 teaspoon fresh tarragon, chopped

¼ cup grated Parmigiano cheese

Several dashes paprika for garnish

continuously. Add the wine and a bouillon cube. Simmer briefly adding a little water if the mixture starts to dry out.

Add the bechamel sauce and tarragon to the cauliflower. Stir and simmer together for a few minutes to allow flavors to combine. Taste and adjust seasoning.

Boil the pasta in 4 quarts salted water. Two minutes before it is ready, drain, saving a little pasta cooking water. Combine the pasta and half the cauliflower sauce in the pasta cooking pot. Add a little pasta cooking water to help coat the pasta if necessary.

Preheat oven to 300 degrees. Butter a casserole dish large enough to hold all the pasta. Place a layer of pasta in the bottom, sprinkle with some grated cheese and spoon over a layer of the cauliflower sauce. Continue to layer pasta, cheese and sauce. Finish with cheese on top and, if desired, some paprika as garnish. Cover with foil and bake for 20 to 30 minutes at 300 degrees .

Makes 5 to 6 servings

Lasagne
Lasagna

1 tablespoon olive oil

1 lamb shank (about 1 pound)

½ onion, chopped

2 cans (32 ounces each) plum tomatoes

1 small can (5 ounces) tomato paste (optional)

2 to 3 sprigs, fresh basil

2 bay leaves

Doria Guadagnoli's cooking has changed little since she moved from the small mountain village in Italy at age 19 to the Big Apple, settling with her new husband in Brooklyn. With 4 children and now 5 grandchildren to keep her young, this energetic lady still cooks up a storm for large family gatherings. One summer when the whole clan was visiting us at our unfinished summer cottage by the lake, we all succumbed to a virulent case of food poisoning (from poorly refrigerated chicken) - except for Doria. She had abstained from the offending fowl - opting for one of the seventeen other dishes we took along to sustain us in the wilderness. Thank heavens she did as she became the nursemaid to a household full of incapacitated family and guests. Lasagna was just one of the many make-ahead foods we had that day. It was so delicious I recall eating a huge portion but the after-effects of the bad chicken kept me away from lasagna for years afterwards. Happily, the bad taste has worn off and I can eat lasagna without twinging. Doria's recipe is superb. It may seem complicated but it is done completely ahead and in easy stages so it's the ideal dish to serve to a large crowd.

Heat the oil in a large pot, add the lamb shanks and brown on all sides. Add the onion and cook briefly until the onion softens. Puree the tomatoes through a food mill and add to the pot. For a dark, dense sauce add the optional tomato paste diluted with an equal amount of water. Add the basil, bay leaves, sugar, salt and pepper to taste. Simmer partially covered for about 1 hour, stirring occasionally. Make ahead and set aside until ready to use. Remove the meat and use for another purpose. For best results, the sauce should not be too thick.

Heat the oil in a skillet, cook the garlic until it softens but does not brown. Add the ground beef, chopped parsley, salt and pepper. Cook, stirring until the meat loses its raw color. Continue to cook, breaking up the clumps of meat, until the water dries out. Add the pureed tomatoes. Simmer until the liquid reduces, about 20 minutes. It should be a very dense mixture. Taste and adjust seasoning. Set aside until ready to use.

Squeeze out excess water from cooked spinach but do not squeeze it dry. Grate the mozzarella on the coarse side of a cheese grater. Set aside about ½ cup for the topping. Combine the chopped spinach and all the cheeses with the egg to form a mushy paste.

To assemble the lasagna, spread a thin layer of tomato sauce on the bottom of the baking pan (see note below for sizes). Lay a sheet of the lasagna dough over top. Drop spoonfuls of the cheese filling over the dough. Follow with a thin layer of meat filling. Spread a few streaks of besciamella sauce over this then several streaks of the tomato sauce. Sprinkle with a little grated Parmigiano. Continue to make layers in this fashion ending with a top layer of cheese and meat and sauces. Sprinkle the reserved grated mozzarella on top and a little more Parmigiano. Cover with aluminum foil and bake in a pre-heated oven set at

½ teaspoon sugar (optional)

Salt and pepper to taste

1 tablespoon olive oil

2 cloves garlic, chopped finely

1 pound lean ground beef

3 to 4 sprigs, fresh parsley leaves, chopped

Salt and pepper to taste

1 can (32 ounces) plum tomatoes, drained, and pureed

¾ cup cooked spinach, chopped

8 ounces mozzarella cheese, grated coarsely

½ pound fresh ricotta cheese

1 egg, lightly beaten

2 to 3 tablespoons grated Parmigiano cheese

Besciamella Sauce (see p. 105)

1 package (pound) pre-cooked lasagna noodles (34 - 7 x 7 inch sheets)

¼ cup grated Parmigiano

350 for about 20 minutes. Uncover and bake for another 5 minutes more to allow the excess liquid to dry. Let the lasagna stand, out of the oven, for a few minutes before cutting.

Makes 10 - 12 servings

Pre-cooked lasagna sheets are available in Italian delis and many supermarkets. The kind Doria Guadagnoli uses are 7 x 7 inch squares and come 16 to17 sheets per package - complete with 2 oven-ready aluminum containers. If using homemade pasta you will need to make 5 eggs worth and roll it out very thinly to make enough 4 x 10 inch strips to fill a 12 x 16 inch pan. If using the dried, factory-made strips, there will be fewer layers as the dough is much thicker. Two packages of 16 strips each should be sufficient. In both cases, the strips should be boiled first until tender but still a little al dente (having some bite). Rinse the cooked lasagna strips in cold water to cool them and dry well before assembling.

Gnocchi di Patate

POTATO DUMPLINGS

2 ½ pounds old potatoes (about 5 cups, cooked and riced)

3 cups all-purpose, unbleached flour

1 teaspoon salt

1 egg

Everyone makes gnocchi throughout Italy. The slight discrepancies in how they are made are due to personal preference and regional habits. In some places egg is never added and the consistency is softer and gummier. Personally, I don't like them to stick to the roof of my mouth so I prefer the firmer consistency that results from mixing an egg into the dough.

Variations of gnocchi abound. Some add cooked, minced spinach, others mix in some ricotta. Yet others are made with different vegetables (see Gnocchi di Zucchini, p. 70) or other flour as in the semolina gnocchi popular in Rome. It may seem confusing (and unpronounceable - it sounds like /ni-oc-key/), but if you mention gnocchi, most Italians will understand you are referring to the basic potato and flour dumpling served, like pasta, with a sauce, as a first course. Gnocchi are undoubtedly one of the all-round, special occasion favorites, judging from the many people who listed them first when asked, "What do you make that is really good?" This could also be because, once you know how, they are very easy to do and can be made ahead and frozen.

The dough is very sticky and not at all like pasta dough. It should be kneaded minimally and cooked very soon after they are made or they will become gummy. The old dictum that the potatoes must be cooked whole, with the skins on, then drained and peeled is based on the theory that the less water the potatoes absorb, the better the dough. For the same reason, you are advised against using new potatoes. I have cooked the potatoes in a variety of ways – boiled whole, baked in the microwave and peeled, cut and boiled. This last method works just as well as the other two, provided the potatoes are not overcooked. They should be well drained, put back in the cooking pot and set on a warm burner for a few minutes to dry out.

Boil whole potatoes until tender. Drain, allow to dry in a colander. When cool enough to handle, peel and put through a ricer onto a floured surface.

While the potatoes are still slightly warm, spread them out on a board and cover with 2 ½ cups of the flour. Beat the egg lightly with the salt and pour over the potato and flour. Use your hands to combine the ingredients, massing them together to form a ball of dough. It may seem that it will not cohere, but it will as you keep pushing it together. The dough will feel very soft and have no elasticity. Once all the potato and flour is gathered together in a ball, lightly knead in the remaining flour, using only enough to be able to shape the gnocchi. To test this, roll a small piece of dough into a coil about ½ inch in diameter. If the coil holds its shape without breaking, the dough is ready to shape.

Flatten the ball of dough to a disk and cut into 1-inch-wide strips. Keep the dough covered with a cloth. With lightly floured hands, roll one strip into a long coil about ½ inch in diameter. (Do not flour the working surface at the beginning of this rolling process or the coil will slide and not roll). Cut the coils diagonally into 2-inch lengths. Dust the cut gnocchi generously with flour and lay carefully on a floured tray so that each one is separate. Continue shaping and cutting the remaining dough.

It is sometimes helpful to cook the gnocchi in batches because of their fragility. In this case, as the gnocchi float to the top, lift them out with a large, slotted spoon into the pasta bowl that has some sauce in the bottom. Continue cooking them in this fashion till they are all done. Dress with more sauce and some cheese.

To make ridged-shape gnocchi, roll the dough into slightly fatter coils (about ¾ inch in diameter) and cut horizontally into 1-inch lengths. Flour your hands and the gnocchi. Pick up one at a time, press it very gently but quickly against the tines of a fork, rolling it off the end to form ridges on one side and a small indentation from your fingertip on the other side.

Gnocchi must be cooked as soon as they are made. Cook just as for pasta, in 4 quarts boiling, salted water. They take only about 2 minutes, and are done when they float to the surface. Drain well, place in a pasta bowl that has some sauce in the bottom. Spoon on more sauce and some cheese and toss very gently, as they are quite fragile.

Serve gnocchi dressed with a Basic Tomato Sauce (Meat Base) (p. 103); or Tomato and Sausage Sauce (p. 104). They are also very good with Gorgonzola Sauce (p. 108) though a smaller portion may be appropriate because of the richness of cream sauces.

To freeze gnocchi, place them on a well-floured tray in one layer. Freeze until solid. Transfer frozen gnocchi into freezer bags and seal. To cook, do not thaw first. Put frozen gnocchi directly into boiling, salted water.

Gnocchi di Zucchini

ZUCCHINI DUMPLINGS

10 cups diced zucchini

½ onion, chopped

3 tablespoons butter

Salt and pepper

1 chicken bouillon cube, crumbled

2 eggs, lightly beaten

Mariucci Vatri learned to make these from her niece who has a restaurant, Ristorante al Tirasegno, in San Danielle, Friuli. They used to make them with "zucca," the big orange squash popular in Northern Italy. If you are adept at handling a piping bag, these gnocchi are not difficult to prepare. They can be made ahead and are a pleasant change from the regular potato gnocchi. It is also a good way to use up great quantities of zucchini if you happen to grow them. Zucchini is one of those vegetables that doesn't know when to stop growing. It will get bigger and bigger, if you let it, but will not be as tasty when very large. Mariucci says to put a small amount of the paste into the piping bag - enough that can be held and squeezed out with one hand, leaving the other hand free to cut off each dumpling with a knife or pair of scissors.

If the skin is tough, remove a thin layer of green skin from the zucchini, and dice finely. In a large skillet, slowly cook onion in butter until it starts to soften. Add the zucchini and season with salt and pepper. If it doesn't all fit, do this in batches. Once the zucchini starts to release some liquid, add the crumbled bouillon cube and cook for about 30 minutes or until the mixture is very soft. Pass through a food mill and let cool. There should be about 2 ½ cups.

Add beaten eggs to the zucchini mixture and mix well. Stir in the flour a little at a time until the consistency is like a thick paste but holds its shape when scooped between 2 spoons. Place a small amount of the paste in a piping bag fitted with a ½-inch plain tube.

Bring to a boil about 3 quarts of water and 2 teaspoons salt. Squeeze 1-inch lengths of the dough from the piping bag directly into the boiling water, pressing the tip of the piping bag against a knife to cut each dumpling. Squeeze out only as many as will fit comfortably in the pan. Cook for about 1 minute. When gnocchi rise to the surface, remove with a slotted spoon and place, in one layer, in a well-buttered shallow casserole.

Melt the butter very slowly with about 10 sage leaves torn into small pieces. Season with a little salt and pepper to taste. Allow the butter and sage to steep for 5 - 10 minutes and then pour over the gnocchi in the casserole. Toss gently to coat them evenly. Sprinkle the grated cheese over top and put under the broiler for about 2 minutes or until the gnocchi are quite hot and the cheese forms a nice brown crust. Serve immediately.

Makes 4 servings

2 ½ cups flour

Piping bag with ½-inch plain tube

½ cup Parmigiano cheese, grated

⅔ cup butter

10 fresh sage leaves, torn into small bits

Salt and pepper to taste

Crespelle con Ricotta e Spinaci

CREPES WITH RICOTTA AND SPINACH

1 cup flour

1 ¼ cup milk

4 large eggs

Salt and pepper to taste

Pinch of nutmeg

2 heaping tablespoons fresh parsley, finely chopped

1 to 2 tablespoons oil

2 cups ricotta cheese

⅔ cup cooked spinach, squeezed dry and chopped

½ cup grated Parmigraino

2 tablespoons bread crumbs

½ teaspoon salt

Pepper to taste

2 to 3 pinches nutmeg

2 ¼ cups mozzarella, coarsely grated

2 cups Basic Tomato Sauce (p. 100)

1 cup water

1 tablespoon butter

1 tablespoon flour

Instead of using pasta dough to enclose this rich, creamy filling, Gianni Ceschia uses a batter of egg, flour and milk cooked like a crepe, then topped with sauce the same as with cannelloni. It is a very rich, elegant dish and especially good for make-ahead occasions. Serve this on its own, instead of a pasta course, and follow with a salad of mixed greens.

You will need an 8-inch crepe pan or the equivalent, a brush for greasing the pan and a spatula. The batter must be allowed to sit, covered in the refrigerator for at least 2 hours or overnight. The crepes should be as thin as possible and will look like lacy handkerchiefs speckled a pretty green.

When assembling the crepes in overlapping layers in the baking pan, make sure each one is thoroughly coated with sauce.

In a bowl, beat together the flour, milk and eggs until well-combined. Season with salt, pepper and nutmeg. Refrigerate for 2 to 3 hours covered with plastic wrap. Stir in parsley just before cooking. Grease an 8-inch crepe pan lightly with some oil and set over high heat. When hot but not smoking, add slightly less than ¼ cup of the batter. Tilt the pan to spread the batter evenly to edges. Cook for about 1 minute or until the edges start to brown. Flip the crepe with a spatula and cook the other side. Remove from pan and set aside until ready to fill. Repeat the process, lightly brushing the pan with oil if the crepes start to stick.

If the ricotta is very moist, drain in a wire mesh colander to remove excess water. In a bowl, mix together the ricotta with the next 6 ingredients for the filling. Taste and adjust the seasoning. Add more bread crumbs if the filling appears to be too moist.

Lay one crepe on a flat surface with the parsley-speckled side facing down. Spread 1 tablespoon of mozzarella in the center keeping 2 inches around the circumference free. Put 1 heaping tablespoon of filling over the grated mozzarella. Fold the crepe in half, making sure the filling is mounded in the middle and has not spread to the top or side edges. Fold each side over the middle, overlapping them to make a pouch measuring about 4 x 4 inches. Fill all the crepes in this manner. (Some filling may be left over.)

Combine the tomato sauce and water to get a slightly thinner sauce. In a saucepan, melt the butter, add flour and cook, stirring for about 1 minute. Add the milk and cook at low heat, stirring until the sauce thickens. Season with salt, pepper and nutmeg. Stir this into the heated, thinned tomato sauce.

Spread several tablespoons of sauce over the bottom of an oven casserole large enough to contain all the filled crepes in a single layer. Lay the crepes in the casserole, folded side down, overlapping each one slightly. Spread some sauce evenly over each crepe and sprinkle the grated Parmesan over top. In a preheated oven set at 350 degrees, bake the filled crepes, uncovered, for 10 to 15 minutes or until the sauce is bubbling. Serve immediately.

Makes 15 to 16 filled crepes

1 cup milk

Salt, pepper and nutmeg to taste

¼ cup grated Parmigiano

TIP

Filled pasta dishes that have been made ahead and kept in the refrigerator will require a longer time in the oven to reheat. It is advisable to cover the baking dish with foil at the beginning to keep the pasta and sauce from drying out. To brown the top, remove the foil and set the pan under a hot broiler for about 1 minute just before serving.

DRIED PASTA

Conchiglie al Tonno e Caperi

PASTA SHELLS WITH TUNA AND CAPERS

Emilia Buscarioli made this for us one summer when she came to stay at the cottage by the lake. There wasn't much in the pantry except for some canned goods and, fortunately, there was still a jar of capers in the refrigerator. She only needed some fresh parsley which Dad always grew even in the sandy soil near the lake, so we had all that was needed. This oil-based sauce is usually served on long, thin pasta like spaghettini or linguine and without grated cheese. The tuna always falls to the

6 tablespoons olive oil

½ small onion

4 to 5 anchovy fillets, chopped

2 cloves garlic, finely chopped

1 7-ounce can tuna packed in oil

¼ cup white wine

¼ teaspoon crushed chili peppers
(optional)

1 tablespoon capers, chopped

Salt and freshly ground pepper to
taste

3 tablespoons chopped, fresh parsley

1 pound conchiglie pasta shells

NOTE

Capers are the pickled buds from the
caper shrub and come in two forms.
The smaller type, called "non-pareil,"
are considered superior and can be
used whole. The larger capers should
be chopped before adding to a sauce
as they are too intrusive if left whole.

bottom of the pasta bowl when it's on long pasta, so now I serve it more often with medium pasta shells. That way the tasty little bits of tuna and capers can lodge in the crevices. This is a handy, quick type of pasta great for impromptu meals.

In a large skillet, heat the oil and cook the onion slowly until it softens. Remove the pan from the heat and add the anchovies. Cook slowly over low heat. Add the garlic and cook until it softens but does not become colored. Add the tuna (with or without the oil in the can depending on your preference) and break it up with a fork. Cook for a few minutes until the tuna becomes a homogeneous, rather coarse texture; add the wine and optional chili peppers. Continue to cook until the wine reduces slightly. Stir in the chopped capers. Taste and season with a little salt and lots of freshly ground pepper. Add ½ cup of the pasta cooking water, to thin out the sauce should it appear dry. Stir in the parsley just before using.

In the meantime, cook the pasta shells in 4 quarts boiling, salted water. Stir occasionally to keep it from sticking. When tender, drain and immediately toss the pasta and sauce together making sure to coat the pasta well. Serve hot with more freshly ground pepper.

Makes 4 to 5 servings

Ditali e Finocchio

DITALI WITH WILD FENNEL

I was carrying my treasured wild fennel greens along to the nearby butcher where Mrs. Teresa Stalteri, upon seeing them, immediately launched into how they used to cook them in her town. She is from Reggio Calabria, the region at the very tip of the Italian peninsula and a short boat ride away from Sicily. Wild fennel grows along both coasts in great abundance. This pasta dish is so simple and clean-tasting, it needs no embellishment other than grated cheese. The slightly chewy texture of the wild fennel leaves is quite pleasant, but if that doesn't appeal to you, chop the leaves more finely.

Wash the wild fennel, trimming away the tougher stems, but reserve them for the pasta water. Drain and dry the leaves and chop finely. Bring to a boil 4 quarts salted water for the pasta, add the thin stems of fennel and cook until tender.

In the meantime, in a skillet, heat the olive oil, add the garlic and cook very slowly. When the garlic starts to color, add the chopped fennel leaves, 1 cup of the pasta water (used to cook the fennel stems), and season with salt. Cover and simmer the greens until they soften (about 3 minutes). Remove from heat.

Remove and discard the fennel stems from the pasta pot, add the ditali and cook, stirring for about 8 to 10 minutes or until tender. Drain, saving a little of the cooking liquid. Pour the pasta and sauce back in the pasta pot, and toss with a little olive oil, some pasta cooking water and several spoons of grated Romano cheese. Serve immediately with extra cheese at the table and some freshly milled pepper.

Makes 4 to 5 servings.

---

1 bunch wild fennel (4 cups, chopped finely)

3 to 4 tablespoons olive oil

2 large cloves garlic, chopped

Salt to taste

1 cup pasta water (flavored with stems from wild fennel)

1 pound ditali pasta

½ cup Pecorino Romano, grated

Freshly milled pepper

NOTE

Do not try to substitute leaves from fennel tops for the wild fennel. Those leaves may resemble wild fennel but the taste is insipid and grassy.

Fennel or "finocchio" was traditionally served around Christmas. It was cut into pieces, like celery sticks, put into ice water to get crisp and set out along with the fried fish that was customarily eaten at this time of year. When most Italians think of fennel, they picture the vegetable with a feathery top like dill and a whitish-green bulb that tastes of anise.

So when I heard Sicilians talk about its wild counterpart, I imagined the two to be interchangeable. This is not so. Wild fennel is a key ingredient in the traditional Sicilian dish "Pasta con Sarde" (Pasta with Sardines) and without it, the dish would not be the same. It grows everywhere along the coastline of Sicily where it thrives in the dry soil and the sea air. In North America, everyone I asked said you can't find wild fennel in stores. Those Sicilians fortunate enough to have acquired some seeds grow it in their back yards. Then the green, leafy herb is blanched and kept frozen.

When I finally tasted some cooked, frozen wild fennel on a dish of Pasta con Sarde, it confirmed what my Sicilian acquaintances had been saying for many years about its distinct characteristics. It has a unique blend of flavors, reminiscent of lemon, mint, fennel and perhaps dill. I was given some seeds by Mrs. Genua, who grows her own and supplied me with the frozen herb. I have passed them around to several gardeners, professional as well as home gardeners in order to be assured a small harvest and more seeds. I was anxious to experience the taste again and experiment but, alas, I had to wait for the seeds to grow before I could have more. But, the planets must have been aligned in the right way because it was very soon after I received the seeds that I happened upon a momentous discovery. This, in turn, led me to a most unexpected and fascinating hunt.

By pure chance one afternoon, I went into the small fruit and vegetable store in the center of Toronto's old "Little Italy" on College Street and saw some greens that looked like dill, but were indeed, wild fennel. My curiosity, and gluttony, compelled me to search out the grower of this uncommon herb. The hunt led to some fascinating conversations and surprising revelations.

My search led me to the Ontario Food Terminal where Joe Melara of King and Raphael Produce was extremely forthcoming - as most food people are when the conversation turns that way. Joe has been in the food wholesaling and distribution business most of his life as was his father who used a horse and cart in his hauling business in Calabria before he emigrated to the new world around 1918. After a few years in Australia, Mr. Melara senior moved on to Vancouver and Toronto where he established a grocery store and a wholesale operation. Currently, Joe's clients include large food stores, but it is mostly the small greengrocers who come to him asking for certain unusual produce which he gets for them whenever possible. The wild fennel came from Vineland, New Jersey, which is one of several sources for his produce along with Texas, Florida and, of course, California. Next stage, Vineland, N.J.

Vineland, New Jersey, sprawls for over 69 miles and has two main industries: glass and agriculture. It is the hub of distribution for many growers who bring their goods in to be auctioned off. The wild fennel was supplied by Ralph Dauito and Son who have been in the business for over 75 years. Sharon Dauito explained that Canada is a big consumer of their produce - especially Montreal and, of course, Toronto which has one of the largest Italian populations in North America. Expecting to get the name of a local grower, I was surprised to hear from Sharon that their source for wild fennel was in Virginia. Another name and phone call led me to the ultimate source.

When Mr. Leo Ayres at Jack Duer Produce picked up the phone one afternoon, I am sure he was not expecting such an unusual call. I wanted to get the name of the grower who supplied the wild fennel and, assumed it would be a person of Italian descent. Not so. "Nobody grows it," according to Leo, "it's wild so it grows on its own. It comes up along the coast. We cut about 25 or 30 boxes of it and send it up to the market in Vineland where they ship it to whoever needs it." We talked a little more about cultivating greens. "If you plant it in the field, then it wouldn't be wild any more 'cause we'd be out there tending it and fertilizing it and it would be tame," says Leo, who explained that it was the same with watercress and dandelion. Wild watercress, known as gordon crease, tasted much better than the cultivated watercress sold today. The same is true for dandelion. His yard is full of it, but when people start planting it in the field, it's not the same. Mind you, when asked if he ate dandelion greens, Leo replied with a definite, "No! As bitter as they are!" but he does make a good dandelion wine. As far as he *knows, the folks in his town use wild fennel for decorating plates and a few - "them that don't know any better" - use the wild fennel over fish. Quite an interesting coincidence considering how the Sicilians love to combine it with sardines.*

The climate of Virginia's north shore is similar to that of Sicily and Reggio Calabria. There must be other locations on both coasts where this herb grows freely, undisturbed and waiting to be appreciated by local gourmands. If so, finding bunches of wild fennel at your greengrocer every spring could become a regular event which one can look forward to with same anticipation as the first asparagus shoots or fresh cherries.

Farfalle con Fegatini di Pollo

BOW-TIE PASTA WITH CHICKEN LIVERS

¾ pound chicken livers

4 tablespoons olive oil

1 tablespoon butter

1 large red or Bermuda onion, chopped into pea-size pieces

5 to 6 sage leaves, torn or crumbled

2 to 3 sprigs thyme, crumbled leaves only

Salt and pepper to taste

½ cup port (red vermouth, dry marsala, or red wine)

½ pound dried farfalle pasta

Freshly grated Parmigiano or Grana

Inspired by a pasta tasted in a renovated 90's-style restaurant, my friends liked it so much, I decided to create my own version which adds some herbs and port. A good fall or winter dish. Rich, warm flavors. Sweetness of the onions balances the pungent flavor of the liver. For those who don't or won't eat liver, the amount of onions can be increased, and the livers may be cut into larger pieces so they can easily be removed from the abstainer's plate. Livers should not be cooked too long or they turn hard, but they must cook at high heat to brown nicely. This is a fast pasta dish and livers should be cooked only when the pasta is almost done. Red or white wine may be used in this sauce, but the port is really superb.

Trim the chicken livers and remove gristle. Cut each one into small pieces and set aside. Start boiling the water for the pasta.

In a skillet, heat oil and butter, add chopped onion and cook at medium heat till it softens. Season with salt, pepper and herbs. Continue to cook at low heat until onions are quite soft. Start cooking the pasta.

When pasta is almost ready, push onions to one side (or remove from skillet temporarily), turn the heat up and add the chicken livers. Cook briefly just until browned on all sides but still pink in the center. Season with salt and lots of pepper. Add port, return onions to pan and simmer for one minute - just until the flavors have combined. Check the seasoning. Drain the pasta, place in the skillet with the sauce and toss gently to coat the pasta well. Serve in warmed pasta bowls with grated Parmigiano and freshly ground pepper.

Makes about 3 servings

Fusilli con Carciofi

FUSILLI WITH ARTICHOKES

When several of my relatives referred to Delia Tetini's superb cooking, I hastened to contact her to find out what she does to impress them so. The answer was not hard to discover. Delia is very adept at adjusting her cooking style to new requirements. Her family eats less meat these days, so she has created interesting ways of preparing pasta with seasonal vegetables. This light dish with artichokes, and Penne with Asparagus (p. 84), are a refreshing change from the standard pasta in tomato sauce. Borrowing from a different culinary style, Delia uses a wok to cook the vegetables then tosses the cooked pasta into the wok for a brief, communal simmer - as if it were a big pasta bowl. There is only a hint of garlic in the pasta recipe below. By leaving the clove intact, it can then be easily removed for those who don't like to bite into a whole piece of garlic. Of course, for those can't bear to eat pasta without garlic, add more and chop it finely.

Trim the artichokes and cut into thin slices. Wash and cut the zucchini into matchstick slices. In a large wok, slowly cook the onion and whole garlic in 2 to 3 tablespoons of the oil. When the onion starts to wilt, add the sliced artichokes and the zucchini, season with salt and pepper and cook for about 10 minutes, stirring occasionally. Add the dissolved bouillon cube, cook another

5 small, fresh artichokes, trimmed and sliced thinly

2 small zucchini, cut into matchstick slices

1 small onion, chopped

1 clove garlic, whole

3 to 4 tablespoons olive oil

Salt and pepper to taste

1 cup frozen peas

1 chicken bouillon cube dissolved in 1 cup hot water

⅓ cup white wine

2 tablespoons fresh, chopped parsley

1 pound fusilli or shell pasta

½ cup grated Parmigiano cheese

5 minutes. Add the frozen peas and simmer until the vegetables are completely tender. Just before the sauce is finished, add the white wine and the parsley and cook another minute or two.

In the meantime, cook 1 pound of pasta in 4 quarts of boiling, salted water. Stir regularly. When the pasta is tender, drain it, saving a little of the pasta water. Toss the pasta into the wok with the vegetables. Pour the remaining olive oil over top and add a little pasta cooking water. Over low heat, cook together just long enough for the pasta to absorb the flavors. Serve immediately with some freshly grated Parmigiano at the table.

Makes 4 to 5 servings.

NOTE ON HOW TO TRIM ARTICHOKES

Artichokes come in sizes ranging from very small to large; the small ones are about the size of limes and the largest ones about the size of grapefruits. In both cases, the tough outer leaves, stem and tips must be discarded. It will seem like a lot of waste, but these parts are quite inedible. Very small artichokes do not have a choke in the center to worry about, so they may be simply sliced and cooked once they have been trimmed. The larger ones have a purplish-yellow feathery choke in the center which should be scraped away. As soon as an artichoke is cut, it will start to discolor. To prevent this, rub the cut parts with the exposed part of half a lemon, or dip the artichoke in lemon water.

Orecchiette con Cimo di Rape

"LITTLE EARS" PASTA WITH RAPINI

Though Andrea Stucovitz considers himself a born and bred "Romano," he loves this pasta which his "nonna pugliese" (grandmother from Apulia) used to make. Nowadays, few people make their own hand-shaped orecchiette (see p. 58) and use commercially made dried varieties which are available in many Italian grocery stores. If your store does not carry them, the rapini dressing works very well on ridged shell pasta. The cavities in the shells are perfect for capturing the savory greens.

Trim the tough ends from the rapini stalks and discard. If the stalks are thick, they can be peeled and boiled along with the rapini tops. Wash the rapini in several rinses of cold water to remove all the sand. Cook, uncovered, in 3 to 4 quarts of lightly salted, boiling water, making sure to keep pushing the greens down into the water if they float above the water as they boil.

When the rapini is tender (after about 10 minutes), remove with a slotted spoon and drain. Keep the cooking water to boil the pasta, adding more water and salt to make up 4 quarts. When greens have cooled, squeeze out the excess water and chop coarsely.

Heat oil and chopped anchovies slowly in a large skillet. Stir to dissolve the anchovies. Add garlic and cook till lightly colored. Add the chopped cooked greens cooking only long enough for the flavors to combine. Taste for salt.

Cook pasta in the boiling, salted greens water. When tender, drain well and immediately toss with the greens and oil mixture to coat the pasta well. Stir in several spoons of the grated cheese. Serve in individual rimmed soup bowls or in a large, warmed pasta bowl with extra grated cheese and freshly milled black pepper.

Makes 4 to 6 servings

2 bunches rapini (4 cups cooked)

½ cup olive oil

8 anchovy filets, chopped

2 cloves garlic, minced

Salt to taste

1 pound dried orecchiette pasta

¾ cup grated Grana or Crotonese cheese

NOTE

Leftovers of this pasta can be reheated very successfully (some think it tastes even better). Heat a little oil in a heavy skillet, sprinkle a little more cheese on the leftover pasta and fry, stirring, but allowing the pasta to form crispy bits.

Papardelle con Sugo di Fagiano

PAPARDELLE WITH PHEASANT SAUCE

1 pheasant (2 to 3 pounds)

3 tablespoons olive oil

½ onion, finely chopped

2 ounces pancetta, cubed

1 small carrot, finely chopped

1 celery stalk, finely chopped

1 clove garlic, minced

2 tablespoons parsley, finely chopped

1 cup white wine

3 cups chicken broth

Salt and pepper

1 pound papardelle pasta

½ cup grated Parmigiano

Elisa Nenis Ceschia taught her son all about good food. He is now a chef/caterer to a wide community of Italians and he still uses some of his mother's recipes like this one. Farm-raised pheasant are more readily available now, so you don't have to go on a hunting trip to get them. The sauce can be used on fettuccine and gnocchi as well.

Skin the pheasant removing all the fat. Cut into small pieces, wash and dry with paper towels. Heat the oil in a large pan, add the onion and cook for about 5 minutes. Add the pancetta, carrot, celery, garlic and 1 tablespoon of parsley and cook for about 5 minutes. Add the pheasant and brown about 10 minutes. Add the white wine, scrape up the browned bits and cook for 5 minutes. Add 2 cups of the broth and simmer at a low heat, covered, for about 1 hour or until tender. Remove the pheasant from the pan and allow to cool. Pass the cooking liquid and vegetables through a foodmill, return to the pan, add the remaining chicken broth and cook for about 15 minutes or until the liquid thickens. Add more broth if the liquid dries up.

Once the pheasant is cool, remove the meat from the bones and cut into medium-size chunks. Add the meat to the sauce and cook for another 5 minutes. Add the remaining parsley and season with salt and pepper to taste.

Bring to a boil 4 quarts of lightly salted water and cook the papardelle until al dente. Drain well and combine with the sauce in the pan. Toss the pasta and sauce together until well combined. Serve immediately with the Parmigiano at the table.

Makes 4 to 6 servings

Pasta con Sarde

PASTA WITH SARDINES

This is a uniquely Sicilian specialty not found in other regions. The one essential ingredient, apart from sardines, is a fresh herb known as wild fennel which is not available in many supermarkets. It seems that everyone who uses it grows their own from seeds carried over by friends or relatives. Some cooks who make this recipe use canned sauce imported from Italy called Condimento per Pasta con Le Sarde. Mrs. Roselina Genua, who is originally from Trapani, very kindly supplied me with the recipe, some seeds and some blanched, frozen herb so I could taste what the pasta should be like.

There are other versions of this dish, but this fairly simple method with tomato is the most common among the expatriate Sicilians. Mrs. Genua, of course, uses her own very dense, bottled plum tomatoes. Generally, it is much easier to find frozen, whole sardines than the fresh ones. Since sardines are very popular in Portugal, I have found the flash-frozen, Portuguese brands to be very good though it is best to use fresh when they are available.

Wash whole sardines under running water and remove the scales. Gut the sardines, discarding the innards. Bone the fish, reserving the head and backbone, and discard all the other tiny bones along the sides and fins. Rinse the reserved fish heads and backbones well. Place in a pot with the cold water and salt to taste and simmer for 5 minutes. Strain the broth through a fine mesh sieve, discard the fish heads and bones. Stir the optional saffron into the broth.

Cook the fresh wild fennel briefly in some boiling, salted water (use the pasta water). Drain, squeeze it dry and chop finely. In a deep skillet, fry the onion in the olive oil. Once it softens, add the sardine broth, pureed tomato, tomato paste, salt and pepper. Simmer for about 10 to 15 minutes. Add the chopped sardines and the wild fennel and simmer for about 3 minutes. If the sauce appears too thick, add a little more pasta water.

6 whole sardines, (¾ pound) fresh or frozen

1 ½ cups water

Salt to taste

2 packages powdered saffron (optional)

1 large bunch fresh wild fennel, or ¼ cup frozen, chopped

1 small onion, chopped

4 tablespoons olive oil

2 ½ cups imported canned plum tomatoes, pureed through a food mill

1 teaspoon tomato paste

1 teaspoon salt (or to taste)

Pepper to taste

¼ cup plain bread crumbs

1 tablespoon sugar

1 tablespoon oil

1 pound spaghetti (or linguine)

In a separate skillet, toast the bread crumbs mixed with the sugar in hot oil until it becomes lightly colored. Set aside.

Cook the spaghetti in 4 quarts of boiling, salted water until tender. Drain and mix the spaghetti and sauce in the pasta pot. Mix thoroughly to coat the pasta well. Toss in half the toasted bread crumbs. Serve in individual plates or in a large pasta platter with the remaining toasted bread crumbs and the pepper mill at the table.

Makes 4 to 5 servings

Penne con Asparagi

PENNE WITH ASPARAGUS

*2 bunches asparagus
(about 2 pounds)*

1 ½ cups water

Salt to taste

1 medium onion, chopped

1 clove garlic, whole

3 tablespoons olive oil

1 tablespoon butter

*½ teaspoon crushed chili flakes
(optional)*

*1 pound dried, short pasta: penne,
gemelle, mezze ziti*

½ cup grated Pecorino Romano

Freshly milled black pepper to taste

Remove the tough ends of the asparagus and discard. Peel the asparagus stalks from the tip down. Cut off the tips and set aside. Cook the peeled stalks in just enough boiling, salted water to cover them. Boil until they are quite tender, about 5 to 7 minutes. Puree the cooked stalks along with about 1 cup of the cooking liquid in a blender or food processor, or pass through a food mill. Save the rest of the cooking liquid in case it is needed later.

In a skillet, cook the onion and whole garlic in 2 tablespoons of the oil and all the butter. Season with some salt and the optional chili flakes. When the onion starts to soften, add the asparagus tips, cook briefly just until the tips are tender. Add the pureed stalks to the skillet and mix to combine. Turn off heat until the pasta is ready. Just before using, drizzle a little bit of uncooked olive oil over the sauce.

In the meantime, cook pasta in 4 quarts of boiling, salted water, stirring regularly. When the pasta is tender, drain well and combine with the asparagus sauce. Stir in a few spoons of the grated cheese. Serve immediately with the remaining cheese and the pepper mill at the table.

Makes 4 to 5 servings

Spaghetti Integrali con Porcini

WHOLE WHEAT SPAGHETTI WITH PORCINI MUSHROOMS

The increased awareness of the importance of fibre in a healthy diet has prompted several pasta manufacturers to introduce a line of whole grain pasta. The imported brands, made from whole grain durum wheat, give the pasta a firm texture unlike the whole wheat noodles sold in bulk. The lack of gluten in regular whole wheat noodles causes them to break into pieces and turn into a heavy sludge when cooked. Of the imported whole grain pasta, spaghettini and linguine have the most pleasing texture, in my opinion

What to put on whole wheat noodles is an interesting question. Tomato is definitely not popular among my family and friends. However, the slightly nutty taste of whole wheat goes well with the earthy flavor of porcini mushrooms. Whole wheat noodles are very compatible with oriental flavorings - a little soya sauce, sesame oil, ginger, stir fried vegetables. But that recipe can go in another book.

Soak the dried porcini mushrooms in the boiling water for 20 minutes or until they are completely soft. Scoop out the mushroom pieces, rinse briefly and chop. Strain the mushroom soaking liquid through a sieve lined with a damp paper towel to remove all sand.

In a deep skillet, heat 3 tablespoons of the oil and 1 tablespoon of butter. Add the shallots and cook at medium heat until they start to wilt. Add the garlic and cook 1 minute more. Add the strained mushroom broth, season with salt and pepper. Simmer until the liquid has reduced almost by half. Remove from heat.

In another skillet, heat 2 tablespoons of the oil and 1 tablespoon of butter. Add the sliced mushrooms, season with salt and saute at high heat for about 4 minutes. When nicely colored all around, add the cooked mushrooms (including any fat) to the skillet with the porcini. Set aside until the pasta is ready. Reheat, adding the remaining butter and a little more olive oil, if necessary.

4 packages (1 ½ ounces) dried porcini mushrooms

2 cups boiling water

4 to 5 tablespoons oil

3 tablespoons butter

3 tablespoons shallots, chopped

1 clove garlic, minced

Salt and freshly milled pepper to taste

½ pound fresh mushrooms, washed, dried and sliced

1 pound whole grain spaghetti or linguine

½ cup grated Parmigiano cheese

Cook the whole wheat pasta in 4 quarts of boiling, salted water. Stir regularly, and taste to determine when the noodles are done to your liking. Drain, reserving a little of the pasta water. Combine the drained pasta and the mushrooms sauce, mixing well to coat the pasta. Add a few spoons of the pasta cooking water to help spread the sauce. Toss with some grated Parmigiano. Serve immediately in warmed pasta bowls.

Makes 4 to 5 servings

Spaghettini con Aglio e Olio

SPAGHETTINI WITH GARLIC AND OIL

1 pound spaghettini

½ cup extra virgin olive oil

3 cloves fresh garlic, finely chopped

1 small dried chili pepper, chopped in half (optional)

Salt to taste

3 tablespoons soft butter

½ cup grated Pecorino Romano or Parmigiano (optional)

Freshly ground black pepper

The simplicity of this dressing for dried pasta makes it a perfect late night or last-minute meal. It is also the basis for a multitude of variations both cooked and raw. Simple though it appears, there are ways in which it can be ruined. Here are some tips for preparing a perfect Aglio e Olio: be generous with the oil - too little won't coat the noodles and give enough flavor. Besides, the excess oil just stays at the bottom of the serving bowl; cook the garlic (whether crushed or in pieces) very slowly so it flavors the oil but does not burn. You can let it get a bit crisp, as long as it does not go black; use a good quality, dried pasta as the texture of the noodles will be very noticeable since there is not much to mask it. The same goes for the oil and cheese; warm the pasta serving bowl and plates, as oil-based sauces cool down very quickly; and finally, as you lift the dressed pasta out of the serving bowl, allow a moment or two for the oil to drip down the ends of the strands.

Heat oil and garlic very slowly in a skillet. Add the optional chili pepper, and salt to taste. When the garlic has flavored the oil and is lightly colored remove from heat. If it appears the garlic is getting too dark, add a few tablespoons of pasta water.

Cook the pasta in 4 quarts of water for approximately 10 to 12 minutes. Drain the pasta, reserving some of the water, toss with butter in a warm serving bowl and pour the hot oil and garlic on top. Toss pasta well to coat evenly, adding some freshly ground pepper. Serve immediately in warmed pasta bowls with the pepper mill and some grated Romano cheese at the table.

Makes 4 to 5 servings

Fettuccine col Borgonzola e Curry

RIBBON PASTA WITH CURRIED BORGONZOLA SAUCE

No, it is not a spelling error. Borgonzola is a specialty cheese created at Quality Cheese by William Borgo and his father Amerigo who produce some of the finest fresh cheeses in their part of the world. Borgonzola has some of the features of Gorgonzola in that it is a cow's milk cheese pierced to allow blue veins to form. But as it is cured, it becomes veiled in a smooth white mold which prevents the yellowing and surface degeneration - and the resulting waste - that occurs with Gorgonzola. The taste is milder and the texture firmer. If you can't find Borgonzola, you can substitute an equal amount of gorgonzola combined with cream cheese.

Bill told me he had been trying out East Indian cooking and had a jar of curry powder around so he decided to put some on this creamy cheese sauce. His kids love it so much they keep asking for him to make it. It does seem to be popular with the young set judging from the response of my 11-year-old nephew who ate it with great gusto.

Start boiling 4 quarts salted water for pasta. In a large deep skillet, heat the oil and slowly cook the onion. When it starts to soften, add the garlic and curry. Stir and cook until the onion and garlic are quite soft but not brown. Add the cream and salt, simmer for a few minutes. Break up the cheese into chunks and add to the skillet. Cook at a low heat, stirring, to melt the cheese. Add the skim milk and some of the pasta water to thin the sauce a little. Do not boil after this point. Keep warm until the pasta is ready.

¼ cup olive oil

1 medium yellow onion, chopped

1 clove garlic, minced

2 teaspoons medium curry powder

1 cup whipping cream

¼ teaspoon salt

6 to 8 ounces Borgonzola cheese or cheese mixture

½ cup skim milk

3 to 4 tablespoons grated Parmigiano

1 pound ribbon pasta like fettuccine or papardelle

In the meantime, cook the pasta. When it is tender, drain it, saving a little of the cooking liquid in case it is needed to thin the sauce. Combine the pasta and sauce in the skillet. Toss gently over very low heat just until the pasta is well coated. If the sauce seems too thick, add a little more of the pasta water. Stir in the Parmigiano. Serve immediately.

Makes 4 to 5 servings

Personal Profile of a Cheesemaker

Amerigo Borgo is a cheesemaker from around Bassano in the Veneto area. This is near Asiago – a town that has given its name to a wonderful cheese. When he emigrated to North America in 1954 it was because being a cheesemaker was a "poor profession." Walking up the mountain every day to the farm, bringing the cows down for the winter and being tied to the cheese production 7 days a week was a hard life. Fortunately for the other Italians who emigrated in the mid and late 1950's, he returned to his original profession, cheesemaking. There are definitely no mountains to contend with for cheesemakers in Southern Ontario apart from those of financial risk and the hurdles of starting a licensed establishment that conforms to the many regulations of the concerned government agencies. Amerigo and his partner were the first to manufacture fresh ricotta cheese and distribute it to major centers in Southern Ontario where the burgeoning enclaves of Italians stretched from Thunder Bay to Windsor and Toronto.

Linguine con Gamberi

LINGUINE WITH SAFFRON CREAM AND SHRIMP

Powdered saffron in small packages can replace the more costly saffron threads. Both can be found in most Italian delicatessens and grocery stores and in many bulk food stores. Betty Vetere-Laskey says you can leave the shrimp whole, chop or slice them lengthwise, as you wish. There are not a lot of shrimp, but remember, you are eating pasta flavored with seafood not shrimps with a starch filler!

In a heavy skillet, melt butter over medium heat, add garlic and parsley and shrimp. Saute briefly just until the shrimp barely turns pink. Remove the shrimp with a slotted spoon and set aside.

Add whipping cream to the skillet. Season with salt and pepper. Cook, stirring constantly, until the cream thickens. Stir in the saffron diluted in 2 tablespoons of pasta water. Taste and adjust the seasoning.

Cook pasta in 4 quarts boiling, salted water. When the pasta is cooked al dente, drain in a colander set over a small pot. Save 1 to 2 cups of the pasta water. Toss the pasta gently with the sauce in the skillet. Set over very low heat, stirring, for about one minute to allow the pasta to absorb the sauce. Add the shrimp and some of the cooking water to thin the sauce. Sprinkle on the optional Parmigiano. Serve immediately in warmed pasta bowls.

Makes 4 to 5 servings

½ stick unsalted butter (2 ounces)

1 large garlic clove, minced

1 tablespoon parsley, chopped

10 large shrimp, peeled and deveined

1 cup whipping cream, room temperature

Salt and freshly ground black pepper to taste

1 teaspoon saffron threads (or 2 packages powdered)

1 pound dried linguine or thin fettuccine

¼ cup grated Parmigiano cheese (optional)

TIP

To extract the most flavor out of shrimp, keep the shells and make a broth with them and 2 cups water, 1 tablespoon oil, ½ tablespoon butter, salt and pepper to taste, and a dash of cayenne. Bring to a boil, lower heat and simmer till the liquid is reduced by half. Strain well. Add the flavored broth (about ⅔ cup) to the sauce. It's even better if you get whole shrimps with the heads on them. Cook the heads along with the shells. Strain the resulting broth through a sieve lined with dampened paper towels to get rid of any sand.

Penne alla Ricotta

PENNE WITH FRESH RICOTTA

1 pound dried penne or bow-tie pasta

1 pound fresh ricotta, drained (2 cups)

¼ cup flavored olive oil

1 clove garlic, minced (if not using flavored oil)

1 tablespoon dried herbs: oregano, basil and/or sage

½ teaspoon salt (or to taste)

Black pepper to taste

¼ teaspoon crushed, dried chili (optional)

½ cup pasta cooking water

⅓ cup grated Parmigiano or grana-type cheese

Amerigo Borgo described what he and his staff whipped up for lunch one day after a fresh batch of still-warm ricotta was made. The sauce is light and nutritious and requires no cooking. It can be spiced up with seasoned olive oil or you can use plain olive oil and add some extra herbs and garlic to taste. They sometimes use a little a bit of pesto instead of herbs. It is unlikely that you will find ricotta so fresh it is still warm, unless, of course, you can get to Amerigo's cheese factory and retail outlet at the right time. The recipe below has been adapted slightly. Be sure to use fresh ricotta that has a soft, lumpy texture not the smooth, homogenized varieties.

Flavored olive oils are available at Italian delicatessens and gourmet food shops. To make your own, see p. 256

Start cooking the pasta in 4 quarts of salted, boiling water. In a large pasta bowl, place the drained ricotta, the flavored oil, herbs, salt, pepper and optional crushed chili pepper. Mash the cheese and seasonings together to form a thick puree, evenly spiced.

Just before the pasta is ready, stir ½ cup of the pasta cooking liquid into the seasoned cheese mixture to heat it through. Drain the pasta and toss it with the cheese mixture in the pasta bowl, adding the grated grana or Parmigiano cheese. Serve immediately with a little extra grated cheese and freshly milled black pepper.

Makes 4 to 5 servings

Ricotta, *which means "cooked again," is made by heating the whey produced as a by-product of cheesemaking, particularly mozzarella and provolone. When the whey is heated, the protein solids are pulled out and form small soft curds which are separated from the liquid and pressed together. Ricotta has all the nutritional value of the aged cheeses and a lot less fat. (There are only 7.9 grams of fat per 100 grams for ricotta made from partly skimmed milk compared to 30 grams per 100 for Monterey Jack. Creamed cottage cheese has 4.5 grams per 100.) Ricotta is prevalent throughout Italy but particularly in the south where the "pasta filata" cheeses like mozzarella, provolone, cacio cavallo and scamorzze are predominant. Since it is cheaper to make than other cheeses, yet equally high in nutritional value, it became a great source of nourishment for the poor. Ricotta has a slightly sweet, milky taste and will absorb whatever flavors are around it. For this reason, it makes a good filling, whether sweet or savory, when combined with other spices and flavors. It should be stored well-covered in the refrigerator and spooned out with a clean spoon whenever you dip into it to keep it from spoiling prematurely.*

Rigatoni alla Positano

RIGATONI PASTA POSITANO STYLE

Andrea Stuckovitz, a young film apprentice on a temporary work sojourn in Toronto, spoke gushingly about this fabulous zucchini and cream pasta. He first tasted it in Positano, a gorgeous fishing town on the Amalfi coast. His version uses Gorgonzola instead of the goat cheese used in the original version. Either way, it is delicious. If neither Gorgonzola or goat cheese can be obtained, try Roquefort or blue cheese. This sauce goes best on a ridged pasta like penne or small rigatoni. The mixing of olive oil, cream and tomato is not as unusual as might be thought. The oil should be light and fruity. The cream, although rich, is diluted by the vegetable juices and milk. The tomato helps color the sauce a lovely salmon shade. Use fresh tomatoes only if very ripe, otherwise the imported, canned tomatoes are preferable.

½ Spanish onion, chopped

2 tablespoons olive oil

5 to 6 dried sage leaves, crumbled

Salt and pepper to taste

½ pound mushrooms, cleaned and sliced

2 medium zucchinis, halved lengthwise and sliced

½ cup dry white wine

2 to 3 plum tomatoes, skinned, seeded and chopped

1 cup whipping cream

⅓ cup milk

6 to 8 ounces Gorgonzola

1 pound dried rigatoni or penne pasta

In a very large skillet or wok big enough to hold all the pasta and sauce, cook onion in oil until it starts to soften. Season with salt, pepper and the dried sage leaves. Add mushrooms and turn up heat. Cook, stirring frequently, until the mushrooms release their juice and start to brown. Add zucchini, season with salt and cook at high heat, stirring.

When nicely colored, add the wine. Cook for one minute and add the chopped tomatoes. Simmer briefly. Add the cream and milk and bring to a boil. Lower heat and add the Gorgonzola broken in little bits. Cook just until the cheese melts. Taste for salt.

Cook pasta in 4 quarts boiling, salted water, stirring occasionally. When tender (approximately 12 to 15 minutes), drain and place in the pan with the sauce. Toss the pasta and sauce together gently in the large pan over very low heat for about 1 minute so pasta has a chance to absorb the sauce. Serve immediately in warmed, rimmed soup bowls. No extra cheese is needed, but if you wish, you may serve some Parmesan on the side along with freshly ground pepper.

Makes 4 to 5 servings

Trenette col Pesto

CURLY PASTA WITH CREAMY PESTO

1 pound trenette, spaghetti or linguine

2 tablespoons butter

1 tablespoon oil

2 cloves garlic, minced

½ cup heavy cream

salt to taste

Names of various dried pastas can be confusing. Ligurians customarily put pesto on homemade long thin pasta called "trenette." The dried, commercial pasta by the same name is a long, thin, wavy ribbon that looks attractive and makes a plain sauce appear interesting. Other types of long, curly pasta which I adored as a child were called mafalda and yolanda - named, according to my mother, after two Italian princesses who both had long, braided hair. Since there is no standard appellation for pasta, (like the DOC for wine) names and shapes change and fall into disuse. Short pasta shapes - as long as they are not too thick - are also compatible with creamy pesto but sometimes, one gets the urge to eat pasta that must be twirled. At those times, short noodles simply don't satisfy.

In a deep skillet, large enough to contain all the pasta, heat butter and oil and gently cook the garlic until it starts to soften. Add the cream and salt, bring to a boil and simmer till sauce starts to thicken.

In the meantime, cook pasta in 4 quarts of boiling, salted water. When the pasta is almost ready, add about ½ cup pasta cooking water into the garlic cream. Stir in the pesto but do not cook it. Drain the pasta, reserving a little more cooking water in case it is needed to thin the sauce later.   Place drained noodles in the skillet with the sauce and toss gently over very low heat just until they are thoroughly coated and the sauce has soaked in a bit. Toss in some grated Parmigiano and a few spoons of toasted pine nuts. Add a little more pasta cooking water, if necessary, to extend the sauce as it is absorbed. Serve immediately in warmed pasta bowls with some extra Parmigiano and whole toasted pine nuts sprinkled over top.

Makes 4 to 5 servings

½ cup pasta cooking water

⅔ cup pesto (see p. 105)

½ cup grated Parmigiano cheese

⅔ cup pine nuts, lightly toasted

Bucatini alla Siciliana

BAKED PASTA WITH EGGPLANT AND PEPPERS

If one could travel back in time, an event I would choose to relive is a meal eaten in an open-air restaurant in Paestum, due south of the Amalfi coast in Campania. We sat under a canopy of umbrella pines in full view of the two beautifully preserved temples of this ancient Greek colony. This was one of those rare occasions when the memory of a dish lingers and is talked about for years and years. "Remember Paestum and the Bucatini and the fresh figs..." We can recreate the taste but not the experience. It must be thick, hollow pasta which has had time to swell as it absorbs the sauce. Rigatoni and penne rigate are also good for this baked dish.

1 large eggplant

2 red bell peppers, seeded and sliced

3 to 4 tablespoons olive oil

2 cloves garlic, chopped

Salt to taste

6 cups Tomato and Eggplant sauce (p.101)

1 pound dried hollow pasta like bucatini or perciatelli

¼ cup freshly grated Pecorino Romano or Crotonese cheese

Peel the eggplant, cut into 1-inch slices, sprinkle each slice with salt and place in a colander; cover with a plate and weight it so the liquid from the eggplant will drain. Leave for about 1 hour. Dry the eggplant slices and cut into cubes. In a large skillet, cook the eggplant and peppers, separately, in oil. Season with garlic and salt and fry until all the vegetables are cooked through and soft.

Heat the tomato and eggplant sauce. Combine half the cooked eggplant and peppers with the sauce. Simmer together for about 10 minutes or until the flavors are blended, taste and adjust seasoning. Reserve the remaining vegetables.

Cook bucatini in plenty of boiling, salted water. Drain and toss together with some of the sauce and a little grated cheese so that the pasta is well coated.

Place a layer of the sauce in a terracotta casserole. Add some bucatini, more sauce, some grated cheese and some of the reserved vegetables. Continue to form layers. Cover and bake in a pre-heated oven set at 350 degrees for about 10 minutes (if ingredients are warm), or 35 minutes (if ingredients are cold). This is best if made early in the day or the day ahead.

Makes 4 to 5 servings

Farfalle all' Aglio, Olio e Pomodori Secchi

BOW-TIE PASTA WITH SUNDRIED TOMATOES

Though Italians, particularly those from the sun-drenched south, were familiar with dried tomatoes, this specialty food was not widely available in North America until the early 1980's. When they were first introduced, their popularity went beyond reasonable use, according to one importer of Italian specialty foods. "People were putting dried tomatoes on everything even if it didn't go together!" Over-exposure can turn people off but this has not been the case. Sales have been steadily increasing every year since the fad died down and now, sundried tomatoes have found a permanent place on grocery shelves. They come in various forms. Some are sold loose in bags. The ones packed in oil with herbs and seasonings are meant to be eaten as an antipasto with bread. As with many "new" products, there are variations in quality. Look for ones that are not loaded with salted and still slightly plump. They are available in Italian cheese and grocery stores and specialty food shops.

In a heavy-bottomed skillet (not cast-iron), cook minced garlic gently in oil. Before it starts to color, add the chopped dried tomatoes, water and the crushed chili peppers. Simmer until the dried tomatoes have softened and most of the water has evaporated. Add the chopped tomatoes, the tomato paste and salt. Simmer for 5 to 8 minutes or until the sauce thickens slightly. Taste and adjust seasoning.

Cook the pasta in 4 quarts boiling, salted water, stirring occasionally. When tender, drain the pasta, dress with the sauce and some of the grated cheese. Toss pasta, sauce and cheese together so that the pasta is well coated. Serve immediately in warmed pasta bowls with the remaining cheese at the table along with some freshly milled pepper.

Makes 4 to 5 servings

2 cloves garlic, minced

½ cup olive oil

½ cup dried tomatoes, chopped

¼ cup water

½ teaspoon crushed, dried chili peppers

1 cup fresh or canned tomatoes, peeled, seeded and chopped

1 teaspoon tomato paste

¼ teaspoon salt (or to taste)

½ cup grated Crotonese or Pecorino Romano cheese

1 pound dried farfalle pasta

Freshly milled pepper

Spaghettini con Vongole e Pomodoro

SPAGHETTINI WITH CLAMS AND TOMATO

1 28-ounce can imported plum tomatoes

½ cup oil (half olive, half corn oil)

1 small onion, finely chopped

1 clove garlic, finely chopped

Salt and pepper to taste

1 cup baby clams (5 ounce can), including broth

2 small celery leaves, chopped (optional)

2 tablespoons fresh parsley

1 pound dried spaghettini or linguine

OPTIONAL GARNISH

Just before pasta is finished cooking, steam 12 clams in 1 cup water. As soon as clams open, remove from pan, rinsing them in the cooking liquid to remove any sand. Before dressing the pasta, set aside several tablespoons of clam sauce. Serve the sauced pasta in individual bowls and garnish with a spoon of extra sauce on top and 2 steamed clams in the shell.

A quick, convenient meal can be made using pasta and canned clams. If you want to dress it up, decorate the plate with some fresh clams. Mrs. Dametto uses her own bottled tomatoes which have been cooked with herbs and seasonings. This slightly adapted version uses good quality, imported plum tomatoes. You can remove seeds and chop coarsely for a chunkier texture or pass the tomatoes through a food mill to obtain a smoother sauce.

Puree the tomatoes through a food mill, or for a chunkier texture, reserve some of the tomato pulp and chop it coarsely.

In a deep skillet, heat the oil and gently cook the onion and garlic seasoned with a little salt and pepper. Once the onion has softened, add the broth from the canned clams and boil until the liquid is reduced by half. Add the pureed tomatoes, ½ teaspoon salt, and simmer for 15 minutes, stirring occasionally. Add the celery leaves, if desired, and half the parsley. Continue to simmer gently until the sauce thickens and oil floats to the surface (about another 10 minutes). Add the clams and the remaining parsley just before using sauce on the pasta.

Cook pasta in 4 quarts water with 1 tablespoon salt, stirring regularly. When done to your likeness, drain and combine the pasta and the clam sauce in the same skillet or the pasta cooking pot. Set over very low heat and toss, allowing the pasta to absorb sauce for a few moments before serving. Serve in warmed pasta bowls with freshly ground pepper on the side. Grated cheese is not ordinarily used on seafood pasta.

Makes 6 servings

SAUCES FOR PASTA

ABOUT TOMATOES AND TOMATO PASTE

Sabina Masci described how her mother, my great aunt, used to make her own "conserva" when the tomato harvest came in. She would use the upstairs porch which got lots of sun. Was the climate in Toronto hotter in those days? Fresh tomatoes were ground and the puree was set on big boards and covered with netting to keep the flies off. It was stirred and eventually became quite dense as it dehydrated through exposure to the sun. It's not a process many modern cooks will be motivated to try but in the early 1920's, it was more of a necessity. "Stores didn't carry all the canned stuff we have today so we pretty much had to make everything from scratch," Sabina says of the "old days."

These days, we can buy tomatoes in many different forms. There are whole plum tomatoes packed in juice; chopped plum tomatoes with no added puree; crushed tomatoes with added puree; tomato paste in tiny cans or in tubes; there is the strained, concentrated tomato puree called "passato di pomodoro" which comes either in vacuum boxes or bottles. Stewed tomatoes, not the plum type, are also found in large cans. But which form should one use?

Canned, whole plum tomatoes packed in juice are the closest thing to fresh or home preserved, provided they are ripe and soft. North American brands usually add a firming agent (calcium chloride) which keeps the tomatoes from breaking down - in fact, unless they are chopped or pureed, they will remain whole for a very long time as they cook. These tomatoes also tend to be under-ripe and watery so, in this case, adding some tomato paste can be a useful thing. Imported brands have only salt and tomato juice added and make a sweeter, thicker sauce.

Canned tomatoes with added puree are generally loaded with tomato paste and can be quite bitter. The colour is dark red and the result is a very thick sauce that clings to the pasta. But the aftertastes can be unpleasant. Many people like the thick, dark sauce and add sugar to compensate for the bitterness. I usually avoid this type.

Canned stewed tomatoes, if they are not the plum variety, have a lot more seeds and are very juicy. These can be pureed through a food mill to remove the seeds and cooked a little longer until they reach the desired consistency.

Passato di pomodoro is extremely smooth, and resembles a very thick tomato juice. Some of the excess water has been removed but it is not as bitter as tomato paste. Nor does it thicken sauces as much as paste. It can be added to watery tomatoes, or to cream sauces when a tomato-cream sauce is desired. When small amounts of tomato are needed in meat or fish recipes, passato di pomodoro can be very handy. Use it either full strength or slightly diluted.

Commercial paste can be bitter if overused. I once watched with silent horror when a woman I knew poured four cans of tomato paste and some water into a pot expecting it to turn into a sauce for the lovely fettuccine I had just shown her how to make. She had the notion that the paste was just like the big cans of plum tomatoes - and a lot easier to carry - all you had to do was add water. That was many years ago and I am sure it is not what she would do today. But it shows some of the misconceptions people had about tomato sauce.

Tomato paste should never be used as a substitute for good, plum tomatoes. Small amounts of tomato paste can be very useful in some recipes as long as one observes certain guidelines and uses the right proportions. If used in moderation and diluted with some water or tomato juice, it can add a depth of color to a sauce and give it a velvety texture. Also, if only watery plum tomatoes are available, the use of a little tomato paste will enrich the tomato sauce without overpowering it - as long as the sauce is made with other flavorful ingredients like meats and sweet vegetables that are first cooked slowly in oil.

When cooking a large amount of meat in a pot of tomato sauce it may be necessary to add water along with the plum tomatoes in order to cover the meat. This extends the cooking time for the meat long enough for it to become tender without reducing the tomatoes excessively. In this case tomato paste will help flavor the extra liquid and give it body. Sometimes, just a small spoon of paste with a bit of water can be added to give color and smoothness to an oil sauce for pasta.

To enrich a tomato sauce with some tomato paste, the proportions are as follows: for each 35 - ounce can of whole, plum tomatoes (28 ounces net), add 1 to 2 tablespoons of paste dissolved in ¼ cup of water. Add this at the same time as the canned tomatoes, which have been pureed or chopped, after the meat or vegetable base has been cooked and thoroughly flavored the oil. Do not add paste to canned tomatoes that have added puree.

Salsa di Pomodoro e Basilico

FRESH PLUM TOMATO AND BASIL SAUCE

On my first visit to Italy one August, many years ago, I was surprised that my cousin, Palma, decided to make a tomato sauce when it was only twenty minutes or so before their usual lunch time. The fresh plum tomatoes she had just purchased were so ripe, they easily passed through the food mill and were simmered briefly with some oil, garlic and fresh basil. The resulting sauce was light and barely coated the pasta. It was just perfect for a hot summer meal. When fresh tomatoes are in season, this quickly cooked sauce is fast and delicious on most types of dried pasta (see also Green Beans in Fresh Tomato Sauce p. 175)

Wash the tomatoes and cut into quarters removing the tough core and any blemished parts. Puree through a food mill. If the tomatoes are not sufficiently ripe, place the quartered tomatoes in a noncorrosive pan and cook at low heat until they soften. Then puree them through a food mill.

In a deep skillet, heat the olive oil and cook the onion so that it softens without browning. Add the garlic and cook briefly. Add the pureed fresh tomato and season with salt and the optional celery leaf or lovage. Simmer for about 10 minutes. Add the basil, torn into little bits, taste and adjust the seasoning if necessary. Simmer another 2 to 3 minutes. Allow the sauce to rest a few minutes before using it on pasta.

Makes about 3 cups

2 quarts very ripe plum tomatoes (3 pounds)

⅓ cup extra virgin olive oil

½ small, yellow cooking onion, chopped

1 clove fresh garlic, chopped

¼ teaspoon salt (or to taste)

1 sprig celery leaf or fresh lovage

5 to 6 large, fresh basil leaves

Salsa di Pomodoro

MEATLESS TOMATO SAUCE

4 tablespoons butter

1 teaspoon oil

1 small onion, finely chopped

1 small carrot, peeled and finely chopped

1 celery stalk, finely chopped

½ teaspoon salt (or to taste)

1 28-ounce can imported plum tomatoes

Of the many varieties of tomato sauces, this meatless one is particularly suited to being combined with cream or white sauce and used on pasta with ricotta cheese fillings. It can also be a base for other sauces or made into a tomato/cream sauce with the simple addition of whipping cream. The method of pureeing the tomatoes after they have been simmered with the vegetables makes it a very dense sauce which may need to be thinned with water or broth before using.

In a deep skillet or saucepan, melt butter and oil and slowly cook onion, carrot and celery. Season lightly with a little salt to draw out the moisture. Cook for 7 to 8 minutes or until the vegetables have softened but not browned.

Chop tomatoes coarsely, add to the pan and simmer, partially covered for 25 - 30 minutes or until the tomatoes have disintegrated and absorbed the flavors. If a thinner sauce is needed, add 1 cup water along with the tomatoes at the beginning of the simmering.

Remove the sauce from the heat and let stand for 15 to 20 minutes. Puree everything through a food mill. Use the sauce as is on dried, short pasta like penne or farfalle (butterfly-shaped pasta), on tortellini or ravioli, or, as a base for other sauces.

Makes 2 ½ - 3 cups

Salsa di Pomodoro e Melanzane

TOMATO AND EGGPLANT SAUCE

In every restaurant and trattorie in Sicily, you will find pasta with this sauce listed on the menu. It is essential to the dish called "Bucatini all Siciliana." According to Richard Dauito, a Florida-based produce wholesaler whose distribution network extends into the northeastern States and Canada, there is a growing interest in Sicilian eggplant. This is a pale, round variety that has a more delicate pulp and fewer seeds than the dark purple, oval shaped eggplant we are more accustomed to. Either one is suitable for this sauce. When buying eggplant, choose ones that are firm and not overripe as they will have fewer seeds and brown spots on the inside.

1 large eggplant

1 to 2 tablespoons salt (or as needed)

5 to 6 tablespoons olive oil

1 small onion, finely chopped

1 clove garlic, minced

2 28-ounce cans plum tomatoes

1 teaspoon dried oregano

Peel and slice the eggplant. Sprinkle each slice with salt and place in a colander with a weighted plate over top to help drain away excess liquid. Leave for a least 1 hour. Dry the eggplant, squeezing out the excess liquid with a towel. Cut the slices into cubes.

Heat the oil in a large pot, add the eggplant cubes and cook, stirring for several minutes. Add the chopped onion, season with a little salt and cook at medium heat until the vegetables become soft. Add the garlic and cook 1 or 2 minutes.

Remove the tough core from the canned tomatoes and chop finely. Add the tomatoes, including the juice, to the vegetables in the pot. Season with oregano and salt to taste (about 2 teaspoons). Simmer, partially covered for about 40 minutes, stirring occasionally. Puree the tomatoes and vegetables through a food mill. Taste and adjust the seasoning and consistency, adding a little more salt, oil and water if needed. (For a baked pasta, the sauce should be neither too thick nor too watery.) Use it on dried pasta (Bucatini alla Siciliana p. 93), or baked stuffed pasta (Cannelloni with Eggplant).

Makes approximately 6 cups

Salsa di Carne tipo Bolognese

BOLOGNESE STYLE MEAT SAUCE

1 onion, finely chopped

3 tablespoons olive oil

3 tablespoons butter

¾ pound ground veal

¼ pound ground pork

Salt and pepper to taste

4 cups plum tomatoes, seeded and chopped

½ cup red wine

1 cup meat broth (see p. 22)

This is Mrs. Mariucci Vatri's version of that very famous meat sauce which, over the years, was invariably teamed with spaghetti. It became such an established combination that many people (except Italians) still refer to it as spaghetti sauce. In fact, it goes well on many shapes and types of pasta. Though it may have originated in Bologna, every Italian household now makes their own version of it. In southern Italy, there might be a stronger tomato presence and butter would be omitted. Some people use only veal or beef. Others like to add other vegetables like carrot, celery and mushrooms.

This one is from the Friuli region. Mrs. Vatri likes to cook it a long time as she prefers a very dense sauce. She advises that the meat be well-browned before adding other ingredients. Although her sauce is made with her own bottled tomatoes, you can substitute canned plum tomatoes from Italy. This sauce goes well on baked pasta like Lasagna (p. 66) It suits short pasta like penne and bowties, and it is also good with gnocchi and cavatelli.

Cook the onion in the oil and butter for about 5 minutes, then add the ground meat. Season with salt and pepper and brown thoroughly, stirring continuously.

Once the meat is no longer pink, add the tomatoes and cook for about 10 minutes. Add the wine and broth, season again and bring to a boil. Reduce the heat, cover and simmer very slowly for 2 ½ to 3 hours. When sauce has finished cooking remove from heat and let stand for a while before using on pasta.

Makes enough for 1 pound of pasta

Sugo di Pomodoro e Carne

BASIC TOMATO SAUCE WITH MEAT

When Mrs. Elvira Severino's family raves about her pasta, the presence of her own home-canned tomatoes in the sauce makes all the difference. Good quality, imported plum tomatoes can be substituted and will make a very pleasing sauce though it won't be quite like hers.

You can use other cuts of meat such as lamb or kid shoulder as long as there is some bone attached, according to Elvira. She also sometimes puts in some whiskey or beer instead of the white wine. This sauce is good on any pasta, whether dried or homemade egg pasta. It freezes well, too, so you may as well make a large quantity. Pure olive oil is fine for a long-cooked sauce like this one, and often she uses a mixture of pure olive and vegetable oil.

If you have not bottled your own tomatoes, you can substitute three 28-ounce cans of imported plum tomatoes, pureed through a food mill and add 2 tablespoons tomato paste mixed in ½ cup water.

Wash the meat, drain and dry well. In a large pot, heat oil and brown the meat on all sides. (If using dried herbs, put them in now.) When the meat is nicely colored, add the onion and garlic. Season with a little salt and pepper and cook, stirring, until the onion softens and is slightly colored. Add the wine and allow it to boil briefly. Add the pureed tomatoes, season again with salt to taste. Simmer, partially covered, for about 45 minutes, stirring occasionally. Add the fresh herbs and continue to cook at a low heat for another 20 to 25 minutes or until the meat is completely tender and the sauce has thickened. Allow the sauce to sit with the heat turned off for 1 hour or longer. Better still, make it 1 day ahead.

Just before using on pasta, reheat the sauce. To make spooning out the sauce easier, remove the meat, which can be served as part of the second course. Keep it warm and covered so it will not dry out. This sauce can be used on any type of pasta. It is especially good on long, curly pasta like mafalda, trenette or long spirals.

Makes enough for 2 pounds of pasta

2 pounds veal and pork (shoulder, neck bones, etc.) cut into chunks

5 to 6 tablespoons oil (half vegetable, half olive)

1 medium onion, finely chopped

1 clove garlic, finely chopped

Salt and pepper to taste

½ cup dry white wine

3 quarts home-bottled plum tomatoes

1 tablespoon chopped, fresh parsley

1 teaspoon each, fresh or dried rosemary and thyme, leaves only

Sugo di Pomodoro e Salsicce

TOMATO SAUCE WITH SAUSAGE

3 to 4 sweet Italian sausages (about 1 pound)

3 tablespoons oil

2 chunks pork neck bones (optional)

1 small yellow onion, chopped

1 small carrot, chopped

½ stalk celery, chopped

2 28-ounce cans plum tomatoes, imported from Italy

1 small dried red chili pepper

1 sprig fresh rosemary leaves, chopped

3 fresh or dried sage leaves, torn or crumbled

Salt to taste

Classic meat sauce has little tomato in it and is very thick and pale. The one we always made was pourable and had a lot more tomato in proportion to loose meat. It was especially good on gnocchi and on short, dried pasta like rigatoni which was sauced, layered in a casserole with mozzarella and baked. To add texture, some of the tomato pulp can be chopped instead of pureed through the food mill. Occasionally, cooked mushrooms were thrown in as well.

Remove casings from sausages and cut the sausage meat into chunks. In a large pot, heat oil and cook sausage meat, stirring till it releases most of its fat. If desired, add the pork bones and brown. Add the chopped vegetables and cook, stirring, until they soften.

Remove the seeds from 3 or 4 tomatoes and chop coarsely. Puree the rest of the tomatoes through a food mill. Add the pureed tomatoes and chopped tomatoes to the pot with the meat and vegetables. Add the chili pepper, half the herbs and some salt to taste. Simmer, partially covered, stirring occasionally for about 40 minutes. Add remaining herbs. Taste for salt. Cook another 10 minutes or until the sauce reaches the desired thickness.

Allow to sit off the heat for 1 hour for the flavors to mellow. Reheat sauce. Remove the optional pork bones before using the sauce on pasta. Serve over Potato Gnocchi (p. 68) or with baked short pasta, like fusilli, rigatoni or penne. Leftover sauce keeps up to 1 week in the refrigerator or much longer in the freezer.

Substitutions: If Italian sausages are not available, use 1 pound ground pork seasoned with salt, pepper and chopped fresh garlic to taste. Increase the quantity of herbs used.

Makes about 6 cups of sauce

Salsa Besciamella

BASIC BECHAMEL SAUCE

There are many baked dishes that call for this basic white sauce sometimes called Balsamella. The consistency will depend on how the sauce is being used. For a medium consistency sauce, follow the proportions below. The sauce can be made thicker by increasing the amount of flour and butter per cup of milk.

Melt butter in a heavy saucepan. Add the flour and cook briefly, stirring. Do not let the butter and flour brown. Add the milk, all at once, stir until smooth. Season with salt and pepper to taste and the optional nutmeg. Cook, stirring until the sauce becomes smooth and thickens.

Makes 1 cup sauce

1 ½ tablespoons butter

1 ½ tablespoons flour

1 cup cold milk

Salt and pepper to taste

Pinch nutmeg (optional)

TIP

To get a fuller flavor you can scald the milk and let it infuse with some onion, a bay leaf and a few peppercorns for 10 to 15 minutes. Strain the milk. Allow the cooked flour and butter to cool before adding the hot, seasoned milk.

Pesto alla Genovese

BASIL AND OIL SAUCE

More than twenty years ago, after a long, tedious drive in snarled traffic crossing the border from France at the Mont Cenis pass, my companions and I arrived at dusk in Torino. Tired, hungry and irritable from being cooped up all day, we managed to find rooms in an albergo with a pleasantly appointed dining salon. Praying it was not too late to get a good plate of hot pasta, the waiter informed us that unfortunately the kitchen had closed and he could only offer us cold cuts. Our disappointed looks caused him to take pity on us so he agreed to bring a simple plate of spaghetti. We waited patiently while it was being cooked, and in no time, were presented with a steaming plate of spaghetti speckled with green. No red sauce! Our surprise and initial disappointment gave way to contented bliss as we had our first whiff and taste of the heavenly basil and oil tinged pasta which so many people know about and love.

2 cups fresh basil leaves, densely packed

¼ cup pine nuts, lightly toasted

½ teaspoon salt

2 large cloves garlic, coarsely chopped

½ cup light olive oil

2 tablespoons butter

½ cup freshly grated Parmigiano cheese (or a combination of Parmigiano and Pecorino Romano)

Before pesto became known in North America, it was chiefly a Ligurian specialty - this region being noted for the abundance of herbs that grow in its temperate climate. As travellers brought back new ideas, and returning immigrants sampled dishes outside their regional repertoire, more and more new sauces made their way into North American kitchens. These days, pesto has become commonplace on restaurant menus. It is being made with other herbs and greens and even with dried tomatoes and olives. Purists from Liguria might protest, but change and adaptability is the way of world.

Though it is best when fresh, making big batches when basil is inexpensive and storing pesto in the freezer or in jars of oil is a practical way to enjoy it all year round.

Pick basil leaves off the stems. Carefully wash the leaves in cool water to remove sand and dry thoroughly in a lettuce spinner or with paper towels.

In a food processor: combine the basil, pine nuts, salt and garlic. Pulse till most of the leaves are chopped. Start adding the oil, gradually blending it in until the mixture becomes a smooth paste. If using the pesto immediately, blend in the butter and cheeses and taste for salt.

In a blender: grind the pine nuts and garlic separately. Place a few of the basil leaves with a small amount of oil and some of the salt in the bottom of the blender. Blend until the mixture becomes a paste. Add the remaining basil leaves gradually, along with the remaining oil. Mix in the ground pine nuts and garlic, the butter and grated cheese. Taste for salt.

In a mortar and pestle: make half the recipe but do not decrease the oil. Crush the garlic, pine nuts and salt in the mortar until a paste is formed. Gradually add some torn up basil leaves and continue to mash. Continue adding leaves until you have the desired amount of paste. Beat in the oil gradually.

To serve on pasta, use about one heaping tablespoon per serving. Cook pasta al dente. Before draining the pasta, remove a cup or so of the salted cooking water. Add a few tablespoons of water to the pesto to heat it up along with a little more oil. Drain the pasta and place in a warm serving bowl. Toss the pasta with some soft butter to make spreading of the pesto easier. Pour the pesto over the pasta and toss well to spread it evenly. Sprinkle on some extra grated Parmigiano or Romano cheese. Serve immediately in warm bowls.

Makes 1 ¼ cups

How to Store Pesto

Pesto may be stored for several months in the freezer. When making pesto to be frozen or stored, it is better to omit the butter and cheeses. These should be added after the pesto has thawed or just before it is to be used. Make small packages of pesto for freezing (about ⅔ cup). For even smaller amounts, freeze pesto in ice cube trays, and keep the frozen cubes in plastic freezer bags.

You can also store pesto in jars covered with oil. Fill sterilized 1-cup mason jars with pesto to within 1 inch of the top. Pour over good olive oil and seal. Jars must be kept in the fridge and will last 3 to 4 weeks if undisturbed. As soon as the jar is dipped into, however, it runs the risk of forming mold on top and should be finished within a few days.

Salsa di Gorgonzola

GORGONZOLA SAUCE

4 tablespoons butter

½ pound gorgonzola cheese

¼ cup dry white wine

1 cup heavy cream

Salt to taste

½ cup freshly grated Parmigiano cheese

2 tablespoons chopped, fresh parsley

As one friend wisely noted: "Gorgonzola is a cheese you can forgive for having such a strong smell." Not everyone can get past the first impression this blue-veined, soft cheese makes. But once tasted, it has converted many. Do not substitute gorgonzola blends (for example, Torta or Cambozola) as the flavor is not sufficiently pronounced when diluted with cream. Serve gorgonzola sauce over gnocchi or with spinach pasta. It is very rich so the pasta portions can be smaller. Remember to save some of the starchy pasta cooking water to thing the sauce as it soaks into the cooked pasta.

In a deep, heavy-bottomed skillet, large enough to hold the pasta, melt the butter at low heat. Add the gorgonzola in pieces (after removing the wrapping and crust). Allow it to melt at very low heat. Stir in the wine and the cream. Bring to a boil, season with a little salt and simmer briefly.

Start cooking pasta in boiling, salted water. When the pasta is almost done, add to the sauce 2 tablespoons of Parmigiano and some of the boiling, salted pasta water to thin out the sauce, if necessary.

When the pasta is ready, stir in the parsley and a little more Parmigiano. Allow pasta and sauce to sit briefly together so the sauce can be absorbed. Serve immediately in warmed pasta plates.

If using this sauce on gnocchi, toss them very gently when mixing with the sauce as gnocchi are quite fragile. Do not allow them to overcook.

Makes enough for 4 to 5 servings of pasta

Meats, Poultry and Game

Bollito di Manzo

BOILED MEAT

2 pounds beef brisket (with bone)

2 to 3 cups dry red wine

2 whole onions, peeled

2 stalks celery

2 large carrots, peeled

1 veal tongue (about 2 pounds)

½ chicken

2 pound piece lamb or veal shoulder

2 bay leaves

5 to 6 whole black peppercorns

2 to 3 tablespoons salt

This seemingly simple yet full-flavored dish is part of a typical Christmas meal for Andrea Sucovitz and his family. It is started two days before which means fewer last-minute preparations on Christmas Day. Using a variety of meats gives the broth a full flavor and provides the stock for the first course which was typically an elegant broth with meat-filled tortellini. The beef should be a substantial cut with a bone to keep it from falling apart. Either chuck or shoulder can be substituted. Tongue is a very moist, tender meat with a creamy texture, but many people will not try it. You can leave it out and substitute more veal. This may seem like a lot of meat, but, leftovers are always nice to have around. Cold, boiled meat makes delicious sandwiches especially when eaten with Green Sauce (p. 259) Mustard Mayonnaise Sauce (p. 257) or Horseradish Cream Sauce (p. 258).

Two days before, marinate the beef in the red wine for 12 hours. The next day, fill a very large stock pot with cold water (check to make sure that when the meat is added the water will not overflow). Add all the vegetables and bring to a boil. Boil for 15 to 20 minutes.

Remove beef from marinade and pat dry with paper towel. Place all the meat in the boiling liquid. When the water returns to a boil, reduce heat and skim off any froth that rises to the surface. Add the bay leaves, peppercorns and salt and continue to simmer at a very low heat.

After about 1 hour, taste the broth, adding more salt if needed. (Remember saltiness intensifies as liquid reduces.) Continue to simmer another 30 minutes or until the chicken is very tender but still not falling off the bone. Remove chicken and keep it covered. Continue to cook and remove the various pieces of meat as they become tender. It may take up to 3 to 4 hours of very low simmering. Keep the meat covered and moistened with broth.

When the tongue is cooked, remove from the broth and peel away the skin. Cut off and discard the gristly part at the base and an inch or two from the tip. Keep with the other meats.

When all the meat has finished cooking and been removed, strain the broth through a very fine wire mesh strainer. Discard the cooked vegetables. Ladle some broth over the meat to keep it moist. Cover and refrigerate until ready to serve. Store the remaining strained broth in a tall container in the refrigerator overnight. The next day, remove the solidified layer of fat at the top.

To serve the bollito it is easiest to slice the meat thinly when it is cold. Remove any fat, gristle and bone from the beef. Cut it into thin slices against the grain. Similarly, slice the tongue very thinly crosswise. Trim the chicken and lamb and cut into serving size pieces or slices. Arrange the meat on a large, low oven casserole. Spoon several ladles of degreased broth over the meat so it is almost covered. Cover the casserole with foil and place in the oven at 350 degrees for 30 minutes or until completely heated through. Uncover and serve the steaming meat directly from the casserole with sauces.

Makes 8 servings

Brassato di Manzo al Vino Rosso

RUMP OF BEEF IN RED WINE

A great recipe for beef lovers! It is important to use a cut of meat that is marbled with fat and can be tied up. Inner rump works best but bottom round and chuck are also suitable. If prepared the night before and allowed to cool completely, the meat becomes very easy to slice. It can also be served as soon as it is made, but the meat when cut comes out as chunks instead of neater slices. The pot it is cooked in should be only big enough to hold the meat and vegetables so the liquid will cover half the meat. It makes a great winter meal served with mashed potatoes and your choice of vegetables. For a multi-course meal, serve a light soup or brodo to start.

3 pounds beef inner rump, tied in a loaf shape

2 to 3 cloves garlic, cut into chunks

4 ounces pancetta, cubed

2 sprigs fresh rosemary

5 fresh sage leaves, torn

Salt and pepper to taste

3 tablespoons butter

2 tablespoons oil

2 cups red wine

1 cup water

1 large onion cut into four pieces

1 carrot, cut into large chunks

2 celery stalks, cut into large pieces

3 to 4 ripe plum tomatoes, peeled and seeded

Pierce the meat in spots and stuff each hole with little bits of garlic, rosemary, sage and ½ of the pancetta. Season with pepper, place the meat in a covered dish and let stand in the fridge for several hours or overnight. Let meat come to room temperature for 2 hours before cooking.

In a heavy pot, melt the butter, add the oil and the rest of the pancetta. Cook till the pancetta starts to release its fat. Add the meat, and brown on all sides.

Add red wine and cook for a few minutes, then the water, onion, carrot, celery, peeled tomatoes and remaining garlic. Cover and simmer for three hours at a low heat. After 2 hours, season with about ½ teaspoon salt. Turn the meat occasionally.

When a fork pierced into the meat goes in easily, remove the meat from the pan and let it cool. Strain the vegetables (save the cooking liquid) and pass through a foodmill. You may want to remove the pieces of pancetta to puree the mixture more easily. Add 2 ½ cups of the cooking liquid to a pan with the vegetable puree. Check seasoning and cook until you obtain a smooth sauce. The remaining cooking liquid can be saved for other uses.

Cut the meat into ¼-inch slices. In an ovenproof serving platter, spoon some of the vegetable sauce on the bottom, arrange the sliced meat over the sauce and spread the remaining sauce on top. Reheat in the oven at 350 degrees for about 10 minutes or till warm. Garnish with fresh parsley if desired.

Makes 8 servings

Coste in "Fonghet"

RIBS BRAISED WITH LEEK

"Fonghet" is a dialect term from Friuli and refers to a cooking method that makes a sauce of butter, leeks, tomato or tomato paste and some water or broth. When the meat is braised in this mixture, the result is a very rich, flavorful sauce which begs to be sopped up by polenta or good crusty bread. Use only back ribs and cut them into smallish portions as a little serving of this is all you need.

Cut the ribs into serving size pieces, (about 2 ribs per piece). Wash and drain. Place in a large, deep pot and cook at high heat for about 10 minutes until they dry and they start to brown in their own fat. Remove from pan.

In the same skillet, add butter and cook garlic, leeks, onion and half the parsley, seasoned with salt and pepper. Stir and cook until soft. Return ribs to the pan, add the tomato paste that has been dissolved in the broth or water. The liquid should reach about halfway up the meat. Season lightly with salt and pepper to taste.

Bring to a boil, then reduce heat, cover and simmer very slowly for about 45 minutes. Stir and turn ribs to color them all around. Add the remaining parsley 10 minutes before the end. Check seasoning. Allow the meat to rest a few minutes before serving. Serve piping hot with polenta or crusty bread followed by a crisp green salad.

Makes 4 servings

2 pounds pork back ribs

3 tablespoons butter

2 cloves garlic, crushed

3 leeks, white part only, finely chopped

½ onion, chopped coarsely

½ cup fresh parsley, chopped

2 teaspoons tomato paste

1 ½ cups broth (or water)

Salt and pepper to taste

Ossobuco con Salsa di Verdura

BRAISED VEAL SHANK

4 large veal shanks

⅓ cup flour

3 tablespoons butter

2 tablespoons olive oil

1 cup white wine

1 tablespoon tomato paste, diluted in

⅓ cup warm water

1 small Spanish onion, cut into eight pieces

1 clove garlic, minced

1 carrot, diced

1 celery stalk, diced

4 fresh (or canned) tomatoes, peeled, seeded and chopped

2 tablespoons parsley, finely chopped

½ cup of chicken broth

Salt and pepper to taste

For this ossobuco which is cooked on top of the stove instead of in the oven, the veal shanks should be cut into 1-inch thick slices. Ossobuco means bone with a hole and refers to the thick centre bone containing the delicious marrow which should be eaten with a little spoon. You can also use beef shanks which are larger and take longer to cook. Occasionally you might find it helpful to tie a string around the meat to keep it from falling apart once it becomes very tender. Traditionally it is served with either plain boiled rice or, with Risotto Milanese (see p. 37).

Make four small cuts around the outside skin of the veal shanks to prevent the meat from curling. (To help keep their shape, you can tie some string around them.) Dip shanks in flour on all sides, shaking off excess flour.

In a skillet large enough to hold all the meat and vegetables, heat the oil and butter and brown the veal on both sides. Add one cup of wine and the diluted tomato paste and cook, covered, for 15 minutes at medium heat. Add the onion, garlic, carrot, celery, tomatoes and parsley and continue cooking for about 20 minutes. Turn the meat, season with salt and pepper, add the remaining wine and the broth and continue cooking for about 40 minutes.

When the meat is completely tender remove from the pan. Pass the vegetables and the cooking juices through a foodmill, return to the pan and cook for 15 minutes or until reduced to a smooth sauce. Place the meat over the sauce and cook at a medium heat for 5 minutes or just until the meat warms up.

Makes 4 servings

Polpette di Carne

BASIC MEATBALL MIXTURE

In a large bowl, combine all the ingredients, squashing them together vigorously with your hands until everything is evenly blended. Set the seasoned meat aside for a few hours, or mix it the day ahead to allow the meat to absorb flavors.

To make meatballs for a tomato sauce: shape into balls about 1 ½ inches in diameter. Moisten hands with a little water to help form neat, firm balls. The meatballs can be fried in some of the oil used in making the tomato sauce (see p. 100) or roasted in the oven for 15 minutes then added to the sauce.

Makes 12 to 15 meatballs

To make tiny meatballs for soups: you will only need about half the above quantity to make 30 tiny meatballs; the rest can be shaped into patties and kept frozen. Form tiny balls about the size of marbles. Use moistened hands to keep the meat from sticking. Fry very gently in a little oil till cooked through but not dried out. Drain on paper towels and add to a soup.

2 ½ pounds ground veal (or veal and pork)

2 eggs

2 cups bread crumbs

3 cloves fresh garlic, minced

2 tablespoons fresh parsley, chopped

2 tablespoons grated Romano cheese

1 tablespoon oil

Salt and pepper to taste

½ teaspoon dried, crushed chili peppers (optional)

Polpettine Piccanti

SPICY APPETIZER MEATBALLS

To make small meatballs suitable for serving as part of an antipasto or hors d'oeuvre, proceed with the recipe for Basic Meatballs.

Mix well. Let stand a couple of hours before shaping into balls 1 inch in diameter. Fry in a little hot oil until well browned all around. Drain on paper towels and serve hot.

Makes 25 to 30 small meatballs.

Add:

1 teaspoon dried oregano

½ teaspoon cinnamon

½ teaspoon dried, crushed chili peppers (or to taste)

Pinch of grated nutmeg

Meatballs

Every Saturday after grocery shopping, came the ritual of preparing the ground meat for making meatballs for Sunday dinner. Even if another meat like veal cutlets or roasted chicken was to be served, meatballs almost always went into the tomato sauce which we invariably made for pasta after Sunday mass. Seasoning the meat the day before made it especially tasty and whatever didn't go into the sauce, was made into meat patties and fried or used as a filling for pasta or vegetables. In North American style Italian cooking, meatballs (especially combined with spaghetti) became such a cliche that they now rarely appear on restaurant menus. Yet, in home cooking, meatballs have never fallen out of favor.

Meatballs go back a long way to the days of the sumptuous banquets of the early Renaissance. Overwhelming amounts of food and hundreds of courses showed off the power and wealth of the household. As the diners never finished all that was laid before them, the result was a surplus of leftovers. With no means of refrigeration to keep such large quantities, the household staff and minions used the surfeit meat and vegetables to make "polpette" and "polpettone" (small and large meatballs) as well as fillings for ravioli and tortellini. Eventually this everyday fare made its way to the tables of the masters of the house. In modern day Italians in North America, different attitudes towards "polpette" are revealed in the following two individuals' responses.

"Nobody could afford to buy meat in those days in our village in the 30's and 40's. It was only people like Zi' Angiolina and Zi' Riccuccio who made polpette. They had a thriving wine business and acted as brokers to many "forestieri" (outsiders) who came to buy the local wines in bulk. Zi'Angiolina fed these valued clients royally on meatballs. But we only saw meat on feast days and holidays and it was always tough old bits and scraps of whatever meat the butcher had. You would get one finger nail of meat and a big chunk of bread." (From a farmer in rural Abruzzi who lived in Italy from 1913 until 1950 when he emigrated to "L'America".)

"Meatballs? Everybody eats them in Italy. You don't see them in restaurants there because they are considered a poor person's food and made with cheap cuts of meat that aren't good for anything but grinding. You have them as part of the second course, not with the pasta. Though, in some parts, it's common to have little meatballs in a dish of lasagna al forno. In that case, it becomes the only course you would have." (from a woman who lived in Bari, and worked for the local telephone company from the 50's until the late 70's when she decided to spend her retired years with her family in Canada.)

MEATBALLS AND SPAGHETTI

In North America, the land of plenty, the affordability of meat allowed Italians to have a "festa" every day of the week. "Qui, tutti i giorni sono feste" (Here every day of the week is like a holiday.) They could use the leanest ground meat from beef, veal and pork instead of whatever scraps of fat, gristle, meat and sinew were left. Combining starch and protein on the same plate was typical of North American meals so the early immigrants who both adapted and adopted much of what they found, started putting pasta and meatballs together. Later immigrants, those who came en masse and formed large communities of Italians, clung more to the traditional ways of eating and kept the pasta as a separate course. Meatballs were always eaten after the pasta and accompanied by vegetables and/or salad. Leftover meatballs were made into sandwiches (or panini) and were a common lunch item for many Italian workers.

MEATBALLS ON A BUN

When Josephine De Angelis started making meatball sandwiches and veal on a bun in the little butcher shop on Clinton Street in Toronto, she had no idea of the wide following she was going to get. It was plain, everyday food, just like Mama used to make and Italians from all over the city started flocking to "Little Italy" for one of her famous sandwiches. The bar next door allowed customers to bring in their sandwich and grab a quick beer. It's no wonder there were line ups for the 50 cent sandwiches. Luckily, the police seemed to avoid the area during lunchtime so the cars that parked illegally on both sides of the street didn't get parking tickets.

The secret of her success was her love of cooking and people. She used only the best ingredients and prepared them with care, just as she would for her family. She loved to talk to the customers who could see into the spotless, organized kitchen. With more than 450,000 people of Italian descent living in Toronto in 1961, Josephine's clients numbered in the thousands and came from all over the city for her home cooking. Steak, veal, meatball and sausage on kaiser buns, with onions or spicy peppers came wrapped in foil paper. Spicy olives and bottles of soda, Brio or Chinotto were also available. Eventually the butcher shop gave way to the take out business and only a display case of cold cuts and cheeses remained. Josie never tired of the work, but the long hours eventually took their toll and for health reasons, she retired from the business but not from cooking.

The recipes for meatballs are various. Even the name varies - some people call them "braciole." What type of ground meat is used depends on personal preference. Many always use a little ground pork to add a sweet, light flavor. Some people prefer the medium ground meat because the added fat gives more flavor. Breadcrumbs are always used, though sometimes they are the moist type made from soaking dried bread. Using different herbs than the traditional parsley can add an interesting touch - sage, for example. The meatballs can be spicy or mild, garlicky or plain. If chopped onion is added, they make great meat patties, fried in oil or grilled for hamburgers. The previous recipes are meant to be a loose guide, not a rigid formula, so feel free to be creative.

Costolette alla Griglia

GRILLED VEAL CHOPS

The best veal I've ever had was supplied by Zia Erminia. When I asked her what she did to make it taste so good, she replied, "Niente, un po' di sale e pepe, poi limone." Basically, nothing but salt, pepper and lemon. "But it was so tender," I replied, "Where did you get the meat?" Her answer was short and sad. In dialect: "Ah, quella carne nn'z trov' mo." (You can't find meat like that nowadays.) Was it nostalgia and hunger or is this really true? It's hard to say, I'm still waiting for another experience like that.

A dear family friend from Australia - land of the "Let's put some meat on the barbie" - made grilled veal that strongly evoked the taste sensation so vivid in my memory. She kindly wrote out her directions with a little apology to the readers. Here it is.

"I have been invited to submit this Veal Chop recipe. I do so with a feeling of pride but I also feel slightly fraudulent not having a drop of Italian blood (to my knowledge) in my veins. However, Maria's brother and his wife [Oliver and Lorraine Pace] are two of my closest friends and my cooking has definitely been influenced by these wonderful Italians." We joke about the fact that Lynne must have been Italian in another life.

Trim the excess fat from the chops, or score the fat around the outside to prevent curling during the cooking. Place the chops in a flat, glass dish that holds them in one layer. Cover with the chopped garlic and herbs. Pour over the lemon juice and season with salt and pepper to taste. Marinate for 4 to 6 hours, covered in a cool place. Turn the meat from time to time.

Bring the meat to room temperature at least one hour before cooking. Heat the barbecue grill to very hot. Remove the chops from the marinade and grill to desired doneness. Baste with the marinade as they cook. Serve with wedges of lemon and garnish with sprigs of parsley or other fresh herbs.

Makes 4 servings.

4 veal chops, ½ pound each (shoulder cut)

2 lemons, juice only

4 cloves fresh garlic, finely chopped

Finely chopped fresh herbs: (parsley, sage, thyme or tarragon)

Salt to taste

Freshly ground black pepper to taste

NOTE

Many Italians like their meat cooked well done. This is entirely a matter of personal preference and there is not a fixed rule about how long to grill meats. The following are some general cooking guidelines for grilled steaks and chops. The meat should be turned once during the cooking. For 1-inch chops: medium - 8 minutes; well done - 10 minutes. For 1½-inch chops: medium - 14 minutes; well done - 18 minutes.

Oseletti Scappatti

BRAISED VEAL AND PORK SKEWERS

1 pound lean veal (leg or tenderloin)

1 pound pork tenderloin

5 tablespoons oil

Pepper to taste

2 cloves garlic, minced

2 to 3 teaspoons dried mixed herbs

5 to 6 ounces lean, sweet pancetta, sliced ⅛-inch thick

2 tablespoons butter

1 small onion, chopped

1 cup water

¼ cup wine

12 6-inch bamboo skewers

HOW TO CUT VEAL SCALOPPINE

Even without a butcher's skill, you can produce your own perfect veal scaloppine. Use a long, sharp, nonserrated knife. Make sure to cut the meat across the grain as thinly as possible. Then lay the slices on a flat board between two sheets of heavy plastic wrap. Using a smooth, metal, meat pounder or heavy rolling pin, beat the slices to a uniform thickness. If you are freezing the cutlets, do not pound them beforehand. Freeze them with sheets of heavy plastic wrap separating each cutlet.

Being on good terms with the butcher is desirable and one way of achieving this is to buy in quantity. When Mrs. Salute Azzano cooks for her extended family, she buys the entire 3 to 4 pound chunk of veal commonly called "polpa" or "noce." This is from the top part of the leg and is the same cut of meat used to make veal cutlets (scaloppine - or "fettine"). Most Italian butchers will not happily sell you half a piece, but you will earn their admiration and attain the rank of preferred customer if you buy the whole thing and make sure to say, "I only need half but I'll cut my own scaloppine from the rest and freeze them." The pancetta in between each piece adds a lot of flavor and extra saltiness. Use smaller pieces if you want to reduce the salt, but do not leave it out. Substitute thick slices of smoked bacon if pancetta is not available. Mrs. Azzano normally serves something light like a soup first and either peas or a salad with the meat. If there is no first course, pan-roasted potatoes or polenta would be a good accompaniment.

Cut the veal and pork into 1-inch cubes, trimming away any bits of fat or tough membrane. Season with 2 or 3 tablespoons of the oil, pepper and the mixed herbs. Mix to cover the meat thoroughly. Let stand for 30 minutes.

Cut the pancetta slices into ¾-inch squares. Thread the cubes of veal and pork onto wooden skewers, sliding a piece of pancetta between each second piece of meat. There will be about 5 chunks of meat and 3 slices of pancetta per skewer. Continue assembling the skewers in this manner.

In a heavy skillet, heat the butter and remaining oil. Add several of the meat skewers and brown on all sides. Remove to a roasting pan. When all the meat has been browned, add the onion to the skillet and cook until tender. When the onion is soft, add the wine and some water, stir to deglaze the pan. Pour this liquid over the meat skewers which should be arranged in a single layer in the roasting pan.

Cover tightly and set in a preheated, 400-degree oven for about 30 minutes. During this time, check at least once to see if more liquid is needed. When the meat is tender, remove the meat skewers to a serving platter. Boil the braising liquid to reduce it slightly, if necessary, and pour it over the meat. Serve immediately.

Makes 4 to 5 servings

Involtini de Vitello in Umido

STUFFED VEAL ROLLS WITH SAGE

These are very rich so one stuffed roll per person may be enough. Serve 2 for those with larger appetites. The easiest way to present them is whole, over a layer of potato puree or polenta on a platter with the sauce spooned over top. A fancier style of service is to slice each roll diagonally into about 3 to 4 slices, then arrange the slices on a platter or on individual plates with the sauce over top.

Mix together the first 9 ingredients for the filling. Allow to sit for a while for the flavors to blend.

Flatten each piece of veal with a pounder. Trim the veal, if necessary, so that each piece is a uniform shape. Spread filling over each piece of veal leaving a small border clear all around the edge. Starting from the long end, roll up tightly and fasten with a skewer attaching 2 sage leaves to each roll.

Dredge each roll in flour seasoned with salt and pepper. Heat butter and oil in a skillet. Cook the veal bundles in the hot fat for about 3 minutes until browned. Add a little broth to come partly up the sides. Cover and cook about 20 minutes, turning occasionally. When the liquid has reduced to half and the veal rolls are nicely colored all around, remove to a warmed serving platter. Turn up heat to reduce sauce slightly. Strain the sauce over veal rolls and serve immediately.

Makes 6 servings

½ pound ground pork

3 slices prosciutto or pancetta, chopped

1 clove garlic, minced

1 thick slice crusty bread soaked in milk to make 1 cup crumbled

1 egg

1 lemon, grated peel only

2 tablespoons Parmigiano, finely grated

Pinch of nutmeg

Pepper to taste

1 pound veal cutlets (approximately 8 pieces)

16 fresh sage leaves

3 tablespoons butter

½ tablespoon oil

1 cup flour (or as needed)

Salt and pepper to taste

2 cups light meat broth

8 skewers (small metal or wooden type)

Rotolo de Vitello

STUFFED VEAL ROLL

3 ½ pound veal brisket, butterflied

4 to 5 ounces sweet pancetta, thinly sliced

1 ¼ cups cooked spinach, chopped

several gratings of nutmeg

9 to 10 slices marinated roasted peppers (optional)

3 hard-boiled eggs

½ cup flour, seasoned with pepper

2 tablespoons oil

½ cup white wine

1 cup broth (chicken or light meat)

2 sprigs rosemary

salt and pepper to taste

1 roll heavy butcher string

My mother, Anna-Grazia Pace, used to make this fancy roast only on rare special occasions to impress guests— like the time when she invited the pastor of the church for dinner. The egg in the center makes it rather attractive when sliced, but it can be omitted. It was always served hot, but it tastes good cold and looks great on a buffet table. Get the butcher to butterfly the veal brisket so that when it is split almost to the end and laid out flat, it resembles an open book. The smoothest part should be on the outside. Removing the white layer of membrane makes it more tender.

Open the veal and lay the smoothest part face down on the work surface. Lay thin slices of pancetta over the veal, leaving free approximately an inch from the edges. Squeeze out excess moisture from spinach, chop finely and season it with a few gratings of nutmeg. Spread the spinach evenly over the pancetta. Lay the red pepper strips spaced out in 3 even rows along the length of the meat - perpendicular to the direction it will be rolled. Place the shelled, whole hard-boiled egg in a line along the middle.

Roll up the meat as tightly as possible to form a long log about 4 to 5 inches in diameter at the thickest part and tapering slightly at the edges. Use skewers to help keep the meat rolled and tie the roll securely with heavy string.

Dredge the tied roast in seasoned flour and fry in hot oil in a large skillet. Turn the roast to brown it on all sides. Once completely browned (about 10 minutes), remove meat from skillet, discard all but 1 tablespoon of fat and add wine and broth to the skillet. Stir and scrape up any brown sticky bits.

Place browned meat in a roasting pan, add the deglazing liquids from the skillet and a sprig or two of rosemary. Cover with a lid or foil and cook in a preheated oven at 375 degrees for 1 hour and 15 minutes or until a meat thermometer registers 170 degrees. Check the roast occasionally to see if the liquid has evaporated. At the end of the cooking time, add some broth or water to the pan to deglaze it.

Allow the meat to stand in a warm place, covered, for 10 minutes to make slicing easier. Strain the pan juices into a tall container and spoon off the fat that rises to the top. Remove string around roast, slice ¾ of the roast on a board. Arrange the slices and the unsliced portion on a heated platter. Pour some of the degreased juices over top and serve the remaining juices in a sauceboat at the table to put over potato puree.

Makes about 8 servings

HOW TO TIE UP A ROLLED ROAST

To tie any rolled, filled meat for roasting, secure the rolled roast with skewers to keep it together while it is being tied. Leaving about 16 inches of string free at one end, wrap the string tightly around the length first and tie a knot. Lay the 16-inch end of string along the length of the roast, then begin wrapping the bundle of string around the roast, looping it through the taut string and firmly attaching it to the extra piece of string along the length. Continue wrapping the string and securing it to the taut and loose string along the full length of the roll. Tie a knot at the end.

Porchetta

ROAST PORK WITH SAGE

In the gorgeous hilltop town of Guardiagrele, a street festival during ferragosto (a mid August holiday) brought hundreds of extra "villeganti" (vacationers) with appetites and money to spend. Street vendors could earn their yearly income from such events. One in particular, offered just the right kind of fare. Since traffic was jammed as were the restaurants and trattorie, his delicious porchetta sandwiches filled the bill. Thick slabs of juicy, herb - scented roasted pork in crusty buns melted in your mouth, steamy and moist and extremely welcome even on such a hot day. His colorful little cart was surrounded by hungry travellers. When we found out he was going to be in another town for another festa the following week, we seriously contemplated making a special trip just to have another of his succulent sandwiches.

Suckling pig roasted on a spit is a common street food, sold usually from heated trucks parked in the piazza on market days. You sometimes have to be careful that they don't give you more fat than you'd like, but, in general, it's worth the 3000 lira. To make porchetta at home, you do not need to find a huge spit and

4 to 5 pounds pork shoulder

1 bulb garlic, (about 10 cloves) peeled and sliced

10 fresh sage leaves

3 to 4 sprigs fresh rosemary, leaves only

Salt and pepper to taste

1 large piece of pork skin (optional)

roast the whole 25 - 30 pound suckling pig. Shoulder butt and picnic shoulder are two cuts that can be done in the oven. As a roast, the meat falls apart in big chunks instead of slices so I prefer to serve it for a more casual meal in buns. The pork skin turns into crisp crackling and should be eaten while hot, on the side. Strong greens like braised rapini or boiled dandelion go especially well with porchetta as does a robust red wine.

Make an incision along the length of the pork shoulder as well as several individual punctures. Stuff bits of garlic and herbs into the punctures and place the remaining garlic and herbs into the incision. Tie the meat with string to hold the filling in. Sprinkle with salt and pepper and place on a rack set in a roasting pan.

If you are using the pork skin, remove any excess fat from the inner part. Score the exterior side with a sharp knife making intersecting crosswise and lengthwise cuts (like a checkerboard pattern). Wrap the pork skin loosely over the roast in the pan tucking it under the roast if it reaches that far. If it does not, secure it to the meat with some skewers. Pork skin is available from many butchers at sausage-making time around January and February.

Set the pork roast, uncovered, in a pre-heated oven set at 350 for 3 ½ to 4 hours. The roast should be checked occasionally. If the fat in the bottom of the pan starts to get too dark, add a little warm water to the roasting pan. The meat is done when it can be pierced easily with a fork and the pork skin has turned into crisp, crackling. The internal temperature of the meat should register 165-185 degrees. Remove the roast from the oven and let it stand for 15 minutes before carving. Remove the pork skin, which has turned into crisp crackling, and cut it into pieces.

Remove the string from the meat. Cut the roast into chunks, trimming away any excess fat. Serve on a platter, garnished with boiled or braised greens like dandelion or rapini. Accompany with split crusty rolls for people to make their own sandwiches.

Makes 8 servings

Salsicce di Carne (Basic Recipe)

FRESH PORK SAUSAGES

One whole 18-pound pork shoulder with bone and skin removed will yield about 15 pounds of ground sausage meat. Equipment you will need are a handcranked or electric meat grinder, a sausage stuffing attachment, piece of sturdy string, a fine pin for pricking the casings, freezer bags or 1-quart mason jars, and vegetable oil to fill the jars.

If you don't have a meat grinder, ask the butcher to bone the meat and grind it, including the fat, through the coarse sausage grind. Combine the ground pork and seasonings in a large bowl. Using your hands, squish the meat and seasonings together until everything is well combined. Fry a small amount of the meat in a skillet and taste to check the seasoning. Adjust if necessary. Allow to sit several hours or overnight.

Sausage casings usually are sold cleaned and salted. Before attaching them to the tube, rinse them well in cold water to remove excess salt. Squeeze out excess moisture. Check for holes by blowing through one end. Attach the stuffing tube to the end of the meat grinder. Pull one entire length of rinsed casing onto the sausage stuffing tube. Tie the end of the casing with string. Push the seasoned sausage meat through the grinder. As the meat fills the casing, prick the starting end to allow air to escape. This is a two-person job as it needs one person to stuff the meat and crank the grinder and another to hold the casing and control the filling so that there is just the right amount of pressure. When you get almost to the end, tie some string tightly around casing to close in the meat. Prick the entire coil.

Tie small pieces of string loosely around the coil to form sausages of about 4 inches in length. Drape the coils of sausage around a pole suspended from the ceiling in the cantina or in a cool room (about 48 degrees F) for 2 days or up to one week. Sausages shrink a little as they dry. Cut into lengths and remove the pieces of string before storing in freezer bags. If storing in

7 ½ pounds pork shoulder, (approximately half a shoulder)

5 teaspoons salt (or to taste)

3 teaspoons pepper

1 teaspoon crushed chili pepper

1 teaspoon garlic granules (optional)

18 to 20 feet small size sausage casing

oil, cook the sausages briefly in a little hot oil. Pack the jars with the fried sausages. (You may need to cut them in half to help them fit more tightly in the jars.) Fill the jars with fresh vegetable oil to cover the sausages completely. Seal and store in a cool cellar. In oil, they keep for about 3 to 4 months.

Makes about 30 to 35 4-inch sausages

Salsicce di Fegato e Carne

FRESH LIVER AND PORK SAUSAGE

7 pounds ground pork shoulder, medium ground for sausage

7 pounds pork liver, coarsely ground

2 oranges, peel only

2 cups extra fat scraped off the skin

1 3-inch piece skin, boiled

2 ½ bulbs fresh garlic

8 to10 teaspoons salt, or to taste

4 to 5 long, red, dried chili peppers, chopped

3 teaspoons crushed chili (or to taste)

Liver sausage is a specialty of Abruzzo and is particularly well made in my father's town. One Christmas when visiting relatives, we made a taste test of sausages from varying butchers. Even the butchers of Sulmona, the larger market town near by, claimed their liver sausages were just the way they are done in Pratola. Often this meant being very hot. Personally, I prefer them with less fire so you can taste the distinctive flavoring of orange rind.

Go to a butcher who will grind everything for you. The liver should be at a very coarse setting. The meat should be ground somewhat finer but not as fine as for minced meat. If you buy the whole shoulder, use half the meat for regular sausages, the other half for the liver and meat sausage. Make sure you get the skin for the extra fat.

If you are grinding the meat yourself, cut the shoulder into strips and use a meat grinder fitted with fine holes. Cut the liver by hand into very small pieces, as generally grinding in a non-commercial meat grinder makes it too mushy. Grind together the extra fat, boiled pork skin, orange rind and garlic. Combine this with the ground meat and liver. Season with salt, and chilies. Mix thoroughly. Check the seasoning by frying some of the meat mixture in a little hot oil. Adjust seasoning, if necessary. Allow meat to sit for several hours or overnight in the fridge.

To stuff and store liver and meat sausages, follow the directions given in the recipe for basic sausage. Note that these sausages will not be as firm as regular meat sausages.

Yields approximately 15 pounds

Variation: For juicier sausages, the amount of fat can be increased. Replace 2 pounds of pork shoulder with 2 pounds pork belly or uncured bacon. Remove the rind, boil and grind it in as well. Also, 2 small pork hearts can be added - cut into small pieces not ground.

SAUSAGE MAKING

Since the time of the Romans, pigs have been slaughtered and preserved by salting and curing. In Italy, this happens usually once a year, around Christmas time or soon after. Pigs that have been fattened over the course of many months reach their peak size and meet their destiny in the form of either salami, prosciutto or sausages of some form. It was always a family ritual and the sausage making time evokes vivid memories for many Italians. As a child, I recall with a mixture of horror and fascination the images and smells of the huge half of a pig carcass hanging from a hook in the basement. It was often cheaper to buy the whole animal and split it with someone rather than buying just the legs and shoulders.

Fewer and fewer Italian families are keeping up this tradition, particularly as pork and fatty meats have fallen out of favor. Recently, there seems to be a trend to re-establish the old rites as people search for new ways to control the quality and content of what they eat. Homemade sausages will have none of the fillers and chemicals used in commercial varieties. Nitrates are essential for making sausages commercially, but for home use there are no government regulations to control the ingredients. The regulations are in place to protect the consumer against hazardous bacteria.

In past centuries, this was done by using an inordinate amount of salt in proportion to meat. A recipe for sausages in the 15th century manuscript of the highly esteemed Renaissance cook, Martino, recommends " se la carne e deci libri, metteve una libra de sale..."

(and if the meat is 10 pounds put in one pound of salt). At that ratio, the water consumption after a feast of Martino's sausages must have been very high.

The seasonings have not varied much since Martino's day - fennel and coarsely ground pepper are what he used. These are the common seasonings for sausages throughout the varied regions of Italy with a few minor variations. In Friuli, they omit the fennel and add cinnamon. In Calabria, hot chili pepper is added. In Abruzzo, a liver and meat sausage is seasoned with orange peel and garlic. If making your own sausages, you can try different kinds of meat - lamb, for instance - and season them with herbs like rosemary and marjoram or sage.

The basic method for making and stuffing sausages is the same. Often, fresh sausages were kept stored in lard or hung to dry. These days, most people freeze them or put them in jars of oil. Whatever the chosen method, remember that the sausages taste best when mixed with a certain percentage of fat. One expert suggested a 70/30 ratio of lean meat to pure fat. The less fat used, the drier the sausage. Let your taste buds guide you and if concerned about fat, remember, a very small portion with some good crusty bread and a glass of red wine can satisfy the craving for this deliciously sweet meat.

Sopressata

DRIED SAUSAGE

Making sausages, both fresh and cured, was part of the ritual of the seasons for most Italian who came from rural centers. It is no longer so. These days, not too many people make their own salami, prosciutto, pancetta and cacciatore sausages. This is partly because people don't have the time or space. But it's also because it can be a risky venture as sometimes they don't turn out. Mrs. Elvira Severino is one person who goes through the annual rite of preparing sausages and salume and makes a most delicious "sopressata" sausage. This is a flat, cured sausage that has been pressed down with a weight (hence the name). It is then hung to dry and allowed to "ripen." With suitable air circulation, temperature and good luck, it will develop the right kind of white mold needed to give it a full, mellow flavor. Though she has made sopressata successfully many, many times, Mrs. Severino is hesitant about putting down a recipe because sometimes, it just doesn't turn out right - even for her. She was concerned that people might have bad luck and if it didn't turn out the first time they would have wasted their time and money.

The laws about commercially made salami products are quite strict and at this time, imported cured meats are not allowed in all parts of North America. Local meat-processing plants are checked regularly by government inspectors to ensure public safety. Large commercial producers are also concerned about contamination since if there is any trace of spoilage in a batch of cured meat, the inspector can close down the entire operation. There is, as well, the practical consideration of having a long shelf life. The addition of nitrates, though not strictly necessary if the cured meat is to be sold within a very limited period, makes it easier for the producers to have a commercially viable product.

Making your own cured meat allows you to control the amount of salt and additives. It is important to note, however, that a certain proportion of salt is absolutely necessary for the meat to undergo the transformation and to keep it from discoloring or going bad. It would be best to try making salami with someone who has done it before successfully and in a location that has the right conditions. The temperature should be cool and dry.

The description below is Mrs. Severino's personal account of the process. The measurements and proportions of seasonings are general instead of specific as these depend on the size of the leg and your personal tastes.

Mrs. Severino tells how she makes her famous "sopressata"

"I use one whole fresh pork leg and take the meat away from the bone. Keep the fat but not the skin. That can be used for sauce. Then I grind it very finely, but you can get the butcher to do that for you. I add a lot of salt. For every 2 or 3 loaves (sausages), I put in a big handful of salt - with both hands. Then some black pepper, ground and crushed goes in. A little paprika and, if you like it hot, a little cayenne pepper can go in too. After everything is mixed really well, you have to taste it. Put a little in a fry pan and cook it to see if you like it. When the taste is right, let it sit for a few hours before stuffing.

"For these sausages you need the big intestines not the small ones used to make regular fresh sausages. These should be cut into 8 or 9 inch lengths. I tie one end with some string, then stuff the meat in as best I can with a spoon. When the casing is full, I tie the other end tightly with string to form a fat log. Then it has to be pressed. I put a kitchen towel on a wooden board and set the stuffed sausages on the towel. Then I cover them with another towel and put a heavy weight over the top. The weight stays on all night then I hang the sausages in the cellar. This happens for 2 or 3 days, putting the weight on at night and hanging the sausages in the day. Eventually the sausages become more compact.

After a minimum of two pressings, you can let the sausages hang in a cool cellar with good air circulation for about 3 to 4 weeks or just under a month (depending on the dryness of the air). As time goes by, a film of white mold will appear over the sausage. This is a good sign. It means the sausages are going to develop the right flavor. As the white powdery coating appears, wipe it off with a dry cloth.

Once the sopressata has been sufficiently cured, it will be firm and a little hard. The sopressata should be wrapped in foil and stored in the refrigerator once it has been cut."

Spezzatino di Agnello alla Pugliese

LAMB STEW WITH RICOTTA AND CHARD

At 76 and 82, Maria Donato Ruggiero and her husband are still a going concern. They make their own prosciutto, preserve vegetables and even supply some unique herbs for Lucia and Roberto's delightful Italian restaurant (Grano). Although meat does not have a dominant place in Pugliese cooking, some of the best lamb in Italy comes from animals that have grazed on wild oregano and other herbs that proliferate on the hillsides in Apulia. Your local lamb may not have the same diet and subsequent flavors, but it can be transformed into this delicious casserole. The seasoning in this dish is extremely simple so the taste of the lamb broth, chard and ricotta can be appreciated. You can add some carrot and celery if you wish to sweeten the broth. Not only does it taste wonderful, it looks beautiful with its puffy, golden-white crust.

Place the lamb chunks in a large pot. Add enough water to cover the meat entirely. Season with salt. Cover and simmer very slowly for about 45 minutes or until the lamb is quite tender and the liquid is reduced to about halfway up the meat. Add the cut-up swiss chard and cook it in the broth with the meat.

Transfer the meat, chard and remaining cooking liquid to an oven casserole. Beat together the ricotta, eggs and Parmigiano. Season with salt to taste. Pour this over the meat and chard. It should sit in a layer on top. Bake in a preheated oven set at 350 degrees for 10 to 15 minutes or until the cheese and egg mixture puffs. Serve in soup bowls with some crusty bread.

Makes 6 to 8 servings

3 pounds spring lamb shoulder, including bones cut into chunks

Salt to taste

2 bunches swiss chard, washed and chopped

1 pound ricotta cheese

3 eggs

2 to 3 tablespoons grated Parmigiano cheese

Fegato all Veneziana

LIVER VENETIAN STYLE

1 ½ pound veal liver

2 to 3 large yellow cooking onions

3 tablespoons olive oil

⅓ cup dry white wine

2 tablespoons homemade tomato puree

⅛ teaspoon cinnamon

Salt and pepper to taste

2 tablespoons butter (optional)

This is one of those classic recipes that go back several centuries and is so simple it hardly needs any instructions. Nevertheless, Adriana Dametto has given it her personal touch, adding a hint of cinnamon. It was a common practice to add lots of spices like cinnamon, cloves, nutmeg and ginger to meats in the days before refrigeration. These days, it has fallen out of use. The suggestion of sweetness cinnamon gives has the effect of tempering the strong flavor of the liver. This could be a plus for those who need coaxing before they will eat this organ meat. The amount of onion can be increased as can the amount of wine if more sauce is desired. A heavy cast iron skillet works best to brown the meat and make a good, dark sauce. If you don't have home bottled tomato puree, you can leave it out, adding a little water instead. Or, cut up one large, ripe tomato, microwave it for 30 seconds and puree it through a food mill.

Trim any gristle from the liver and cut each slice on the diagonal into 1-inch wide strips. Peel the onions and cut in half, lengthwise, then horizontally into thin slices.

Heat the oil in a large skillet that can contain all the liver comfortably. Add the onions and cook, stirring, for about 8 minutes or until they have softened and turned a golden color. Push the onions to one side, or remove from the pan temporarily, turn up the heat and add the sliced liver. Cook at fairly high heat for about 3 minutes. Turn the pieces to brown them on both sides. When the meat is well colored and no longer pink in the middle, add the wine. Cook the liver and onions in the wine for about half a minute. Add the tomato, cinnamon and salt and pepper to taste. Simmer for one more minute until the flavors are combined. Add the optional butter. Serve immediately with crusty bread and cooked greens.

Makes 4 servings

Pollo con Erbe

CHICKEN BRAISED WITH HERBS

One summer while we were staying at Zia Agostina's in the little mountain village where my mother was born, we left to visit other relatives in Chieti, only 1 hour away. We were feted royally and lavishly all day so by the time we rolled our bloated bodies back to the coolness of the mountain air, we had no notion of eating - ever again! But Zia Agostina had prepared some chicken for us, not knowing how late and how full we would be. Zia was always very persistent when it came to offering food and despite many protests, she wouldn't take no for an answer. Usual etiquette for Italians demands that you refuse the food at least three time before you finally give in to having a little taste. The host must also offer at least half a dozen times to make sure you really can't eat. Saying no amounts to a social and personal snub so visitors must come prepared with a big appetite or have a strategy to deal with the generous onslaught of food. The chicken had, by that time, been simmering such a long time with the herbs and garlic that the meat simply fell off the bone. The fragrant scent and sticky, caramelized garlic lured us into eating more and more until it was all gone. Zia Agostina was vindicated once again in her determination to feed us hungry North Americans who, by her reasoning, must be very deprived when it came to good food. Succulent is the best way to describe this chicken. Whether it was the chicken itself or the wonderful herbs collected on the mountainside or just the long slow simmering, it's hard to pinpoint the secret. Lorraine Pace's adaptation below comes as close as I've ever gotten to the tastes.

Separate the chicken legs and thighs. Remove the skin, setting aside 2 or 3 pieces and discard the rest. In a deep skillet with a good lid, heat the oil and add the chicken pieces along with the reserved chicken skin. Cook briefly just until the chicken loses its raw color and the skin has given off some fat. Add half the garlic and simmer for 2 minutes. Tear the herbs into small bits or cut with some scissors and add to the chicken. Season with some salt and pepper. Cover with water (or broth) just so it

6 medium chicken legs with thighs attached

3 tablespoons olive oil

6 to 8 large cloves garlic, lightly smashed

Several sprigs fresh herbs: rosemary, marjoram, savory, basil

Salt and pepper to taste

2 cups water (or chicken broth)

⅓ glass white wine (optional)

reaches half way up the chicken. Cover with a tight-fitting lid and simmer at very low heat for about 45 minutes. Check periodically to make sure the liquid does not dry out.

When the chicken is tender, remove the lid, add the remaining garlic and the wine and boil it down. Continue to cook at medium-high heat reducing the liquid in the pan until the chicken pieces are quite brown and the garlic starts to darken and caramelize. (Do not let it blacken, however.) Serve immediately with a little bread to soak up the oil left in the pan.

Makes 4 to 6 servings

Pollastrini alla Griglia

BROILED CORNISH HENS

2 Cornish hens

4 cloves garlic, cut into quarters

1 teaspoon rosemary, crushed

2 tablespoons parsley, finely chopped

½ cup soya sauce

3 tablespoons teriyaki sauce

Salt and pepper to taste

Dash of tabasco, optional

There is no Italian translation for Cornish hen. The closest is pollastrini - the diminutive form of pollastra or pullet. Both pullets and Cornish hens are plump and round but Cornish hens are smaller. They are fed a special diet to fatten them so they can be killed after 21 days. Pullets are 12 weeks old when killed and can weigh from 3 to 6 pounds.

Sergio Rossi's cooking style is eclectic as he mingles in mainly non-Italian circles. Blending oriental sauces with Mediterranean herbs is not unusual to him. He is a barbecue whiz and cooks this usually on an outdoor grill but it can also be done under the broiler in the oven.

Cut the Cornish hens in half, removing the extra fat. Wash them in cold water and drain in a colander. In a large bowl, combine the garlic, rosemary, parsley, soya and teriyaki. Add the tabasco, if desired. Place the Cornish hens in the marinade, toss, cover and let sit for 2 hours in the refrigerator. Turn the hens a few times while they are marinating.

Preheat the broiler or grill. Remove the Cornish hens from the marinade, season with salt and pepper, and place them breast side up on a baking dish (or breast side down if they are being grilled). Cook for 8 minutes on each side. Turn and broil for another 6 minutes or until well browned.

Makes 4 servings

Quaglie alle Erbe Aromatiche e Vino Bianco

QUAIL BRAISED WITH HERBS AND WHITE WINE

This recipe comes from Assunta Rossi whose husband was a hunter so fresh quail was always used. If only frozen quail is available, thaw it in the refrigerator overnight. Traditionally quail is served with polenta which makes a perfect vehicle to absorb the delicious juices from the braising process. One 4 ounce quail served with polenta and a vegetable might be sufficient for one person if the meal starts with a pasta course. For larger appetites, or if one main course is being served, count on at least 2 quail per person. Sauteed peas are the usual vegetable "contorno" (accompaniment).

Wash and dry the quails. Combine ¾ of the pancetta with the chopped herbs and garlic. Stuff the cavity of each quail with this herb filling, adding a small dot of butter to each one. Tie the legs together with pieces of string.

In a deep skillet large enough to hold all the quail (or use two skillets), heat the oil and the remaining butter and cook the chopped onion and the rest of the pancetta for 5 minutes. Remove this with a slotted spoon leaving the fat in the pan. Add the quail and brown on both sides. When nicely colored, add the wine, cook briefly, stirring to dissolve the brown sticky bits. Return the onion mixture to the pan, add the water and cook at a very low heat, covered tightly, for about 1 hour.

8 fresh 4 ounce jumbo quails

8 medium slices pancetta, chopped

5 tablespoons fresh parsley, chopped

3 sprigs fresh rosemary, leaves only, chopped

4 fresh sage leaves, chopped

2 to 3 cloves garlic, minced

4 tablespoons butter

½ onion, chopped

⅓ cup oil

½ cup dry white wine

1 cup water

Salt and pepper to taste

Turn the quail twice during this time. Add a little more water if the sauce starts to dry out. When the quail is very tender and browned all over, remove the pan from the heat and let the quail rest, covered, a few minutes. Cut away the string. Serve the quail on a platter, over a base of plain polenta with the pan juices spooned over top.

Alternate serving suggestion: Remove quail and most of the sauce from pan, cover and keep warm. Fry slices of cold, firm polenta in the same skillet adding a little of the braising sauce. Garnish quail with several slices of fried polenta.

Makes 4 servings

About Quail

"Jumbo" quail, like jumbo shrimp, may seem like an oxymoron. But when you compare the tiny quail with the larger ones that are almost three times the size, the term is perfectly reasonable. According to Mary Richmond, who supplies quail along with other specialty "wild" meats and game (pheasant, guinea hen, boar and venison), the demand for the very small sized birds has dropped off almost entirely. Quail come in small, large, extra large and jumbo sizes. The small ones are only about 1 ½ ounces compared to the 3 to 4 ounces of the jumbo birds which are allowed to grow for longer. There is a lot of bone on these lean birds so unless you have a mania for picking (as some of us do), search out a source for the extra large or jumbo size. If you can only find the packages of frozen, small quail, count on at least three per serving and let them thaw in the refrigerator before cooking.

A suggestion for quail lovers and film buffs: devote an evening one fall or winter to a supper party featuring quail on the menu then watch the old Alfred Hitchcock suspense classic "Frenzy" for its hilarious vignette on quails done in the French style with grapes.

Coniglio in Umido

BRAISED RABBIT

Rabbits were raised in Friuli and eaten every Sunday. According to Assunta Rossi, the thyme is very important in this dish and using lard or bacon makes it tastier. The delicious sauce from the braised vegetables and cooking juices goes well with polenta or over potato puree. If made ahead, reheat it slowly adding a little water or broth to the pan. Be careful of tiny pieces of bone that may break off.

Remove the liver, heart and kidneys from the rabbit and set aside for another use. Wash the rabbit well in cool water. Combine the next seven marinade ingredients, tearing the fresh herbs into little pieces. Set the whole rabbit in a glass or ceramic bowl. Pour the marinade over the rabbit. Cover and marinate for several hours or overnight in the refrigerator.

Take rabbit out of the marinade and remove as much of the thin membrane covering the flesh as you can. Cut into serving sized pieces, place in a deep, heavy-bottomed skillet and cook at high heat for about 3 minutes (without any fat) until it dries and starts to color in places.

Remove the rabbit pieces from pan temporarily, add oil and butter to the pan and cook the pork (or bacon) until it gives off some fat and starts to brown. Add garlic, onion, carrot and celery and cook gently. When the vegetables have softened, add the rabbit and half the herbs. Cook for about 10 minutes, uncovered. Add the wine and water and season with salt and pepper to taste. Lower the heat and simmer, covered, stirring occasionally.

After about 45 minutes, add the remaining fresh herbs and a little more water if needed. Continue to cook for another 20 to 30 minutes.

The meat should be very tender and the vegetables will have turned into a dense, chunky sauce. Allow to the meat to rest for a few minutes in the pot, covered, with the heat off before serving. Serve with polenta or potato puree.

Makes 6 servings

1 rabbit (3 pounds without the head)

1 onion, chopped

1 clove garlic, chopped

1 cup of milk,

½ cup of vinegar

Sprigs of rosemary and thyme

A few sage leaves

Enough water to cover the rabbit

¼ cup of oil

2 tablespoons butter

3 tablespoons chopped pork belly (or slab bacon)

1 clove garlic, chopped

1 onion, chopped

1 carrot, finely chopped

1 celery stalk, finely chopped

4 sprigs fresh rosemary, leaves only

4 to 5 fresh sage leaves, torn

2 to 3 sprigs thyme, leaves only

⅓ cup parsley, chopped

1 cup dry white wine

½ cup water

Salt and pepper to taste

The rabbits carried by many butchers and supermarkets these days are a domesticated, farmed variety with a mild, pleasant taste that makes a nice change from chicken. They are also leaner than chicken. Ask your butcher to remove the head, if it offends you. Otherwise, all parts of the rabbit are delicious, including the liver, heart and kidneys. These can be trimmed, diced and cooked with a little oil, onion, sage, salt and pepper. If only frozen rabbit is available, thaw it overnight in the refrigerator.

To cut up a whole rabbit, sever the front and back legs at the joint. Chop the back (the saddle), crosswise, into 3 or 4 pieces using a heavy knife or cleaver. Removing the thin membrane covering the flesh is optional, but it has a better appearance if you do.

It is not absolutely necessary to marinate these farm-raised rabbits as one always did the wild rabbit which had a gamy taste and tougher flesh. However, marinating will add a richer, more full-bodied flavor to a braised rabbit.

Trippa in Umido

STEWED TRIPE

Tripe always evokes a strong reaction - it's something you either love or hate. Tripe lovers will enjoy this version. Adriana Dametto got this old recipe from her mother but it originated in her uncle's osteria in the town of Sequals, north of Trieste on the Adriatic Sea. It is traditionally a winter dish, served often on New Year's Eve with polenta. Adriana prefers using beef, not veal, tripe as the latter tends to be overly soft and mushy. Make sure to remove all the fat after the tripe is boiled. Turn leftover stewed tripe into a soup by adding some chicken broth.

Wash the tripe. Cut off and discard the excess fat and cut into 5-inch squares. Rinse well. Fill a 5-quart pot with cold water, add the tripe and bring to a boil. Add 1 tablespoon of salt, the onion, carrot, celery and bay leaf. Boil for 15 minutes. Drain, set aside the tripe and discard the vegetables. Rinse tripe, scraping off the excess fat. Rinse again and cut into ¼-inch strips.

Dry the tripe in a large soup pot over high heat for about 5 minutes. Remove from the pan and add the oil and butter. Cook the onion till it starts to soften. Add the leek, carrot and celery, season lightly with salt and pepper and cook for another 5 minutes.

Add the wine, rosemary and bay leaf and cook at medium to high heat till wine evaporates. Add the peeled tomatoes, bouillon cube and broth to cover. Cook at a low heat for about 2 ½ to 3 hours. Check seasoning. Ten minutes before serving, stir in the Parmigiano.

Makes 4 servings

2 ½ pounds beef tripe

1 tablespoon salt

1 onion, whole

1 carrot

1 celery stalk

1 bay leaf

⅓ cup oil

2 tablespoons butter

1 onion, finely chopped

1 leek, (white part only) cleaned and finely chopped

1 carrot, grated coarsely

1 celery stalk, diced

⅓ cup white wine

1 bay leaf

½ teaspoon rosemary leaves, finely chopped

Salt and pepper

3 to 4 peeled tomatoes, seeded and chopped

1 chicken bouillon cube

3 cups chicken broth

⅓ cup grated Parmigiano

Fish and Seafood

Insalata di Stoccafisso

STOCKFISH SALAD

2 ½ pounds stockfish

2 to 3 cloves garlic, minced

1 cup olive oil

Salt and pepper

Lemon and parsley as garnish

Since the days when the dietary laws required abstaining from meat, fish, has been a staple of the Italian diet. Since refrigeration was not available, salted or dried fish - particularly "merluzzo" (cod) - became the preferred choice for "magro" (lean) days. Assunta Rossi usually makes this for Christmas Eve dinner and on Good Friday when meat is traditionally not eaten. She comes from a part of Friuli where you can, in one day, be within reach of both the sea and the mountains. In spite of the proximity of fresh fish, this air-dried cod, softened then pounded just as it would have been done three centuries ago, is a traditional, family favorite. She does not soak the fish in water as one does baccala (salted cod). When asked why she replied, " We have always done it this way - ever since I can remember. The man at the fish store says it can be soaked for a day to soften it but I don't have any confidence in doing it differently." When everyone raves ecstatically about Assunta's stock fish salad served with polenta, why should she change her tried and true method. To make the pounding more effective, she uses her husband's cement mallet. The fish is softened in a dampened cloth which also protects it during the pounding. The end result is tender flakes of fish with a creamy consistency. Though Assunta usually serves it with warm polenta, it also goes well on crusty bread.

Three days before serving, wrap the fish in a damp kitchen towel and keep in a cool spot for 2 days. Redampen the tea towel from time to time. After the second day, while the fish is still wrapped in the cloth, pound the fish with a heavy mallet or a meat pounder, starting at the tail and working your way up to the head. Continue pounding for about 30 to 45 minutes or until it is flexible enough to be folded in half. If it is not supple enough to bend easily, it should be pounded longer. Unwrap the fish, fold it in half. Tie the ends together with a string and soak in cold water overnight.

The next day, fill a large pot with enough cold water to cover the fish. Place the fish in the pot and bring to a boil. As soon as the water boils, take the pot off the heat and allow the fish to cool in the water.

Once the fish has totally cooled, drain well. Discard all the bones, leaving the skin on. Using your hands, break the fish into chunks and place in a bowl. Pour in the olive oil a little at a time stirring constantly. Add the garlic, and season with salt and pepper. Allow the fish to marinate for several hours before serving. Garnish the serving platter with lemon wedges and sprigs of parsley. Serve with polenta or crusty bread.

Makes 8 small servings

Branzino al Forno

BAKED SEA BASS

Rosanna Canella loves to cook and enjoys experimenting. After nearly choking to death on a fish bone many years ago, she was reluctant to try whole baked fish. It was while she was on vacation at her brother's condo on Margarita Island off the coast of Venezuela that she changed her attitude. Luciano felt like having fish so they went to the local outdoor market and picked up a beautiful sea bass, freshly caught. Cooking supplies on the island were not always available so she used what they had on hand. Luckily she had brought a few things with her: "... garlic, because the garlic there is so small you can hardly peel it. Lemons too, they only have limes there. And some bay leaves. Onions, they had. It was so delicious. And the fish was not at all spiny."

The freshness of the fish is what counts. This one weighed about 4 pounds and had flaky white flesh. If whole sea bass is not available in that size, get two smaller ones. The same method works with other whole fish like whitefish or snapper. Rosanna advises not to use a glass baking dish as this makes the fish steam and doesn't yield as good a sauce as a metal roasting pan.

4 pounds sea bass, scaled and gutted

½ cup oil

1 cup dry white wine

1 large onion, sliced

6 cloves garlic, sliced

6 bay leaves

2 tablespoons peppercorns

2 to 3 lemons, sliced

Salt and pepper

Sprigs of parsley and lemon wedges
as garnish

Depending on where it is caught in the Mediterranean, bass is known by different names - "spigola" is one and "dentice" is another similar variety. In North America, white bass from the Pacific coast or the black sea bass from the Atlantic are similar to the Italian "dentice." There is also freshwater bass from the Great Lakes and filets from the large Chilean bass have been appearing regularly, both fresh and frozen.

Leave the head on the fish (or remove it, if desired). Wash thoroughly, dry and place the fish in a 12 x 14 inch roasting pan.

Rub some of the oil on the fish. Pour the remaining oil and white wine over fish. Scatter the onion, garlic, bay leaves, peppercorns and lemon slices over the fish. Season with salt and pepper.

Cover the pan with foil and bake at 350 degrees in a preheated oven for about 25 minutes. Baste the fish occasionally. Turn up the oven temperature to 375 degrees, remove the foil and bake for another 10 minutes or until the fish is tender.

Transfer the fish to a board. Remove the skin and lift pieces of the fillets from the bone structure. Arrange the fillets on a platter. Place the roasting pan on top of the stove and cook at a high heat. Strain the vegetables and juices over the fish. Decorate the platter with sprigs of parsley and lemon wedges.

Serves 4 people

Merluzzo Fritto

FRIED WHITING

Diane Terrano told me that her Sicilian mother-in-law, Paola, makes wonderful fish. I went to visit with the idea of finding a few good fish recipes and learning some of the secrets of her good cooking. It was like trying to count the drops of water in a waterfall. The generosity tumbled out in profusion and in the end I was drenched in the possibilities for what to do with fish. Cooking is such a natural and spontaneous process for Paola, it hard to recreate what she does exactly without standing over her shoulder and watching her every day. This was, at first, disappointing until I eventually realized the secret to preparing fish is determined by various factors that change daily; the condition and size of the fish, the menu, the ingredients in your fridge or pantry, your mood and, finally, who is going to be eating the fish.

In the end, there are no big secrets to cooking fish - other than don't overcook it. Buying good quality fish is the other crucial factor. Apart from that, fish can be fried or baked, cooked with tomato in a zuppa or simply grilled with a little salt. Good fish needs very little done to it so feel free to do the minimum.

Clean and butterfly all the fish. Mix together flour, garlic granules, dried mint, salt and pepper. Coat the entire fish inside and out with the flour mixture shaking off the excess.

Heat oil in a skillet so that it measures about ¼ inch. When a pinch of flour dropped into the hot oil sizzles, the fish should be placed, skin side up, in a single layer in the pan. Cook for about 2 minutes at moderately high heat. Turn and brown the other side. Add half the fresh mint and chopped garlic. When the fish is done, lift it gently out of the pan with a spatula, drain on paper towels. Remove any small bits of garlic that have fallen into the oil in the pan and cook the next batch of fish. Serve hot or at room temperature garnished with lemon wedges.

Makes 6 portions

6 whole whiting, cleaned and gutted

1 cup flour

1 teaspoon garlic granules

1 teaspoon dried mint (or parsley)

½ teaspoon salt

Pepper to taste

8 to10 fresh mint leaves, chopped

2 cloves garlic

Oil for frying (about ¼ inch deep in skillet)

Lemon wedges for garnish

Whiting is part of the cod family of fish. When they are very small, they look a little like large, long smelts. They have a delicate white flesh that falls off the bone easily. They are often cooked whole - with or without the heads - and you just eat around the bones. Or, they can be easily butterflied. Get the fishmonger to trim and gut the fish first. Rinse the gutted fish and pat dry with paper towels. Cut the opening of the belly extending it all the way to the tail. Starting at the tail end, pry the spine bone from the flesh. Work your way up on one side with finger and knife tip. Do the same on the other side. When the spine is completely loosened up to the gills, sever the spine at the tail and top, discarding the head as well. The fish should be able to lie flat, ready for stuffing or frying.

Trota Salmonata in "Toccietto" alla Veneziana

SALMON TROUT IN LEEK SAUCE

2 pounds trout (lake, salmon, rainbow, golden)

3 tablespoons olive oil

2 tablespoons butter

4 leeks, white part only, washed and sliced

1 cup white wine

½ cup homemade tomato puree

Salt and pepper to taste

¾ cup flour

5 tablespoons vegetable oil for frying

3 to 4 tablespoons fresh parsley, chopped

Mrs. Adriana Dametto learned this method of braising fish from a Venetian friend more than 40 years ago. The general method is more important than a strict adherence to the proportions given in the recipe as you need to adapt quantities to the size and amount of fish you catch. If you fished at the local fish store and found trout the size indicated below, you'll have no problems. But if someone brings home freshly caught lake trout or several rainbow trout or salmon trout, the proportions will need adjusting. In this case follow your instincts and keep these points in mind. You should make enough leek sauce to cover the bottom of the pan. If the fish will not fit in one skillet, use two and increase the amount of sauce. Adjust the cooking time for different size fish - allowing about 10 minutes per inch measured from the thickest part - and don't forget to include the browning as part of the total cooking time.

Don't discard the fish heads. Cook them along with the chunks of fish as they enhance the flavor of the sauce. Also, some people like to pick at the delicate meat on the heads.

1 clove garlic, minced

4 lemon wedges for garnish

If you keep those few precepts in mind, you will be rewarded with a delicious, moist fish, complemented by a dense, flavorful sauce. Mrs. Dametto insists you must add the parsley and garlic garnish at the very end and not cook it. Some people may find the raw garlic too strong a presence in which case they could mix the garlic into the sauce and garnish the fish with fresh, chopped parsley.

Wash trout and cut crosswise into 2 ½ to 3 inch pieces. Do not debone it. Dry with paper towels.

In a skillet with a good lid, large enough to hold all the fish, heat olive oil and butter. Cook leeks gently for about 5 minutes until they soften. Add the white wine and tomato puree, season with salt and pepper and simmer partially covered, at a very low heat for 20 to 30 minutes. Add a little more wine, or water if the mixture starts to dry up.

Season fish pieces with salt and pepper. Dredge in flour and in a separate skillet, fry in hot vegetable oil until nicely colored on both sides (about 3 to 4 minutes). Remove from pan and place over the sauce in the other skillet. Cover and cook at moderate heat without turning the fish at all - just shake the skillet occasionally and check that the sauce is not drying out. Cook for about 10 to 12 minutes. Just before serving, sprinkle with fresh chopped parsley and garlic. Garnish with lemon wedges. Serve hot with either polenta or warm potato salad.

Makes 4 servings

Fritto Misto

MIXED FISH FRY

15 baby squid

1 pound tiger shrimp

1 pound bay scallops

1 pound monkfish or orange roughy

2 crab legs

2 lemons, juice only

2 eggs, beaten

2 tablespoon parsley, finely chopped

1 clove garlic, minced

1 cup flour

2 cups oil

Salt and pepper

Lemon wedges and parsley

1 cup olive oil

½ teaspoon chili pepper

1 clove garlic, minced

1 tablespoon parsley, finely chopped

Everyone in Italy eats "fritto misto." It's as natural as having watermelon in the summer and nuts at Christmas. When you come from a town near the Adriatic, as Grace Di Julio does, a meal of fried fish is a regular occurrence. In the Di Iulio household, Grace is the chief cook, but she says her husband, Pal, is the one who maintains the family traditions and is her best critic. According to Pal, it was a tradition in Molise to serve an orange salad with fritto misto as a way of refreshing the palate. Grace likes to include crab legs in her fritto misto but the choice of fish and shellfish is personal.

Wash and clean the squid. Remove the head and tentacles of the squid and pull them away from the body. Cut off the tentacles, discard the head and the ink sac. Remove the ball of cartilage attached to the tentacles. Pull out the clear, plastic bone from the body of the squid. Peel off the skin. Rinse the body and the inside of the squid. Cut up the body of the squid into ⅛-inch rings.

Shell, de-vein and wash the shrimp. Wash the scallops. Bone the monkfish and cut up into 1-inch pieces. Cut up the crab legs into 3-inch pieces.

Fill 5 separate bowls with water and lemon juice and place each fish into the separate bowls. Soak for about an hour. Remove the fish from the bowls and pat dry with paper towels. Season with salt and pepper and place the fish in a colander.

Beat the eggs with the parsley, garlic and season with salt and pepper. Dip the fish into the beaten egg except for the crab. Lightly flour all the fish except the crab legs. Shake off the excess flour before frying. In really hot oil, fry each fish individually until lightly colored and crispy. Place the fish on paper towels, then transfer it to an oven dish and place in a warm oven.

Combine the oil, chili pepper, garlic and parsley. This dressing should be served on the side for those who want to add a little zing to the fritto misto. Serve the fritto misto on a platter with lemon wedges and sprigs of parsley.

Serve with an Orange Salad. Combine 4 oranges, peeled and thinly sliced, 3 tablespoons olive oil and freshly ground pepper.

Makes 4 to 6 servings

Calamari Ripieni e Piselli

STUFFED SQUID AND PEAS

Twice a week, calamari and seppie (cuttlefish) were brought from Lignano, a seaside resort town only 20 kilometers away from the village where Mrs. Nenis Elisa Ceschia lived in Friuli. Squid is very popular throughout Italy whether it is fried, boiled and marinated in a salad, or stuffed as in this recipe. It was also the least expensive item you could get from the fishmonger. In Italy, the best time for them was in the winter. In North America, frozen squid are available year round. The frozen 3 or 5 pound boxes are a great bargain. The only drawback is that you have to clean them but this goes quickly after the first few. Check the size of the squid if buying them in boxes as they may be too small for stuffing.

Wash and clean the squid. Remove the head and tentacles of the squid pulling them away from the body. Cut off the tentacles and set aside. Discard the head and entrails in the sac. Pull out the clear bone from the body of the squid. Peel off the skin. Rinse the body and the inside of the squid and dry on a paper towel. Chop the tentacles for the stuffing.

In a large bowl, combine the bread, chopped tentacles, fillet of sole, garlic, parsley, eggs, Parmigiano, and season with salt and pepper. Mix well. Stuff each squid with the filling leaving some space at the top. Do not overstuff them. Secure with a toothpick. Season with salt and pepper.

Heat oil in a large skillet and cook the celery, carrot, parsley, and gar-

10 large squid

4 slices white bread, crushed in food processor

½ pound fillet of sole, cut up into tiny pieces

1 clove garlic, minced

2 eggs

4 teaspoons Parmigiano cheese, grated

2 tablespoons parsley, finely chopped

⅓ cup olive oil

1 celery stalk, finely chopped

1 carrot, finely diced

1 clove garlic, minced

1 tablespoon parsley, finely chopped

1 cup white wine

2 cups frozen peas

Salt and pepper

Toothpicks

lic for a few minutes adding some water if needed. Add the squid and cook until they color lightly. Add the white wine and simmer, covered, for about 15 to 20 minutes. When the squid is cooked a fork should easily go through it. Transfer the squid to a serving platter and keep warm. Add the peas to the pan, season with salt and pepper and cook for 2 to 3 minutes. Pour the peas over the squid and serve hot.

Makes 4 servings

Zuppa di Pesce con Frutti di Mare

SEAFOOD STEW

6 to 7 mussels

10 littleneck clams

4 to 5 cleaned squid

4 to 5 cleaned cuttlefish

1 large piece skate (2 to 3 pounds), skinned

½ pound small shrimp

½ pound large shrimp

1 Alaska king crab leg, (frozen)

1 lobster tail, (frozen)

3 tablespoons olive oil

¼ large onion, finely chopped

1 28-ounce can plum tomatoes

Salt and pepper to taste

Water or fish broth as needed

2 to 3 cloves garlic, minced

2 to 3 tablespoons fresh parsley, finely chopped

Coming from Francavilla al Mare, an Adriatic resort town in the Abruzzo region, Delia Tetini loves all kinds of fish and seafood. But her daughter cannot eat fish with bones, so Delia prepares her "zuppa di pesce" with moluscs, crustaceans and skate. It is a special occasion meal as the ingredients are quite costly. At the local fish warehouse, they clean and chop everything to her specifications. When questioned about the clams, Delia confessed that they are mostly for decoration as the quality is inconsistent. If you are fortunate enough to be near the sea or have access to fresh, affordable, top quality clams, use more of them. There is no fixed rule about the type of seafood or fish that can go into a "zuppa di pesce" - just take care that the longer cooking ones go in first. A final tip from Delia: use a wide, heavy skillet and shake, do not stir the stew.

Scrub the mussels and clams. Wash the squid and cuttlefish and cut into rings or strips. Cut the skate into small pieces. Peel and devein the shrimp. Use a cleaver to cut the crab leg and lobster tail into serving size pieces if the fishmonger has not already done so.

Place the mussels and clams in 2 cups lightly salted water in a skillet. Cook, uncovered, and as they open, remove them from the skillet. Discard any that do not open. Set the rest aside. Reserve the cooking liquid, and strain it through a sieve lined with a coffee filter to remove the sand.

In a wide, heavy skillet, heat the oil and cook the onion very slowly just until it starts to soften. Chop the tomatoes finely, add to the skillet and cook at medium heat for about 5 minutes. Season with salt and pepper to taste.

Add the squid and cuttlefish to the skillet and simmer for 20 to 25 minutes. As the sauce becomes dense, add the cooking liquid from the mussels and clams. Add the skate pieces and cook 5 to 7 minutes. Check that the sauce does not dry out, adding more water if necessary. Add the crab and lobster pieces. Lastly, add the mussels, clams and shrimp. Combine the chopped garlic, parsley, capers and olive oil, stir into the stew and simmer for a few minutes. Serve with thick slices of grilled, crusty bread.

Makes 6 servings

4 to 5 tablespoons olive oil

1 tablespoon capers

Zuppa di Cozze e Vongole

MUSSEL AND CLAM SOUP

This is usually served on Christmas Eve in Regina Casciata's family, as it is the custom to eat no meat on this occasion. It was originally made with just mussels, but Regina thinks it tastes better when mixed with clams. Of course, as she lives in San Francisco close to great markets, the molluscs are guaranteed to be fresh and wonderful. Don't try to make it unless they are. The secret, is to soak the clams all day, rinsing them often and scrubbing them well to rid them of all sand. Regina told me of a trick she picked up from her sister – to remove the beards from mussels she uses a pair of pliers.

Early in the day start soaking the clams in a large tub. Change the water and rinse several times. Scrub well to remove all sand. Remove the beards from the mussels and rinse.

In a Dutch oven pot, heat some of the oil and cook the onion along with 3 or 4 cloves of minced garlic. When the onions have softened, add the tomatoes which have had the tough stems

8 dozen littleneck clams

2 to 3 pounds cultivated mussels

½ cup olive oil

1 onion, chopped

6 to 8 cloves garlic, minced

3 35-ounce cans plum tomatoes, including the juice, stems removed

½ cup dry white wine

⅓ cup parsley, chopped

Hot pepper flakes to taste

Salt and pepper to taste

removed but are still whole. Season with salt and pepper and simmer for about 30 minutes.

In another large pot, heat a little of the remaining oil, add the clams and mussels, cover and cook for about 5 minutes. (Do this in batches.) Add the remaining garlic and the white wine to the last batch and cook for about 3 minutes with the lid on. Combine all the shellfish in one pot. Add the simmered tomato sauce and the fresh parsley, cover again and cook at medium heat for about 15 minutes. Check the seasoning. Serve in rimmed soup bowls with crusty bread.

Makes 6 to 8 servings

Cozze Ripiene

STUFFED MUSSELS

20 large cultivated mussels
(or 30 small ones)

1 egg

¼ cup bread crumbs

½ pound (1 cup) mortadella,
finely chopped

4 tablespoons olive oil

1 medium onion, finely chopped

3 cloves garlic, minced

1 ½ cups plum tomatoes, peeled,
seeded and chopped

⅓ cup parsley, finely chopped

1 ½ cups white wine

Salt and pepper

Carla Rossi learned this dish from her aunt who originates from Ameglia, a resort town in Liguria. Stuffed mussels can be served as an appetizer or as a main part of the meal. Strangely enough mortadella is added to this recipe, but that is common in many Ligurian dishes.

Thoroughly wash the mussels, scrubbing them with a brush if necessary. In a large pot, bring 1 cup water to a boil, add the mussels, cover and simmer for 3 to 5 minutes or until mussels open. Drain the mussels and discard any that do not open. You may want to save the broth, strain it and add it to the sauce.

To make the filling, beat the egg, adding the bread crumbs and mortadella. Mix until well-combined and moist. Press 2 teaspoons of the filling firmly into the bottom half of each shell keeping the top shell attached. Fill all the mussels.

To make the sauce cook the onion in the olive oil in a deep skillet until it softens. Add the garlic, tomatoes and parsley and cook uncovered for 5 to 7 minutes at a medium heat. Add the wine and simmer for another 10 to 15 minutes until it thickens slightly.

Transfer the sauce to a roasting pan large enough to hold all the mussels. Spoon a little sauce over each filled mussel. Lay the filled mussels over the sauce. Bake, covered, in a 350 degree oven for 15 minutes or until heated through. If the sauce dries up, add a little water or mussel broth to the roasting pan. Transfer to a platter and serve hot with some crusty bread to soak up the sauce.

Makes 4 servings

One-Dish Meals

Uova in Fonghet

EGGS IN LEEK SAUCE

3 tablespoons butter

2 tablespoons oil

2 leeks, white part only, finel
chopped

½ cup parsley, finely chopped

⅓ cup water

2 tablespoons tomato paste

1 ½ cups warm water

6 eggs

Salt and pepper

In Friulano dialect, this dish is called "Us in Fonghet" with a circumflex accent over the U. It used to refer to a sauce that was made with mushrooms "funghi" - hence the name. These days, "fonghet," inexplicably, no longer uses mushrooms of any kind. It refers to a sauce made with leeks, tomato and parsley. This is often eaten for breakfast or as a light lunch with a radicchio salad. Carla Rossi says the dish looks better and is easier to serve if there is less white around each egg. When she makes it, she always discards some of the white before putting the egg on the vegetable mixture. To do this without accident, it is advisable to break each egg into a separate bowl first and pour off a little of the white.

Heat the butter and oil in a large skillet and cook the leek and parsley for about 15 minutes. Add ⅓ cup water half way through the cooking. Dissolve tomato paste in the remaining water, add to the skillet and continue cooking for another 15 minutes.

Break each egg directly over the vegetable mixture and season with salt and pepper. Cover tightly and cook over low heat for 5 minutes or until the eggs are done. Cut around each egg before serving.

Makes 3 servings

Frittata di Cipolla

OMELETTE WITH ONIONS

On her many visits to the small mountain village in Abruzzo, Lorraine Pace had many opportunities to watch Zia Agostina turn out a delicious, fluffy frittata - with a lightly browned crust top and bottom. She has now become the official family frittata maker as she does it so well. A few little tricks, like adding sugar and oil to the eggs, were developed over the years.

In a nonstick skillet, heat ¼ cup of the oil, add the onions, season with salt and pepper and cook for about 10 minutes or until they are quite tender and wilted.

In a bowl, combine the eggs, milk, 2 teaspoons of oil, parsley, garlic, sugar, salt and pepper to taste. Beat until light. Add to the onions in the skillet. Cook over medium-low heat, constantly scraping the eggs in from the edges of the pan using a wooden spoon or plastic spatula. Eventually, the eggs will start to set and form a cohesive pancake that is a little moist on top. Slide the frittata out of the skillet onto a large, flat, oven dish or 10-inch pie plate. Sprinkle the Parmigiano on top and set under a very hot broiler for about 2 minutes or until the frittata puffs and forms a light golden crust. Serve hot or at room temperature.

Makes 4 to 5 servings

2 cups sliced onions

¼ cup plus 2 teaspoons oil

Salt and pepper to taste

8 to 10 eggs

¼ cup milk (optional)

1 teaspoon fresh parsley, minced

½ teaspoon garlic granules

¼ teaspoon sugar

2 to 3 tablespoons grated Parmigiano cheese

Frittata di Zucchini al Forno

BAKED ZUCCHINI PIE

2 pounds zucchini

3 tablespoons oil

1 onion, finely chopped

8 ounces mozzarella, grated

8 slices mortadella, finely chopped

5 eggs

6 tablespoons Parmigiano

Salt and pepper

Zia Paola Pavero's answer to "what am I going to do with all the zucchini in the garden?" is a Northern Italian version of a zucchini casserole. It has no tomato and uses mortadella. This dish can be served cold or hot accompanied by a green salad. Vegetarians can leave out the mortadella.

Slice zucchini into rounds. Sprinkle with salt and leave for about 1 hour in a colander.

Heat the oil and cook the onion in a frying pan for about 5 minutes. Add the zucchini and cook for about 15 minutes or until tender, stirring continuously. Allow to cool.

In the meantime beat the eggs with half of the Parmigiano and season with salt and pepper. Combine the zucchini with the egg mixture. Preheat oven to 350 degrees.

Grease a 9-inch spring-form pan and heat in oven for about 5 minutes. Place half the zucchini mixture in the heated pan. Add the mozzarella, mortadella and the rest of the zucchini mixture. Sprinkle the top with the remaining Parmigiano. Bake for about 40 to 45 minutes or until the pie is cooked through and a light brown crust is formed.

Makes 6 servings

Frico con Patate

MELTED CHEESE AND POTATO PIE

This Friulano specialty resembles an omelette but has no eggs. It is held together solely by the cheese. Emily Malisani usually serves this dish as a main course for a light supper accompanied by a salad of strong greens and perhaps pickled beets. Originally, it was made with a medium hard, mild cheese like Montasio (also called Friulano by local manufacturers.) It works extremely well with brick, Gruyere or a medium provolone as well, but not with mozzarella or cream cheeses. To add a little zing, you can mix in a small amount of Gorgonzola or blue cheese.

Heat some oil in a nonstick skillet about 9 inches in diameter. Gently cook the onion until it starts to soften. Season with salt and pepper.

Cut the peeled potatoes into very thin slices. Add to the onion, season again and cook for about 15 minutes turning continuously. When the potatoes are tender, stir in the grated cheese including the Parmigiano. Cook on both sides until the cheeses melt forming a cohesive pancake. Slide the pie onto a serving plate, place under a hot broiler briefly to lightly brown the top. Cut into wedges and serve hot.

Makes 4 servings

3 tablespoons of oil

1 small onion, chopped

Salt and pepper to taste

4 large potatoes, washed and peeled

½ pound cheese (Friulano or Gruyere), coarsely grated

3 tablespoons grated Parmigiano

Anello di Riso con Prosciutto e Vitello

RICE AND PROSCIUTTO RING WITH VEAL

1 ½ pounds Provimi veal shoulder

5 tablespoons oil

3 tablespoons butter

1 onion, finely chopped

1 clove garlic, minced

Salt and pepper

Pinch of nutmeg

Pinch of cinnamon

¼ cup white wine

2 to 3 tablespoons parsley, finely chopped

1 pound mushrooms, cleaned and sliced

FOR THE RISOTTO:

1 onion, finely chopped

4 tablespoons butter

2 tablespoons oil

2 ½ cups Arborio rice

¼ cup white wine

1 cup water

6 cups chicken broth (as needed)

Salt and pepper to taste

½ pound prosciutto, thinly sliced

Start the meal with a light brodo then follow with this attractive rice and veal combination and finish with a crisp salad. Elizabeth Giacometti uses a ceramic bundt pan to mold the rice but a plain ring mold will also do. For a simpler, everyday version, you can serve the delicious braised veal over unmolded risotto. For those who want to cut down on the richness of the dish and perhaps who don't care for warm prosciutto, you can omit lining the ring mold. In that case, decorate the rice ring with a little chopped parsley. Make sure to use milk-fed, Provimi veal for this.

Trim the fat from the veal and cut into small pieces about ½ inch square. Heat half the oil and butter in a large skillet, and gently cook half the onion and garlic for about 5 minutes, stirring. Add the veal, season with salt, pepper, nutmeg and cinnamon and cook for about 5 minutes at high heat. Add white wine and some parsley, cover and simmer at low heat for about 45 minutes or until the meat is tender.

In a separate skillet, add the rest of the oil and butter, and cook the remaining onion, garlic and parsley until the onions have softened. Add the mushrooms, season with salt and pepper and cook for about 20 minutes. When the veal has finished cooking, combine it with the mushrooms. Taste and adjust the seasoning. Set it aside, off heat.

In a large pot, gently cook the onion in half the butter and all the oil until onion is translucent. Add the rice and cook for 2 minutes, stirring. Add the white wine and the water. Once this has been absorbed start adding the hot broth gradually. Follow the instructions for making basic risotto (p. 36). Add salt and pepper to taste. When the rice is tender and all the liquid has been absorbed, stir in the remaining 2 tablespoons of butter.

Line a well-greased bundt pan (or ring mold) with slices of prosciutto so that they overlap and hang over the edge. Spoon the risotto into the pan, pat it down and fold the ends of prosciutto over the top to enclose the ring. Place the bundt pan over a pot of boiling water and cook for about 10 minutes, or cover and bake in a pan of water in the oven at 350 for 15 minutes.

Take the pan off the heat and let it stand for 5 minutes. Invert the mold onto a large serving platter. Place the hot veal/mushroom mixture in the middle of the mold and also around the edges. Serve immediately.

Makes 8 servings

Sformato di Carciofi

ARTICHOKE PIE

Martha Muzzi gave us her recipe for an artichoke loaf which her mother, Mary, used to make whenever there was a barbecue and she was asked to bring something along. It tastes delicious cold. She uses the baby artichokes that do not have a choke. There was no problem with supply - they had "carciofi" at their back door as they lived on the farm. Martha says that "the weather along our foggy, warm and sometimes frosty coastline is perfect for the globe variety." Artichokes that have been "frost-kissed" look a little like someone with a peeling suntan and may not be as pretty as an all green one, but the taste is excellent. If you have trouble finding as many artichokes as the recipe calls for, you can substitute the boiled, canned ones - but not the ones in oil. In that case you need only 24 artichokes and should cut them into quarters. This can be baked in loaf pans or in a large 9 x 13 inch pan and cut into squares.

3 dozen baby artichokes

2 lemons

1 loaf, day-old Italian bread soaked in milk and water

6 small cloves garlic, finely chopped

8 eggs, beaten well

1 ½ cups grated cheese (Asiago and Parmigiano)

⅓ cup bunch fresh parsley, chopped finely

Salt and pepper to taste

1 tablespoon fresh herbs (sage, thyme), optional

Wash and trim the artichokes. As you do each one, plunge the artichoke into a bowl of cold water into which you have squeezed one lemon in order to keep them from discoloring. When all the artichokes are trimmed, drain and place in a large pot, cover with cold water about 1 inch above the artichokes and add the juice of one lemon, including the lemon peel. Bring to a boil and simmer about 20 minutes until tender.

Squeeze the milk and water from the bread, breaking it up into a paste. Add the garlic, eggs, grated cheeses, parsley, salt and pepper to taste and optional herbs to taste. Mix well.

Grease a 9 x 13 inch oven pan with a little oil, margarine or vegetable spray. Spread layers of the bread mixture and the boiled artichokes alternately in the pan, starting and ending with the bread mixture.

Bake in a pre-heated 350 degree oven for 45 to 50 minutes. Serve hot or cold cut into squares. This can be made the day ahead.

Makes 4 to 6 servings

FAMILY PROFILE

Every morning at 5 am, Dominic gets up and surveys with pride the growing, tending, packing and shipping of the produce distributed by the family run company. He speaks about the satisfaction of seeing the process from the beginning when the fields are prepared and seeds are planted, to the end, when the produce arrives on the store shelves in neat packages. Dominic and Martha Muzzi, co-owners of Watsonville Produce, Inc. CA, come by their devotion to supplying quality produce honestly. Both were raised in families that farmed in Italy and in California.

When he was 8 years old, Dominic left Calabria (province of Catazaro) with his parents and seven brothers and sisters. They moved to Welland, Ontario, made their way to the west coast and eventually down to California where he started farming with his family. Martha's father, Giuseppe Giannini, deserves a special place in the history of agriculture in California for his innovations to the way artichokes are grown. The account of her family's background is an interesting illustration of one common pattern of immigration to and from Italy in the early part of the century. Italian workers came, often without their families, as short term laborers, going wherever there was work, sometimes as farm workers or in the mines. When the work was finished they would move on or return to Italy. Martha's father was born in Jackson, California but, when he was a year and a half, his parents decided to return to Colle di Compito, in the province of

Lucca, Tuscany. But at age 17, Giuseppe decided to return to America and started farming. He was one of the first to start growing artichokes. According to Dominic, his father-in-law was a perfectionist. Martha relates the history of her father's agricultural innovations.

"When I was born, Dad had a brussel sprouts farm, and three years later purchased a 30-acre parcel of land in Pescadero, California where he began growing artichokes. My father, Giuseppe Giannini, decided to experiment with what he referred to as "stumping" artichoke plants. Stumping is done by hand with a machete knife and is the process of removing the dried out stalk that has produced the artichoke buds, and that can't produce any longer. By doing this the plant still produces shoots to grow artichokes and does so year round. Not only did he have production all year long, he almost doubled his production per acre. The heaviest producing season is in late winter and early spring, but the globe artichoke is produced twelve months of the year providing mother nature doesn't send surprise floods."

The farming tradition carries on with the third generation as son and daughter, Dominic and Lisa, now partners in the family business, continue to grow, pack and ship fresh produce throughout North America - from strawberries, brussel sprouts and zucchini to spinach, spring mix lettuces and celery hearts. Whenever I buy vegetables from the local grocer, I imagine them growing in the lush misty valley overlooking the ocean where people like the Muzzi family carry on the tradition of living and working close to the land. Let us sing the praises of those who tend to the quality of the foods we consume and provide us with means of nourishing our bodies.

Melanzane e Zucchini al Forno

EGGPLANT AND ZUCCHINI CASSEROLE

2 medium eggplants, peeled and cut into ¾ inch slices

¼ cup oil

Salt and pepper to taste

3 medium zucchini, cut into ½-inch cubes

1 onion, finely chopped

2 celery stalks, diced

1 clove garlic, finely chopped

4 ripe tomatoes, peeled, seeded and chopped

6 tablespoons grated Parmigiano

2 tablespoons fresh parsley, chopped

½ cup mozzarella, coarsely grated

½ cup seasoned, toasted bread crumbs

SEASONED BREADCRUMB TOPPING

To make seasoned toasted bread crumb: Grind 1 or 2 large slices of stale white bread in food processor to make coarse grains the size of peppercorns. (Do not use dark crusts). Season with salt, pepper, garlic granules and parsley to taste. Moisten with 2 tablespoons oil (melted butter or lard) and toast in a 350 degree oven until golden and crunchy. This makes about 1 cup.

This Italian version of ratatouille makes a light, meatless meal served with just a vegetable salad and bread. It even tastes good cold or at room temperature if you leave out the mozzarella. Elizabeth Giacometti likes cooking all the vegetables together for a longer time which gives the dish a more homogeneous texture, almost like a puree. By cooking the eggplant and zucchini separately, the vegetables retain their individual character. Do not worry about the amount of salt used to draw out the water from eggplant as much of the saltiness drains away along with the brown liquid. Making your own seasoned bread crumbs gives a nice crunchy topping, unlike the fine, commercial breadcrumbs which tend to have a gritty, sandy texture when toasted or fried. Sprinkle salt generously over each slice of eggplant, place in a colander and let sit for 1 hour to drain the excess. Rinse, dry with a towel, and cut into1-inch chunks.

In a large skillet, saute the eggplant in 2 tablespoons oil. Season with salt and pepper. Do this in batches in order not to crowd the pan. When the eggplant is cooked through and lightly colored, remove to a bowl. Add more oil to the skillet and saute the zucchini, in batches, until tender and lightly colored. Season with salt and pepper.

In a separate skillet, cook the onion and celery in 2 tablespoons oil until they start to soften. Add the garlic, season with salt and pepper and cook for another minute. Add the chopped tomatoes with the juice and simmer for about 5 minutes or until the tomatoes form a thick sauce. Combine the cooked eggplant and zucchini and the tomato mixture. Simmer, covered, just long enough for the flavors to blend. Taste and adjust the seasoning.

Just before serving, preheat the oven to 375 degrees. Stir the Parmigiano, mozzarella and half the parsley into the vegetable mixture. Spoon it into a casserole dish and top with the seasoned toasted bread crumbs. Bake for 5 to 10 minutes. When the casserole is heated through and the cheese bubbles, serve immediately with the remaining parsley on top.

Makes 6 servings

Sformato di Spinaci

SPINACH MOLD

In the dead of winter in a quaint "Locanda" (inn/restaurant) in Tuscany, we were served a "sformato di spinaci" to accompany little boiled meatballs after a plate of steaming, home-made ravioli. Since we were the only patrons, we got the prized table by the fireplace which was a blessing. The place had been closed until the day before and the heating system had just been turned on. Warmth had not yet penetrated the thick stone walls which gradually started to drip with condensation. The owner/cook brought us our dinner wearing a ski jacket over her apron. Never did plates of hot food make such a steamy and dramatic show as in the fire and candle-lit atmosphere of this old, vaulted dining room.

According to Giuseppina, my source for this recipe, there are two ways of preparing a sformato. In Emiglia Romagna, they enclose it in a pastry casing in which case it is called a Torta. In Tuscany, it is made with extra egg and baked in a high oven casserole or mold. It resembles a souffle that does not rise.

In a saucepan, melt the butter, add the flour and cook a few minutes without allowing it to brown. Gradually add the cold milk stirring to form a smooth sauce. Season with nutmeg, salt and pepper. Cook, stirring, until the sauce thickens. Allow it to cool.

Wash the spinach several times to remove all traces of sand. Discard the tough stems. Cook in a covered pot for 5 minutes with just the water that clings to the leaves. Allow the spinach to cool and squeeze out the excess water. Chop very finely with a mezza luna chopper or a good, sharp knife. Combine the chopped spinach with the whole eggs, the grated Parmigiano and bread crumbs. Season with dry Marsala, salt and pepper to taste. Stir in the cooled white sauce. Add more bread crumbs if the mixture seems too soft. It should be fairly thick.

In a separate bowl, beat the whites until stiff peaks form. Fold these into the vegetable mixture. Pour into a well buttered 2 or

2 tablespoons butter

2 tablespoons flour

1 ½ cups cold milk

⅛ teaspoon grated nutmeg

Salt and pepper to taste

20 ounces spinach

4 whole eggs plus 4 extra whites

⅓ cup grated Parmigiano

¼ cup bread crumbs

¼ cup dry Marsala

TIP

To get the sformato to cook slowly and not form a crust as it baked, Benizia used to line the sides of the pan with oiled paper (parchment can be used). She also covered the top to keep the sformato flat.

3 quart oven casserole or souffle mold. Bake for about 30 minutes in a preheated oven set at 350 degrees. The sformato will rise like a souffle but then fall again. Remove from the oven and allow to set a couple of minutes before unmolding it onto a serving platter. Cut into slices and serve hot.

Makes 4 servings

DINING IN STYLE

Giuseppina's mother, Benizia Battitori, not only taught her how to cook, she instilled in her a wonderful attitude and approach to food. Benizia worked as a cook to a certain Contessa Mafalda and was well versed in the art of cooking required by the aristocracy. For Benizia, eating is like saying a prayer. It must nourish the soul as well as the body so meals must be eaten in the right way, sitting down with the table beautifully set. There was no such thing as eating standing up or having food on the run in her household. Even for the simplest food, the table was set with the white linen that Benizia favored. At the Contessa's, the food itself was simple but the style of presentation was elaborate. Everything went on beautiful platters and the table was always set with silver. Care was taken to serve vegetables of the suitable color for the meat or fish so that everything was visually pleasing. "L'occhio deve avere la sua parte" (the eye must have a part to play) was a favorite expression often repeated by Benizia.

It is not surprising that Giuseppina developed an eye for beautiful things and deals in antiques, jewelry and tableware. Wherever Giuseppina has travelled, from Livorno where she grew up to New York, Florida and Toronto, where she has operated, she carries with her that special interest in style and graciousness that her mother instilled in her around the dining table.

Torta di Zucchini Calabrese

ZUCCHINI CASSEROLE CALABRESE STYLE

Maria Arturi's family has been making this casserole for many years. This versatile Calabrese dish is great hot as a meatless main course or a one-dish meal. It is good cold too and can be taken along on a picnic or used as a delicious sandwich filling for lunches.

Cut the zucchini diagonally into ⅛-inch slices. Salt and let the excess moisture drain for1 hour. Pat dry with paper towels. Beat the eggs with the parsley, 2 tablespoons of Parmigiano, and salt and pepper to taste. Marinate the zucchini slices in the egg mixture, letting them sit for about 30 minutes, turning occasionally.

Combine the flour with the bread crumbs and ⅓ cup Parmigiano. Coat each zucchini slice in the crumb mixture, patting it down on both sides. Deep fry in hot oil about 2 minutes or until golden brown. Drain on paper towels.

Combine the mozzarella, boiled eggs and 2 tablespoons of the Parmigiano. Spread a little tomato sauce on the bottom of a 12 x 9 inch casserole dish. Cover with a layer of the zucchini slices and sprinkle some of the mozzarella and egg mixture over the zucchini. Repeat the layers ending with a thin layer of tomato sauce. Top with the remaining Parmigiano. Bake in a preheated oven set at 350 degrees, uncovered, for about 25 minutes. Let cool before cutting into squares. Serve warm or room temperature.

Makes 6 servings

---

15 medium zucchini (3 pounds)

Salt and pepper to taste

3 eggs, beaten

2 tablespoons parsley, finely chopped

¾ cup Parmigiano, grated

1 cup flour

1 ½ cups bread crumbs

2 cups mozzarella, grated

4 hard boiled eggs, minced

1 ½ cups Basic Meatless Tomato Sauce (p. 100)

2 cups oil for frying

Tip

To use less oil, the zucchini can be shallow-fried in a nonstick skillet. If the oil darkens too much, discard it. Clean the pan and add fresh oil.

Vegetables and Salads

Carciofi Bolliti

BOILED ARTICHOKES

4 large globe artichokes

1 lemon, juice only

½ cup olive oil

3 to 4 tablespoons red wine vinegar

Salt and pepper to taste

1 clove garlic, minced

As anyone who has ever been to the bustling Ontario Food Terminal knows getting the best produce for you money requires courage, stamina and a lot of hard work. You rise with the birds to get there before the best stuff gets snapped up by the other buyers - mostly small grocers, chefs, caterers and the occasional food fanatic. Since the growing season in Southern Ontario is so short, everyone in the food business is almost totally dependent on this source for their supplies. Joe Melara of King and Raphael Toronto Ltd. is a produce wholesaler in a city with one of the largest Italian communities outside Italy. He is constantly on the go calling all over North America - from California to Florida, from Texas to Vineland, New Jersey - to make sure the trucks are loaded with fresh vegetables and herbs to meet the particular needs of his clients. He can source just about anything that grows It was from him that my local Italian green grocer acquired some wild fennel. Joe and Elaine Melara love all vegetables, especially the big globe variety of artichokes. This simple way of eating them will appeal to everyone. It makes a slow, sociable start to a casual dinner party and the dressing goes well with other braised or raw vegetables. Balsamic vinegar can also be used along with or in place of regular red wine vinegar.

Soak the artichokes in warm water. Cut off the stem and break off the very tough outer leaves. Trim the pointed tips with scissors. Place trimmed artichokes in a pot, cover with cold water and the juice of one lemon. Bring to a boil and cook for about 20 to 25 minutes or until a fork inserted into the center goes in easily. Drain them and set them upside down.

Combine the olive oil, vinegar, salt and pepper and garlic. Divide the dressing into 4 small ramekins. Serve the artichokes, standing upright on a plate with the dressing on the side. To eat, pull off the leaves, one at a time, and dip the bottom tender end into the dressing. As you get close to the center, scoop out and discard the fuzzy choke. The bottom may be sliced and eaten with some of the dressing spooned over.

Makes 4 servings

Carciofi Ripiene

STUFFED ARTICHOKES

Giuseppina stuffed artichokes are meatless and have a light, fluffy filling. She uses only the small artichokes with little or no furry choke. Braising in a light tomato sauce makes them very tender and also yields a delicious tomato sauce for pasta. There is a wonderful efficiency to this kind of dish that produces two courses at once particularly since the leftover artichokes taste just as good reheated in a microwave. It is lucky that Giuseppina's husband Joe loves the artichoke part while her two sons prefer the stuffing.

In a deep skillet, large enough to hold the artichokes, heat the oil and cook the onion until it starts to soften. Add the tomatoes which have been pureed through a food mill. Season with salt and pepper. Set aside until the artichokes are filled.

Mix together the bread crumbs, cheese, parsley, garlic, salt and pepper. Add the eggs and milk, mixing everything together to form a soft, wet paste, about the consistency of very fresh ricotta cheese. If the mixture seems too heavy, add a little more milk or water.

Trim the artichokes, removing all the tough outer leaves, the tips and the stem. Rub the cut parts of the artichoke with lemon to avoid discoloration. Open up the leaves to make space for the filling. Use a knife to cut around the purple leaves and, with a spoon, scoop out the prickly leaves and the hairy fibres of the choke. Stuff with the filling mixture, mounding it slightly.

Place the filled artichokes, standing upright, in the skillet with the tomato sauce. Simmer, covered, for about 40 to 45 minutes. Check during the cooking, adding up to 1 ½ cups of water if the sauce becomes too dense.

When the artichokes are tender, remove from the skillet with some of the tomato sauce. Keep them warm as part of the second course. Use the tomato sauce over pasta as the first course.

Makes 4 to 5 servings

¼ cup oil

1 small onion, chopped

3 cups canned or fresh plum tomatoes, pureed

½ teaspoon salt

Pepper to taste

¾ cup bread crumbs

¾ cup grated Romano and Parmigiano cheese (combined)

3 eggs

½ cup milk

2 tablespoons fresh parsley, chopped

2 cloves garlic, minced

Salt and pepper to taste

8 medium artichokes

1 lemon, cut in half

Asparagi Affogati

BRAISED ASPARAGUS

2 bunches asparagus (allow 4 thick
stalks per serving)

3 tablespoons extra virgin olive oil

2 tablespoons shallots, finely chopped

Salt and pepper to taste

¼ cup water

Lemon wedges to garnish the plate

Emilia Buscarioli showed my father her favorite way of
preparing broccoli which is to make it "affogato" with garlic. Affogato means drowned or smothered. Ever since then,
this is his preferred way to cook greens both because of the flavor and his strong sense of economy. Vegetables cooked in this
manner have a more pronounced flavor. The usual method of
cooking soft green vegetables is to boil them in lots of water
then cook them again with oil, garlic and seasonings. This softens the intense taste of the vegetable. Furthermore, it uses up a
lot of electricity or gas, which is wasteful according to Papa who
never boils more water than is absolutely needed because he
lived through the war and hard economic times and appreciates
the value of our modern resources. So, if you want to be ecolog-
ically correct and like a deeper flavor of vegetables like broccoli,
rapini, fennel and asparagus, prepare them the "affogato" way.

Break the tough ends off the asparagus and discard. If the
asparagus are thick, peel the stalks from the base of the tip to
the ends.

VARIATION

At Easter time when asparagus are at
their best, they are traditionally
served with slices of hard boiled egg
decorating the serving platter. Omit
the lemon and spoon some of the
braising juices over the egg slices as
well as the asparagus.

Heat the olive oil and cook the shallots at a very low heat just
until they start to soften. Add the asparagus and the water.
Season with salt and pepper. Cover tightly and simmer at a low
temperature for 5 minutes if thick, 2 minutes if thin. Place the
asparagus on a serving platter, pour the cooking juices with the
shallots over top and garnish with lemon wedges. Serve immediately.

Makes 4 servings

Nonna Nunziata used to start each winter day by lighting a fire in the huge fireplace that was used for cooking and heating. Then she would set a big cauldron of beans over the fire to simmer very slowly and steadily. In this particular village in a very lush valley in Abruzzo, beans were a staple almost as much as pasta and bread. It is a local tradition at Christmas to serve "le sette minestre" (the seven soups) which included seven different legume dishes: lentils, chickpeas (garbanzo), lupini, romano beans and white beans sometimes alone, sometimes as a soup or perhaps combined with greens.

Tuscany may be famous for its white cannelini beans cooked in a flask, but beans are also a staple in many other localities throughout Italy. This is not surprising since beans are very nourishing and when combined with another grain, like pasta or bread and a little cheese, they provide all the amino acids of a complete protein. A big bowl of pasta and beans with some grated Parmigiano is a meal in itself. A plate of beans and rapini served with crusty bread and followed by a piece of cheese and fruit was a typical evening supper - with, of course, a glass of robust red wine.

Fresh beans are available for only a limited time and dried beans need lots of time to cook so canned beans are most commonly used by Italians in North America. The chief varieties of canned legumes used by Italians are romano (or cranberry) beans, white and red kidney beans and chickpeas. Fava and lima beans are generally sold frozen. If substituting canned beans for fresh or dried, they should be drained and rinsed before they are used. They will be quite adequate in some dishes, such as soups, but if time permits, it is well worth making the effort to cook up the dried beans or, better still, freeze bushels of the fresh ones when they are in season.

To freeze fresh beans, after shelling them, they should be blanched for about 2 minutes in boiling water. Drain well and allow to cool. Place in freezer bags and remove as much air as possible from the bag using a straw. Seal and freeze. Fresh beans and blanched, frozen beans take much less time to cook. Depending on the type, cooking time is from 15 to 20 minutes. Three pounds of beans in the shell will yield approximately one pound of shelled beans.

Fagioli Bianchi

WHITE BEANS

1 pound dried white beans (kidney or great northern)

2 teaspoons salt

Kidney beans, being larger will take more time to cook than the smaller great northern. Do not let beans cook at a rolling boil as this will cause their skins to break unattractively. This method can be used to prepare other colored beans like romano or cranberry beans and red kidney beans. Use these for any of the recipes that call for cooked white beans.

Cover beans with plenty of cold water and soak overnight. The next day, drain and rinse.

Fill a large pot with cold water, add the beans and bring to a boil. Reduce the heat, season with salt and simmer very gently for about 2 to 2 ½ hours or until the beans are tender. Drain and cool in a colander. Store in the refrigerator until needed.

Makes 6 cups

Fagioli e Cipolle

BEANS AND ONIONS

2 medium cooking onions, sliced

3 to 4 tablespoons olive oil

Salt and pepper to taste

2 cloves garlic, chopped

4 cups cooked white beans, kidney or romano

Fry the onions gently in 2 tablespoons olive oil. Season with salt and pepper. When the onions have softened, add the garlic and cook until it starts to color lightly. Add the beans, stirring to coat them with the oil. Taste and adjust the seasoning, adding a little more oil if necessary. Cook just until the beans are heated through and well-flavored. Serve as a vegetable (contorno) with sausages, lamb, or pork.

Makes 6 servings

Insalata di Fagioli

BEAN SALAD

While the cooked beans are still warm, combine with the ½ cup olive oil, garlic, mint, parsley, pepper and onions. Allow to sit for 2 hours, turning the beans occasionally. Fifteen minutes before serving, mix in the wine vinegar, taste and adjust the seasoning adding a little more oil if needed. Serve at room temperature.

Makes 8 servings

4 to 5 cups cooked white beans

½ cup olive oil

1 clove garlic, minced

5 to 6 fresh mint leaves, torn into bits

1 teaspoon fresh parsley, chopped

Freshly milled pepper to taste

3 green onions, chopped finely

¼ cup wine vinegar

"Le Tigarelle" con Salsa di Pomodoro

GREEN BEANS AND FRESH TOMATO SAUCE

As a child, whenever my mother made this using the green beans and tomatoes from the garden, she served it in the big, oval pasta platter as a first course. This is great idea for a light summer meal but I was always disappointed because it wasn't pasta. Fortunately, children's tastes change. Now, I love green beans in any shape and form, but then, pasta topped my list of favorite foods. Generally, she used long, flat beans known as "corallo" which have a bigger bean inside a flat, green pod. They also have a string running down one seam which gets tough particularly as they get bigger. This string should always be pulled off along with the tips. Regular green beans can also be used.

Wash the beans and break off the tips, pulling along any tough string that is attached. Bring 3 to 4 quarts water to a boil with salt. Add the beans and simmer for about 15 minutes or until the beans have softened a little but are not finished cooking. Drain well, saving a little of the cooking water.

1 ½ pounds corallo or regular green beans

1 tablespoon salt

3 cups Fresh Plum Tomato Sauce (p. 99)

3 tablespoons freshly grated Parmigiano

Make the Fresh Tomato Sauce (see p. 99). Combine the partially cooked beans and the sauce. Cook the beans in the sauce, partially covered, until the beans are very tender. Add a little hot vegetable water if the sauce starts to thicken too much. Add the fresh basil leaves at the end. Serve hot with some Parmigiano sprinkled over top.

Makes 4 servings

Bietole Saltate

SAUTEED SWISS CHARD

2 bunches swiss chard

Salt to taste

2 thick slices sweet pancetta, cubed

2 teaspoons oil

1 small yellow cooking onion, chopped

3 tablespoons butter

¼ cup grated Grana Padano cheese

VARIATION

Bietole Gratinate con Besciamella
(Gratinee of Swiss Chard with Bechamel)
Prepare the swiss chard as for Sauteed Swiss Chard (above) but do not add the butter and cheese at the end. Instead, mix the sauteed swiss chard with 1 cup (unsalted) bechamel sauce (p. 105), top with the grated Grana cheese and place under a hot broiler for 2 minutes or until the cheese browns slightly.

This recipe from Dina Giacomaso is a richer way to serve cooked greens and goes well with plain boiled meats, grilled or baked fish. As a one-dish meal, it is delicious served over plain polenta. Pancetta can be replaced by thick-sliced slab bacon.

Separate the stalks of swiss chard and wash in several rinses of cold water. Trim away any bruised or discolored parts. Cut the stalks in half, separating the leaves from the long, white stems. Cut the white stems into chunks. Cook the leaves and stems in 3 quarts lightly salted, boiling water for about 5 to 7 minutes or until tender. Drain, allow to cool and squeeze out the excess water.

In a large skillet, cook pancetta in hot oil till it releases most of its fat but is still soft. Add chopped onion and cook at low heat till it softens and pancetta just starts to brown.

Chop the drained chard coarsely, add to the skillet with the pancetta and onion. Cook, stirring, until the chard is heated through and flavored. Stir in the butter and the grated cheese.

Makes 6 servings

Cicoria e Cipolla Saltate

SAUTEED DANDELION AND ONION

Gathering wild foods was part of everyday life for Italians from rural regions. Whether it was wild fennel growing by the salty coastline of Sicily and Reggio Calabria or the new dandelion shoots that dot the fields in early spring or mushroom gathering in the woods, the lure of eating things that grow wild has deep roots. The attraction is not merely due to the fact that it is free. In fact, the labor involved in gathering enough greens to make a small bowl of four servings would bring the cost to an astronomical level if we consider time is money. But the taste makes it all worth it. Now it is no longer necessary to go to parks and grassy plains to have a meal of dandelion greens as most green grocers and supermarkets carry the cultivated variety. Those who are real afficionados claim that the taste is not the same. Since dandelion is a very strong, slightly bitter green, don't even think about serving it to uninitiated guests. Children don't like it much either. But, those who do will benefit from the salutary effects it has on the circulation system.

Trim the root off the dandelions. Wash the leaves in several rinses of cold water to remove all dirt. Drain. Bring to a boil 2 quarts lightly salted water. Add the cleaned dandelion leaves and boil for about 8 to 10 minutes or until the leaves are completely wilted and tender. Keep pushing the greens down if they float above the boiling water. Drain and allow to cool.

Squeeze out the excess moisture from the boiled greens. The dandelion will be greatly reduced in volume. If using long-leafed, cultivated greens, chop them. The small greens collected in the wild will not need to be chopped.

In a skillet, heat the oil and cook the onion over low heat until the onion softens. Season with salt. Add the garlic and cook a little longer. Add the greens and cook just until the greens absorb the flavors and are heated through. Taste and add salt if needed. Serve hot. Dandelion goes will with rich, fatty meat like sausages or porchetta.

Makes 4 servings

2 large bunches cultivated dandelion (or 50-60 wild dandelions)

2 tablespoons olive oil

1 small onion

1 clove garlic, chopped

Salt and pepper to taste

Melanzane Ripiene

STUFFED EGGPLANT

3 large purple eggplants

½ pound ground pork

2 slices of bread

⅓ cup milk

3 tablespoons parsley, finely chopped

3 tablespoons Romano or Parmigiano cheese

1 clove garlic, minced

2 eggs

Salt and pepper

3 tablespoons oil

2 cups Basic Meatless Tomato Sauce, (see p. 100)

This is an old family recipe which Maria Arturi's mother used to make in Calabria. Since it great hot or cold and is better when made the day before, she normally bakes this dish for picnics. It is also a good filler for sandwiches and panini. Advice from Maria to those who like to vary recipes is, "Don't substitute veal or beef for the pork; it won't taste the same." She also recommends that the tomato sauce not be too dense.

Preheat oven to 350 degrees. Wash the eggplants and cut off the top step. Cut them in half lengthwise and cook in boiling water for about 5-7 minutes. The eggplant should be firm but soft enough to remove the center pulp. Drain and run cold water over them and allow to cool. Scoop out some pulp making a well for the filling. Chop the pulp finely and reserve.

Soak the bread in the milk, squeeze it dry and chop finely. Combine the pork meat, bread, reserved eggplant pulp, parsley, cheese, garlic and eggs. Season with salt and pepper. Squeeze the excess water from the eggplant shells and sprinkle with salt. Stuff the eggplant with the filling. Grease the bottom of a 9 x 12-inch oven casserole with the oil and place the eggplant in the pan. Bake uncovered for half an hour. Spoon some tomato sauce the eggplant and bake for another half hour. Serve immediately.

Makes 6 servings

Patate Arrostite con Rosmarino

ROASTED POTATOES WITH ROSEMARY

To get that wonderful brown, crispy crust on roasted potatoes, use enough oil, high oven temperature and a good pan. Certain pans are more effective. Aluminum is what works the best for me so I use a basic, 12 x 16 inch heavy baking sheet. The shallow, enameled, cast iron roasting pans are fine, as are the thinner blue-speckled enameled ones, though these tend to cause the potatoes to stick more. Louise warns against using glass or ceramic roasting dishes as they tend to steam the potatoes rather than roast them to a nice brown color.

Preheat the oven to 425 degrees. Wash, peel and dry the potatoes. Cut them in half lengthwise, then cut each half into 2 or 3 long wedges. Place the cut potatoes in a shallow roasting pan and pour the oil over top. Season with the garlic granules, rosemary, salt and pepper. Use your hands to rub the oil and seasoning into the potato pieces to coat them thoroughly.

Place the pan in the middle of a preheated oven. Roast uncovered for about 30 minutes. Using a flat, metal spatula, turn the potatoes at least twice to brown them all around. When the potatoes are cooked through and have browned nicely, lift them out with a slotted spatula letting some of the oil drain off before putting them in a serving bowl. Serve immediately.

Makes 4 large servings

Some cooks would never dream of using anything processed when fresh is available. There are times when fresh garlic is not the most convenient way to impart a garlic flavor. Garlic granules or dehydrated garlic is very useful for its ability to season certain foods more thoroughly. Breadcrumb and seasoned flour coatings, for example, are enhanced greatly by the use of garlic granules, whereas minced garlic spreads unevenly. Using fresh, chopped or even whole pieces of garlic when roasting potatoes runs the risk of getting charred little bits that taste bitter. Many cooks will prepare garlic oil ahead of time and use that, but if you do not have any flavored oil, garlic granules (not the cakey powder or garlic salt) can work wonders.

8 medium potatoes (4 pounds)

½ cup olive oil

2 teaspoons garlic granules

2 to 3 sprigs fresh rosemary, leaves only

Salt and pepper to taste

Patate al Forno

CRISPY BAKED POTATOES

6 medium potatoes, whole, washed

½ cup oil

Garlic granules to taste

Galt and pepper to taste

Baked potatoes in Abruzzo in the old days, usually meant potatoes thrown into the fireplace under a metal dome covered with hot coals. Grandfather would toss them around and everyone would break into them, fingertips burning, releasing the steamy vapor which was particularly welcome on a cold winter's night. I haven't met anyone who makes baked potatoes that way over here, although these from Donnie Belissario come the closest. So if your fireplace is out of commission, do this instead.

Wash the potatoes well and dry them but do not peel. Heat the oven to 450 degrees. Place the potatoes on a foil-lined baking sheet. Rub the oil all over them and season generously with the garlic granules, salt and pepper. Bake for about 1 hour and 15 minutes or until tender when pierced with a knife. Brush more oil over them during the baking. The skin will become very crispy and browned all over when they are done.

Makes 6 servings

Sartu di Patate

POTATO AND CHEESE PIE

8 large potatoes

¼ pound butter

1 cup milk

Salt and pepper to taste

2 tablespoons fresh parsley, chopped

Alba Di Cesare, who comes from near Naples, couldn't tell me the meaning of the name for this baked potato dish. There is a famous Neapolitan rice dish known as "Sartu di Riso" which is an elaborate rice timbale baked with meat, vegetables, eggs and cheese. Alba's sartu is made with potatoes instead. When this dish comes out of the oven, it should be golden on top and look like a pie or torte. As it is quite rich, she serves it with vegetables like broccoli or rapini.

Peel the potatoes, and boil in lightly salted water for 25 to 30 minutes until tender. Drain and mash well or pass through a potato ricer to make a smooth, lump-free consistency. Mix in the butter, milk, salt, pepper and parsley. Allow the mixture to cool slightly then add the eggs, mozzarella and some of the Parmigiano. Stir until all is well combined. Sprinkle some more Parmigiano over top. Bake in a pre-heated oven set at 350 degrees for about 20 minutes or until the cheese melts and a light golden crust forms on top. Serve hot.

2 eggs

½ pound mozzarella, grated

½ cup grated Parmigiano

Makes 6 servings

Insalata Mista con Pomodoro Giallo

SALAD WITH GOLDEN CHERRY TOMATOES

Greens, preferably just plucked from the garden, have always been a mainstay of Italian meals. That latest wave that has overtaken the produce shelves is the lovely mixture of baby greens known as Mesclun, Spring Mix or California Mix. The tender, fragile leaves of exotic lettuces and other greens are harvested when they have just sprouted and have not been sprayed for bugs. Deanne Dobler, who works at Frank Capurro and Son in Watsonville, CA, explained that there are 14 varieties of leafy vegetables in the spring mix grown and packed by the Capurros. Some have an oriental origin and others are Mediterranean or local. The names are fascinating: lollorossa, little gem, tango, red oak, red perella, cocarde, tat soi, arugula, red mustard, mizuna, red chard, radicchio, frisee. If you plan to grow your own spring mix, keep picking the young shoots and more will sprout. You can dress up a meal instantly with a salad of these decorative and very tasty greens (and reds) adding a few golden cherry tomatoes and the dressing suggested below.

1 head, regular leaf lettuce (green or red)

4 large handfuls mesclun or spring mix

15 to 20 golden cherry tomatoes

4 tablespoons olive oil (or to taste)

1 teaspoon balsamic vinegar

½ lemon, juiced

Salt and pepper to taste

½ cup crumbled blue cheese (optional)

Wash and spin-dry the leaf lettuce. Tear it into small pieces and place in a large salad bowl. Add the mesclun. No washing is needed as it is prewashed and dried before it is mixed and shipped. Wash the cherry tomatoes and split them in half. Add to the bowl. Dress the vegetables with the olive oil, balsamic, lemon juice, salt and pepper to taste. Toss well. Serve with the blue cheese crumbled on top or put it on the side for each person to add if desired.

Makes 4 to 5 servings

Insalata Estiva di Papa

DAD'S SUMMER SALAD

½ cauliflower, cooked until tender

½ broccoli, cooked until tender

2 beets, cooked, peeled and sliced

1 10-inch piece seedless cucumber, peeled and cubed

2 large ripe tomatoes, cut into wedges

1 small bulb onion, sliced thinly

1 clove garlic, chopped

Salt and pepper to taste

½ cup olive oil

2 tablespoons wine vinegar (optional)

Dad is very proud of his showy rose garden, but it's the vegetable patch in the back yard that gives him the most satisfaction. Though he has cut back on the number of items he now grows, there are a few he will not do without; onions, garlic, beets, tomatoes, cucumbers and parsley along with a row of raspberries and strawberries. He prefers his greens cooked and his vegetables tender, not crunchy, so his salads generally combine cooked and raw ingredients. With some bread and a piece of cheese, this salad makes a complete summer meal. He often keeps some cooked cauliflower or broccoli and boiled garden beets on hand. Then, when lunch comes around, all he has to do is step out to the back yard to collect the rest. Remember to chill freshly picked cucumbers before cutting into them.

Cut the cauliflower and broccoli into smaller pieces and arrange on a platter along with chunks of cucumber. Chop the tomato into wedges and distribute evenly on the platter. Arrange slices of beets around without blending them in too much. Scatter the sliced onion and garlic over top. Season with salt and pepper and drizzle olive oil generously over the vegetables. Allow the salad to stand 10 minutes or so at room temperature. Without disturbing the arrangement of the vegetables too much, tip the platter and spoon the juices over the vegetables. Add the optional vinegar. Allow the salad to stand another 10 minutes and spread the juices around again. Serve with crusty bread, which should be dipped into the dressing.

Makes 4 servings

Insalata di Arance Sanguigne alla Siciliana

SICILIAN STYLE MARINATED BLOOD ORANGE SALAD

Genine Natale described the luscious yet simple salad a Sicilian friend had made with slices of blood oranges. I had often put oranges in other salads, but on their own, blood oranges make a spectacularly pretty display as well as a refreshing palate cleanser especially when served after fried fish. March is the time when the oranges are at their best. They are not as sweet as regular oranges, yet taste less acidic. When buying oranges for slicing, choose the smaller, firm ones as the bigger ones often have a space through the center making it difficult to get whole, attractive slices. Use only the best quality, extra virgin olive oil.

Use a sharp, serrated knife to cut away the peel including all the white pulp of one blood orange. Slice the peeled orange crosswise into ¼-inch slices. Use only the best slices; if any fall apart, set them aside. Lay each slice on a large serving plate, in one layer. Remove the seeds. Continue to peel and slice the remaining oranges until you have about 16 to 18 good slices. Set any unpeeled oranges aside. Drizzle the olive oil over the slices, season with salt and lots of freshly milled black pepper. Let stand for 20 minutes. Spoon some of the oil and juice over the orange slices. Garnish with mint leaves if you like. Serve as a starter or at the end of a rich meal. Or use as a garnish for Fennel and Arugula Salad.

Makes 4 servings

6 small, firm blood oranges

½ cup good quality, extra virgin olive oil

Salt and freshly milled pepper to taste

4 to 5 fresh mint leaves, torn (optional)

Insalata di Finocchi e Rucola

FENNEL AND ARUGULA SALAD

2 bulbs fresh fennel

1 bunch arugula

1 head radicchio

4 stalks fresh parsley, leaves only, torn

Salt and freshly ground pepper to taste

½ cup good quality, extra virgin olive oil

1 tablespoon red wine vinegar

1 teaspoon balsamic vinegar

Juice from half an orange

16 black olives

When you want a crisp, crunchy salad to balance a rich main courses like Polenta with Sausage or Porchetta, this is a good choice to start or finish the meal. It is a great winter salad as fennel is at its best from December to March.

Cut off fennel tops and leaves. Cut into half lengthwise and trim away any bruised parts on the outer sections. Remove a slice from the bottom and cut out the root core. Use a thin blade or vegetable slicer to cut the fennel into very thin slices. Rinse and cover with ice water.

Rinse and dry the arugula and the radicchio. Set aside 8 whole arugula leaves as garnish. Tear the radicchio and remaining arugula into mouth-sized bits. Drain fennel and combine with arugula and radicchio. Add the parsley leaves, torn into small bits. Season with salt, pepper, oil, wine vinegar and balsamic vinegar. Toss well with half the orange juice. Taste, adjust seasonings and toss again.

Arrange 2 to 3 whole arugula leaves on each salad plate. Spoon the dressed vegetables in the middle. Garnish with 2 to 3 marinated orange slices and, if desired, some black olives. Pour the remaining orange juice over each salad.

Makes 4 servings

Breads, Focaccia, Panini and Pizza

SANDWICHES AND PANINI

"Hey, who wants to have a snack?" "I do!" I always replied in the affirmative. Then Ma would say, "O.K. how about you making some sandwiches. There is mortadella and salami in the fridge. And make a nice cup of tea, too." I believe she was anxious that my sister, who never ate enough to convince Ma that she could survive the night, might get sick and starve to death. I, on the other hand, had a vigorous appetite and was always ready to eat. So, naturally, I was the one to volunteer and ended up making sandwiches and tea for everyone.

There was something so very satisfying about biting into thick crusty bread or rolls filled with whatever was on hand. Leftover meat patties, cutlets or chicken, cold cuts and cheese with lettuce, or just tomatoes with oil and salt - anything was possible. Adding onions, or cucumbers, using any leftover cooked vegetables like green beans or cauliflower, or rapini turned this regular evening snack into a game of "let's see what I can surprise them with this time." Instead of playing with building blocks, I constructed sandwiches. Once I amazed the next door neighbor, Auntie Jean, who she was also a cousin by marriage. When she saw me build a sandwich that was about three and a half inches high, she couldn't believe a child my size would be able to bite into it. Somehow, I managed.

Whether it's for "la merenda" (afternoon snack), to put in a lunch bag, to take on a picnic or to have instead of dinner, sandwiches will never lose their appeal. Good quality bread or buns are crucial. Italian bakeries these days are producing a bigger variety of breads and panini than ever before. In the old days, the only kind around were kaiser buns, supplied often by Jewish bakeries. As more Italians got into the bakery business, other types of breads appeared. "Pane a mattone" is a very hard crust, round loaf with a great center. (The chewy crust will tear your gums if you are not careful.) The decorative ring bread, resembling a giant donut, looks great on the table, but it's hard to cut for sandwiches. There are "Calabrese" buns, "spaccatelle" (with a seam down the middle), whole grain rolls (panini integrale) and more.

Specialty breads with olives, herbs, and vegetables, semolina bread, corn breads and flatbreads are some of the newer offerings in certain, upscale bakeries. Personally, I find using specialty breads in sandwiches a waste unless they harmonize well with the fillings. Generally I enjoy them most just on their own with butter or oil.

Italians will go to great lengths to find a bread they are happy with. One baker I know, Mr. Egidio Giuliani at Royal Bakery goes to the trouble to produce a unique crusty rye bun with caraway seeds only once a month for the few who know about it. They get there very early in the morning to stock up and it's usually gone by 9:30 or 10 am. "Some people eat only this bread. I make 100 for a family and they freeze it. It is a healthy bread, too, because it is made from a starter and without the chemicals and dough conditioners." Large scale production is out of the question since Egidio says the rye dough is particularly hard to work with and his employees don't know how to handle it. This bread which is a flat bun with a soft, beige interior is popular in the Alto Adige, the northernmost part of Italy near the Austrian border. It was in Bolzano that Egidio learned how to make it.

PANINI: THE NEW WAVE

The first thing to do whenever driving across a border into Italy, is to stop for refreshment at one of the huge autostrada stops. Not only can you have the gas tank filled and the engine checked, you can re-fuel yourself in the bustling cafeteria- style bar/cafe section. You can also buy all the fixings for a picnic in the grocery/deli section, but you may decide it's not worth the bother to make your own snack when the sandwiches and panini are staring at you so invitingly in display cases. Depending on the region you are in, the offerings will vary from one spot to another. There is always a huge variety of cold cuts. Some bigger locations have an extensive selection of sandwiches with imaginative names like "La Barcellona" or "La Fantasia" displaying the list of ingredients on hand-written signs. Decision-making could be a problem since you'll want to try one of each! But do not dawdle or someone else will be served ahead of you. This is fast food at it's most delicious.

Good news travels fast. Trendy cafes in many North American cities have been quick to pick up on the popularity of these panini and sandwiches particularly in light of the economic environment and the need to downscale. Now, if you walk along the old Italian neighborhood in Toronto where people used to line up for the Meatball Sandwiches or Veal on a Bun for 50 cents, you will see sophisticated clients sitting, cramped yet cheerful, on crowded outdoor patios. They graze on sandwiches and panini filled with grilled vegetables and mozzarella di buffala while they sip on big glasses of "latte" (short for latte macchiato - steamed milk with a shot of espresso). It is worth noting, however, that the old places that sell the veal on a bun still thrive.

Pane Casareccio

COUNTRY STYLE BREAD

2 ½ tablespoons warm water

½ teaspoon yeast

¼ cup unbleached bread flour

1 cup plus 2 tablespoons cool (but not ice cold) tap water

1 teaspoon yeast

Unbleached flour as necessary to form a dough

1 ½ teaspoons salt mixed with one teaspoon water

Very few Italians make their own crusty breads. Wherever there are communities of Italians, there is bound to be a bakery that caters to their daily bread needs. To get a recipe and method for making the sturdy type of bread that, in Italy, is known as "pane casareccio," I went to my associate and friend, Doris Eisen, who has been baking breads at home for over 35 years and teaching the "hands on" bread making classes at The Cooking Workshop in Toronto. Doris is passionate about cooking in general and especially about the process of making bread. Over time, she has meticulously tested and tasted many kinds of breads that she bakes for her family on a daily basis.

Bread making at home is more an art than a precise science, there are so many variables in the types of flour, water and climate from one kitchen to another. It's best to watch someone do it to see and feel the precise texture of the dough at the point when no more flour is needed. For that reason, the exact amount of flour necessary cannot be given. For those who can't operate without a ballpark range, count on starting with about 3 cups of flour at the beginning, and adding ½ cup at a time. Professional bakers weigh everything including the water and use specially blended flours with conditioners in them in order to get consistent results.

This particular bread that I fell in love with, reminded me of the bread I had in my mother's village in the Abruzzi mountains. It had a dense, moist center and dark, chewy crust. It was baked as a huge round loaf and lasted for about a week wrapped in a cloth and kept in a wooden chest. As it became stale, it was still good to eat especially for dipping into soup and soaking up sauces and oil. I could finally understand the practice in medieval times of using trenchers of dried bread as plates upon which food was served.

I don't recommend waiting a week before eating Doris' bread. But, if there is still some around after a few days, it makes wonderful Bruschetta and is perfect for the Panzanella Salad (p. 9). Fifteen hours before preparing the bread, make the starter. Put the warm water in a small bowl, sprinkle in yeast and let it sit 5 minutes. Stir in ¼ cup flour. Cover with plastic wrap, let sit at room temperature for 15 hours.

Put the cool water in a large bowl and sprinkle in the yeast. Let sit several minutes until yeast is dissolved then add the starter. Slowly add flour, spoonful by spoonful, stirring, until a ball of dough is formed. Knead vigorously, adding flour as needed to prevent stickiness for 15 minutes by hand, or 7 to 8 minutes if using the dough hook of a machine. The dough should be medium firm and not very sticky.

In a small cup, place the salt and water mixture and add just enough flour to form a thick paste. Add this mixture to the ball of dough, and knead for a few more minutes to combine well.

On a floured board, press the dough into a somewhat flat disk, then gather the edges in toward the center, pinching the seams together as you go in order to form a ball of dough that is smooth on the bottom and has the seams on top. Flour profusely. Place the dough in a well floured banneton, or a bowl lined with a kitchen towel into which flour has been rubbed. The dough should have its seam facing upward.

The banneton should be 9 inches by 3 ½ or larger. If using a bowl, it should be large to allow for the dough to expand to many times its size. Cover with waxed paper which has shortening spread over it, to help prevent sticking. Loosely place a towel over the wax paper and let rise 4 to 5 hours. Occasionally sprinkle the dough with flour to prevent sticking.

NOTE:

A banneton is a basket (which may or may not be lined with cotton) used to contain and shape a bread dough as it rises. The basket is thoroughly coated inside with flour before the dough is set in it.

About 50 minutes before baking time, heat a baking stone, set in the middle of the oven, to 500 degrees. When the dough has risen, invert the banneton over the baking stone so the dough drops directly onto the stone, and spray the oven with water from an atomizer. Close the oven door, and for the first 10 minutes of baking, spray the oven every 2 to 3 minutes. After 15 minutes, reduce the heat to 475 and cover the bread lightly with a flat piece of foil to prevent excessive browning. After 10 minutes at 475, reduce the oven heat to 400 degrees and bake for 15 minutes more, for a total baking time of 40 minutes. Cool on a rack.

This bread will have a chewy crust and a dense well flavored creamy colored interior. Because it is baked at very high heat, an accurate oven thermometer is advisable for optimum results.

Makes one large loaf

Focaccia con Acciughe

FLATBREAD WITH HERBS AND ANCHOVIES

1 ½ pounds of pizza dough (p. 200)

½ cup light olive oil

2 tablespoon mashed anchovies or anchovy paste

3 cloves garlic, minced

1 tablespoon dried oregano

Freshly ground pepper to taste

Salt to taste (optional)

Vegetable oil (for greasing pan and hands)

"Pizza Bianca" (white pizza) is a flatbread seasoned with just oil and coarse salt and sometimes a few herbs or anchovies. The plain version with oil and salt is sold as a bread, by weight, in Italian bakeries - and they usually run out fast. With bread and pizza doughs being so readily available in North American bakeries and supermarkets, it takes no time to whip up a flatbread to go with an antipasto. The version below is perfect on its own as a pre-dinner appetizer to have with cocktails or an aperitivo.

Note the differences in two ways of stretching the dough. Plain focaccia is stretched in the pan with well oiled hands and coaxed into shape. The top is dimpled with fingertips to make the little indentations to hold the oil and seasonings. The rolling pin method allows you to sprinkle cornmeal into the bottom of the oiled pan thereby giving a crisp, crunchy crust.

Homemade pizza dough should be finished its first rise and be at room temperature. If using a store-bought dough, let it rise and get to room temperature while still loosely enclosed in its plastic bag. When the dough has almost doubled, remove from bag and, with oiled hands, spread the dough on a well-oiled baking sheet. Press the dough with fingertips as far as it will stretch. If the dough is too elastic, allow it to rest, covered with plastic, and stretch again until it reaches the preferred thickness (approximately 1 inch high). Allow the stretched out dough to rise in the pan, loosely covered with plastic until the dough puffs slightly. Press the top gently with fingertips to make small indentations.

Mix together oil, anchovies and garlic. Allow to sit for 30 minutes or more. Just before baking, drizzle a little vegetable oil over the risen dough. Spread the anchovy, garlic and oil mixture evenly over top of dough. Season with oregano and freshly ground black pepper. Add some salt if desired (remember anchovies are quite salty).

Prick the dough all over with a fork and bake in a preheated oven at 475 degrees for about 12 minutes or until browned on the bottom and very lightly colored on top. Brush the edges of the crust with some of the excess oil in the pan. Allow to cool slightly before sliding it out of the pan. Cut into small squares or triangles.

Makes one 12 x 18 inch flatbread

Pane di Pasqua

EASTER EGGBREAD

Easter was always a time of great festivity, even more so than Christmas in Italy. One of the traditional dishes is an egg bread baked with a symbolic egg cradled in the top. In some regions, the egg bread was formed into a dove shape, "La Colombina" and finished with a sweet almond paste glaze. In Milan, they make a tall, rich, very eggy sweet cake, Panetone, which is a fairly involved production. This simplified version of egg bread is made by a "paesan" from my mother's village. Maria Giovanna usually makes about 12 of these loaves at a time and freezes them. The bread takes time to make, as the dough has 3 long, slow risings but the process is straightforward and the kneading is not difficult. You can occupy yourself with other things during the rising times. Maria Giovanna likes to use double yolk eggs from a specialty egg shop to give a deeper color.

1 ⅓ cups granulated sugar

1 cup whole milk

¼ pound unsalted butter

Strips of peel from ¼ lemon

½ package vanilla powder or a few drops of vanilla extract

8 eggs plus 4 to 6 extra yolks

1 tablespoons active dry yeast

¼ cup warm water

7 to 8 cups all-purpose flour, prefer-ably unbleached

1 small egg, beaten with 1 to 2 table-spoons water (glaze)

Usually her breads are finished with a simple egg glaze and a little granulated sugar. The recipe below has been adapted for a smaller quantity and is topped with a variation of the rich, almond glaze traditionally used on the "Colombina." This bread is particularly nice dipped into coffee whether you celebrate or not.

In a saucepan, combine sugar, milk, butter and strips of lemon peel. Heat at a low temperature just until butter melts and sugar has dissolved. Do not boil. Add vanilla and set aside.

Sprinkle yeast over warm water in small bowl or measuring cup so it all falls to the bottom. Once yeast has swollen, in about 3 to 4 minutes, stir into smooth paste. Add yeast to milk mixture. Mix well.

Start beating in flour a little at a time. At first mixture looks lumpy, then looks like batter. Eventually it becomes too stiff to stir and forms a solid mass. Turn out onto floured surface, continue adding flour a little at a time as you knead until dough isn't sticky. Continue kneading until very smooth and elastic, but the dough will still feel a little sticky if you push your finger down into the core.

To make braided rings, divide dough into three portions; shape each portion into 3 long ropes, each about 18 inches long and 1 inch in diameter. Form into a braid, pinching ends together. Form braid into a circle and secure ends by pinching together. Place on parchment-lined baking sheet. Once bread has been shaped, cover with towel and let rise 2 hours at room temperature.

Place dough in large, lightly floured bowl. Cover with plastic wrap and leave in cool place to rise overnight. The next day, punch dough down and knead into uniform round shape on very lightly floured board. Butter and flour 3 to 4 loaf pans (4 x 8 ½ inch), and line with parchment paper, and fill about ⅔ full with dough.

Preheat oven to 300. Once bread has finished its second rising, brush on glaze. Place in oven, lower temperature to 250-275. Cylindrical shapes and pan loaves rise quite high, so place on lower shelf of the oven. Bake about 1 ½ hours or until puffed and colored. Ovens vary in intensity, and these breads will burn on the bottom if the temperature is too high. Check during baking and rotate baking sheet or lower temperature if bottom or top gets dark too quickly.

When bread is done, it sounds hollow on bottom. Place on racks to cool. To freeze, wrap cooled bread in foil first.

Makes about 3 to 4 loaves

Taralli con Vino Bianco e Finocchio

BREAD RINGS WITH WHITE WINE AND FENNEL

Giuseppina Fini flipped the pages of her small spiral notebook for the particular taralli recipe that her husband loves. She makes several different types - sweet ones that are glazed with white frosting; dark, moist ones made with reduced grape juice; pale, crisp ones with a little sugar and fennel. These are more like a tasty bread stick in a ring shape. The more you eat them, the more wine you drink - which, she says, is why men prefer them to the sweet ones. She finally found the right page, smeared and sticky with cooking stains, but legible. One day she plans to rewrite her notes - or perhaps get her son to type them on his computer. But then, she shrugs, it probably won't happen since she doesn't rely on the notes anymore.

Sprinkle yeast into warm water. When the yeast has dissolved, stir in salt. Combine flour, baking powder and fennel seeds. Mound on a board, make a well in the center, pour in the oil, wine and dissolved yeast. Work the liquids into the flour mixture, adding a little more water only if necessary to form a firm dough. Knead for 15 minutes.

To shape the taralli, keep the dough covered while you roll pieces into long coils about ¼ inch in diameter. Cut into 7-8 inch lengths and pinch the ends together. Shape all the dough in this way. The dough will start rising as you shape it but it should not be allowed to rise too much.

Gently place 4 or 5 rings into boiling water. When they float, remove them with a slotted spoon, letting the water drip. Set on a smooth surface (plastic or metal) as they will stick to cloth. Move them to another spot and turn them to dry.

Pre-heat the oven to 350 degrees. When all the dough has been shaped and boiled, bake the fairly dry rings directly on the oven racks for 40 minutes. Turn them to get an even color. When they are colored a golden brown and are quite hard, remove from oven, set on racks to cool. Store in an air-tight container in the freezer.

Makes 5 dozen taralli

1 package dry yeast

½ cup warm water

1 teaspoon salt

2 pounds flour

1 teaspoon baking powder

1 heaping tablespoon fennel seeds

1 cup olive oil

5 to 6 ounces white wine

Tramezzini di Manzo alla Griglia

GRILLED FLANK STEAK AND ARUGULA SANDWICHES

2 cups beer

4 green onions, chopped

¼ cup oil

¼ cup soya sauce

2 tablespoons brown sugar

2 tablespoons honey

2 tablespoons fresh ginger, grated

2 cloves garlic, minced

½ teaspoon salt

½ teaspoon red chili pepper flakes

2 flank steaks (1 ½ pounds each)

12 to 16 leaves fresh arugula

½ cup Shallot and Balsamic Vinegar Spread (p. 259)

1 ½ cups Artichoke Puree (p. 256), optional

Dijon mustard

1 round loaf crusty bread, sliced and grilled

Flank steak is not a cut of meat widely found in Italian butcher shops. Many years ago, when I first tasted a friend's marinated, grilled beef, it was so incredibly good I begged for the recipe. I lost touch with that friend and the original recipe disappeared amidst the turmoil of moving so I created an approximation. The thinly sliced meat served on grilled slices of crusty bread with either mustard, shallot spread or artichoke puree has became a favorite among family and friends. There is nothing remotely Italian about the marinade. But, the intense flavors and tenderness of the meat pleases palates of any origin - even Papa agrees it is "molto saporito."

Combine first 10 ingredients for the marinade and mix well. Place the flank steak in a glass or ceramic dish. Pour the marinade on top and cover. Place in the refrigerator. Let sit overnight or up to two days; turn the meat occasionally.

Drain the flank steak and dry it with paper towels. Preheat the barbecue and spray the grill with cooking oil spray. Grill the flank steak for about 4 to 5 minutes on each side for medium-rare. Transfer to a plate, allow to cool slightly before cutting.

Slice the meat across the grain at a fairly sharp angle to make very thin slices. If assembling individual portions, spread a thin layer of Shallot and Balsamic Spread over slices of warm, grilled bread. Top with slices of meat. Garnish with a spoon of Artichoke Puree or Dijon mustard and arugula leaves. Alternately, you can let guests construct their own open-face sandwiches and serve the meat on a platter garnished with arugula leaves.

Makes 8 to 10 sandwiches

Autostrada Toast

GARLICKY HAM AND CHEESE TOAST

I was introduced to these wonderful places of restoration (the autostrada stops) by my brother and his wife. Whenever we stopped for refreshment early in the morning, Lorraine would invariably opt for a toast with a steaming cup of cappuccino. Feeling nostalgic about those wonderful snacks when we got home, Lorraine used her mother's old sandwich press to create her own embellished version. She laces the mayonnaise with garlic and uses more interesting types of bread. The results, in my opinion, surpass any we tried in Italy.

Combine the mayonnaise, garlic and Dijon, mixing well. Cut the bread into 8 long slices, 3/16 inch thick. Spread the garlic mayonnaise on one side of each of the bread slices. Arrange a ham slice over the bread, then a slice of cheese and another slice of ham. Top with a slice of bread, pressing down well.

Preheat an electric sandwich press. If you do not have one, use a cast iron skillet. Lightly butter the outside of the toasts on both sides as you would for grilled cheese sandwiches. Lay one filled sandwich in the heated press, close down the top lid. Cook for about 1 minute or until the cheese melts and the bread has browned. Cut the sandwiches in half and serve on a platter garnished with crisp radishes, fennel or carrot sticks for a predinner snack with cocktails or in between deals at a cards night.

Makes 16 portions

½ cup mayonnaise

1 teaspoon minced garlic

1 teaspoon Dijon mustard

1 round loaf dense peasant bread, sliced thinly

16 to 18 slices prosciutto cotto or cooked ham

16 slices medium provolone cheese

Butter or margarine for greasing bread

Garnish: carrot sticks, sliced fennel or radishes

NOTE ABOUT THE BREAD

In Italy, toasts are usually made with white bread that has a fine, dense texture and a soft crust. Packaged white bread sold in North America is too flimsy. The crusty loaves with a spongy interior full of air pockets is also not good. The best bread to use for toasts should have a dense center and a crust which is not excessively chewy. Get the bakery to slice the bread for you.

Panino con Verdura alla Griglia

GRILLED VEGETABLE AND BOCCONCINI CHEESE SANDWICH

2 medium-sized zucchini

1 medium-sized eggplant

2 red bell peppers

1 tablespoon Italian seasoning (dried oregano, basil, marjoram)

½ cup oil

2 tablespoons balsamic vinegar

Salt and pepper

4 Calabrese buns or 2 long baguette loaves

4 slices Bocconcini cheese

SERVING SUGGESTIONS:

Serve as an accompaniment to Grilled Veal Chops (p. 119) or any meat course that is cooked on the grill. In the summer you can cook the entire meal on an outside grill without having to cook in the kitchen. Arrange the vegetables on a large flat platter. Season with oil, balsamic vinegar, Italian seasoning or oregano, salt and pepper.

Irma Faverin does her grilled vegetables not on a barbecue but on a stovetop grill pan. It is a ridged, non-stick, cast iron, pan that covers two elements on the stove. She uses no oil on the vegetables before they are cooked, but if you do this on an outdoor barbecue, it is advisable to brush the vegetables with oil first and make slightly thicker slices. The trick to getting attractive brown ridge marks on the vegetables without burning them is to make the grill pan very hot, then lower the heat as soon as the vegetables are put on. You can make your own Italian seasoning with a combination of the following herbs: parsley, basil, oregano, rosemary and marjoram. Irma says she sometimes uses white wine vinegar instead of balsamic which tends to discolor the vegetables. Other vegetables, can, of course, be done in the same way. Try some sliced red onion, portobello mushrooms or sweet potatoes.

Thinly slice the zucchini about ¼ of an inch in an oval shape, salt and let drain for about an hour in a colander. Peel the eggplant, slice into ¼-inch rounds, salt and let drain for about an hour in a colander. Slice the peppers lengthwise (about eight pieces per pepper.)

Heat up a stove-top grill or barbeque. Just before the vegetables go on, lower heat to medium. Grill the zucchini and the eggplant about one minute on each side. Grill the peppers about 1 minute on each side. They will still be crunchy. The vegetables should have a light brown mark from the grill. Be careful not to burn the vegetables.

Slice the buns or baguettes in half lengthwise, spread a little Shallot and Balsamic Vinegar Spread (p. 259) on both sides. Arrange a few pieces of grilled vegetables on the bread. Top with slices of bocconcini cheese. Drizzle some of the dressing from the vegetables over the cheese. Close the top and cut in half. Serve with olives and cherry tomatoes as garnish.

Makes 4 sandwiches

Panino con Salsicce e Cipolla

GRILLED SAUSAGE AND ONION ON A CRUSTY BUN

Whenever a large group of Italians gather for picnics or other outdoor social event, the food is always fast and easy. The smell of grilled Italian sausages fills the air and suddenly it seems that all is well with the world. But you needn't wait for a community picnic. Serve these at a card party or when watching football. This is casual dining at its best. You don't even need knives or forks, just paper plates and plenty of napkins.

In a large skillet, heat the oil and cook the onions over very low heat. Season with salt and pepper to taste. Cook, turning regularly for about 25 to 30 minutes. The onions should become completely soft and slightly golden in colour. Set aside and reheat when ready to serve.

If using homemade sausages, pre-boiling will not be necessary. Commercial sausages can be very salty and may benefit from being boiled first. Place sausages in a skillet and cover with cold water. Bring to a boil. The sausages will give off a lot of froth. Boil for about 5 minutes, drain, discarding all the water. Prick the sausages all over and place on a preheated barbecue. Cook, turning on all sides, for about 10 minutes or until well browned all around and cooked through.

Serve the grilled sausages in the split buns with the sauteed onions and optional roasted red peppers on the side.

Makes 6 servings

2 tablespoons oil

5 cups sliced onions

Salt and pepper to taste

1 cup marinated roasted peppers

6 fresh Italian sausages (about 2 ½ pounds)

6 long crusty rolls (spaccatelli)

Pizza

Pizza is just bread dough that is rolled flat, seasoned and baked on a stone or in a pan. For such a simple dish, it is surprising how many variations one finds in the way it is made. It can be thick and bready or thin and crisp. The top may be a light coating of oil and tomato or laden with cheese and "toppings." Sometimes it is stuffed and rolled or it may be folded into turnovers (calzone). In Tuscany, they put a fried egg on top. In Sicily they bake it four inches high and call it by another name entirely.

Perhaps the most surprising, modern version of pizza I have encountered was discovered one spring while on holiday in Rome. We stumbled upon a small shop in the bustling African Quarter that sold only pizza. Not surprising, you may think, in Rome, but this store was unique. Tray after tray of pizza with toppings that looked like a high tech salad bar sat in display cases ready to be sold by weight. On a sturdy crust with a light tomato and herb topping were piled unexpected raw and cold ingredients: avocado, shrimp, fresh tomato, and slivered yellow peppers was one combination. Another had tuna, tomatoes, black olives and hard boiled egg. Yet another had shredded greens, sliced bocconcini, marinated artichokes and roasted red pepper. I gave up my plans for making supper and bought a slice. It was a little hard to eat, especially while walking down the street, but the awkwardness was worth it. It might make purists cringe but it was totally enjoyable, nevertheless.

The pizza crust was very sturdy. It had a crunchy bottom yet a soft center and the 4 by 6 inch piece did not flop or sag with the weight of the toppings. The tomato topping was moist but did not make the crust soggy. Pizza doughs made at home with all purpose flour would not create a firm enough dough unless they are quite thick and have a crisp bottom. The best dough for this particular treatment is one made with a combination of semolina and all purpose flour. A light coating of cornmeal over the greased pan ensures a nice crispy crust.

Whether you make your own dough or use store bought, as more and more Italians are doing, baking pizza can be a creative and enjoyable adventure in cooking - as long as the end results are pleasing.

THE AFRICAN CONNECTION: SOPHIA'S BRUSCHETTA PIZZA

In a well-known bar/cafe on College Street in Toronto's Little Italy, I encountered a pizza similar to the exceptional one I tasted in the African Quarter in Rome.

By uncanny coincidence, I learned that the creator of this dish was an Eretrian woman. Sophia Vagadia who came to Canada before the flood of refugees started arriving, grew up in an Italian environment in Eretria. She went to an Italian school and speaks Italian fluently. At home, they regularly ate Italian food and followed Italian fashions. When she arrived at the Toronto airport after fleeing Eretria, Sophia asked the cab driver to take her directly to where the Italians live. He brought her to the very corner where she now works and she has lived in the neighborhood ever since.

The food she prepares for the cafe is just like what she cooks at home. Sophia is a creative cook and likes trying out new things for the menu or making up whatever special requests she gets from the regular clients. Her bruschetta pizza was something she dreamed up one day when she was tired of making the same old thing. This is her description of how she assembles her Bruschetta Pizza. "The night before, I make the dough and put it in the refrigerator. In the morning, I roll out the dough and pierce it all over with special roller that has holes; but, at home, you can use a fork. I brush it with lots of oil and bake it. Once the bottom is crisp I take it out and add the toppings: more oil, then fresh garlic and herbs (basil and oregano), chopped red onion, cucumber, fresh tomatoes and crumbled feta. If you want, you can add some olives and jalapeno peppers - but that's up to you."

Pasta per Pizza

BASIC PIZZA DOUGH

½ teaspoon sugar

1 ¼ cups warm water

1 package dry yeast (slightly less than 1 tablespoon)

3 tablespoons olive oil

½ teaspoon salt

3 ½ cups all purpose flour

Cornmeal for dusting the pan

There are many slightly different versions of basic pizza dough. One person insists on adding an egg. Another claims the secret is a little milk. Most people use oil, though in the old days, which means in Italy, lard was often the preferred fat. The dough can be made with slightly less yeast and allowed a slow, cold rise in the refrigerator. The version below is for a fairly fast-rising, rapid dough. Do not use rapid mix yeast or the instant blending kind. Traditional dry or cake yeast works best. Lots of kneading and a final rise in the pan will give soft yet well structured texture. The recipe can easily be doubled, in which case you would not have to increase the amount of yeast or sugar, but allow a slightly longer rising time.

Dissolve sugar in ½ cup warm water. Sprinkle over the yeast and let stand until it starts to froth. In a large bowl, combine the yeast mixture with the remaining water, about 1 ½ tablespoons of olive oil and the salt.

Gradually stir the flour into the yeast and water mixture with a wooden spoon setting aside the last ½ cup or more of flour. When the mixture forms a cohesive, slightly sticky dough, turn it onto a floured board. Knead for 5 minutes or until the dough is smooth and elastic adding the remaining flour. Place in a lightly oiled bowl, turning the dough to coat it with oil. Cover with plastic wrap, let rise for about 2 hours or until doubled in bulk. Punch down the dough and knead a few minutes. Roll it out with a rolling pin on a lightly floured surface. It should be about ½ inch thick.

Grease a 12 x 18 inch baking pan with a tablespoon of oil and sprinkle with a little cornmeal. Place rolled out dough in the pan. Cover and let it rise for about 30 minutes in a warm place until it puffs slightly. Preheat the oven to 425 degrees. Spread on desired topping and prick the top with a fork just before baking.

Makes one 12 x 18 inch pizza

Pizza di Semolina

SEMOLINA PIZZA

In a large bowl, dissolve the sugar in ½ cup warm water. Sprinkle yeast over water and allow to stand 5 minutes until it bubbles. Stir the remaining water, oil and salt into the frothy yeast mixture.

Start adding the semolina to the yeast and water mixture stirring it in to make a granular mush. Once all the semolina has been mixed in, add the all-purpose flour gradually. After about 1 cup, the dough will be firm enough to work on a flat surface. Scrape the dough from the wooden spoon and the bowl with a scraper, gather all the dough together and knead on a floured surface. Gradually incorporate as much as ⅓ cup more flour. Continue kneading for about 10 minutes, dusting lightly with flour only if necessary. The dough will be very springy and slightly sticky when pressed down firmly, but it should come away from your hands easily.

Shape the kneaded dough into a ball, place in a clean bowl cover with plastic wrap and let rise in a warm place (not in the oven). After 2 hours, punch down dough, knead again on a lightly floured surface for 5 minutes until the dough is smooth and elastic. Shape into a ball and place in a lightly greased bowl, coating the dough all around with a little oil.

Cover with plastic and let rise for 2 hours or till dough has doubled. Punch down dough again, knead a few moments and shape into a ball. On a lightly floured surface, flatten the ball to a disk, flip it over once or twice so it does not stick. Using a rolling pin, stretch the dough till it is about ¼ inch thick and approximately 12 x 16 inches or to fit the pan.

Grease a baking sheet with oil and sprinkle with some cornmeal. Gently lay the rolled out dough in the baking sheet, stretching it to the edges. Cover with a towel and let rise for about 30 minutes.

¼ teaspoon sugar

1 ½ cups warm water

1 package (slightly less than 1 tablespoon) dry yeast

2 tablespoons oil

2 teaspoons salt

2 cups semolina (fine ground)

1 ½ cups all-purpose flour

Cornmeal for dusting baking pan

Oil for greasing dough and pan

2 cups Basic Tomato Topping for Pizza (p. 210)

Preheat oven to 425 degrees. After the dough has puffed in the pan, press around the edges of the pan to form a slightly higher border. Spread two cups Basic Tomato Topping for Pizza evenly over the top. Drizzle a little extra oil over top. Prick crust with a fork. Bake in the middle of a hot oven for 20 minutes or until the bottom is lightly colored. Remove from oven and brush a little oil around the crust. Allow to cool slightly before cutting.

Makes one 12 x 16 inch pizza

Pizza con Quattro Formaggi

PIZZA WITH FOUR CHEESES

1 batch Basic Pizza Dough or 1 ½ pound store-bought dough

2 cups grated mozzarella cheese

1 cup finely cubed Friulano cheese

1 cup finely cubed Fontina cheese

½ cup Gorgonzola cheese, cut into small pieces

10 fresh basil leaves

Cornmeal for dusting the pan

2 tablespoons oil

Make the pizza dough, or if using a store-bought dough, allow it to come to room temperature in the plastic bag. When it has puffed considerably, roll it out with a rolling pin on a lightly floured surface. It should be about ½ inch thick.

Grease a 12 x 18 inch baking pan with some of the oil. Sprinkle with a little cornmeal. Place the rolled out dough in the pan. Cover and let it rise in warm place for about 30 minutes or until the dough puffs slightly. Preheat the oven to 425 degrees.

Combine all the cheeses in a bowl and season with the fresh basil leaves torn into little bits. Press along the edges of the puffed dough to form a crust that will hold in the topping. Prick the crust with a fork. Spread the cheeses evenly over the top. Drizzle oil very lightly over the top.

Bake at 425 degrees for about 10 to 15 minutes or until the crust at the bottom is crisp and the cheese is slightly colored. Allow to cool slightly before sliding it out of the pan. Brush the edges of the crust with some oil. Cut into small 2-inch squares and serve.

Makes one 12 x 18 inch pizza

ABOUT PIZZA STONES

Wood-fired brick ovens were the customary medium for cooking breads and pizzas. To replicate the dry, crunchy effect created by this kind of heat, pizza stones or unglazed quarry tiles are sold and touted as being the next best thing to building your own wood-burning oven. Before cooking became a fashionable pastime, Italians were baking pizzas at home in whatever oven and pan they could find. A heavy aluminum roasting pan was the one we used for many years. It doubled as a roasting pan for chicken and was our lasagna pan too. Because it had high, 2-inch sides, the pan contained the pizza dough so it could rise up and puff nicely. We always thought of pizza as a tomato-topped moist flatbread with a crusty bottom. Oiling the pan and lining it with cornmeal made it crunchy and taste great - especially when it was reheated. Of course, reheated pizza didn't usually have mozzarella cheese on it - just tomato and herbs. Or possibly oil and anchovies. We didn't call a pizza without tomato topping focaccia then but "pizza bianca" (white pizza).

Using a stone allows you to cut down on the oil and creates a dry, crunchy bottom crust as opposed to a slightly oily, crunchy one which, I might add, most people still prefer. If you have a stone and a paddle, preheat the stone and remember to stretch your dough and lay it on the paddle before you put the topping on it. Sprinkling cornmeal on the paddle helps the dough slide off onto the stone.

Pizza Ripiena

STUFFED RAPINI PIZZA

3 bunches rapini

⅓ cup olive oil

1 medium yellow onion, chopped

2 large cloves garlic, finely chopped

Salt and pepper to taste

1 pound mozzarella cheese, grated

2 batches Basic Pizza Dough or two 1½ pound store-bought packages

Oil for greasing the pan and brushing the dough

Cornmeal for dusting the pan

TIP

To make a more attractive finish to a pizza crust, brush the edges of the pizza with a little oil as soon as it comes out of the oven.

Whenever Nancy Vetere is invited to a potluck gathering, everyone hopes this is what she'll bring. It usually gets gobbled up so fast she's learned to make at least two of them. Instead of a flat, filled pizza, Nancy often makes this as a roll. She spreads the filling over one rolled out sheet of pizza dough, then rolls it up jelly roll fashion into a long log. The ends are pinched and folded under and the pizza is baked so that the seam is on the bottom. It looks lovely when you take it out of the oven, like a pizza-bread. When it is cut the air comes out and the loaf flattens a little. It still makes an attractive slice when cut on the diagonal. Fillings for any stuffed pizza vary depending on regional preferences. Other greens can be substituted, such as broccoli or cooked escarole or combinations of greens. In some places, ground meat, eggs and tomatoes are used.

Wash rapini in several changes of cold water. Cut off the tough stems especially if they are stringy. Cook the rapini tops in 3 quarts of boiling, lightly salted water for about 4 to 5 minutes or until the greens are tender. Drain well, allow to cool and squeeze out the excess water. Chop the cooked rapini finely.

Heat the oil in a skillet and cook the onions until they become soft. Season with salt and pepper. Add the garlic and cook 1 or 2 minutes, being careful not to let the garlic turn brown. Add the chopped, cooked rapini. Mix thoroughly and cook to let the rapini become flavored. Taste and adjust the seasoning, if needed. Allow the mixture to cool before using.

Preheat the oven to 350 degrees. Grease a large 12 x 18 inch pan with oil. Sprinkle cornmeal over the bottom. Prepare a double batch of pizza dough. Roll out one of the doughs and cover the bottom of the baking sheet. Spread the rapini filling over the dough. Sprinkle the grated mozzarella evenly over the rapini filling. Roll the second dough to the same dimensions as the pan and cover the filling. Pinch the edges of the dough together to form a good seal.

Brush the top of the filled pizza with oil. Prick the crust all over with a fork. Sprinkle with a little salt and freshly milled black pepper. Bake in a pre-heated oven at 350 degrees for about 30 to 35 minutes or until the crust is slightly golden. Allow to cool a little before cutting. Serve hot or at room temperature, cut into 3 x 2 inch pieces.

Makes one 12 x 16 inch pizza

Pizza con Funghi ed Olio di Tartuffo

MUSHROOM PIZZA WITH TRUFFLE OIL

James Savona of Brunello Imports speaks passionately about food and flavors. This was what prompted him to start his thriving importing business that now carries over 30 different types of olive oils as well as gourmet preserves like truffle paste, sun-dried tomatoes and artichoke puree.

Having spent the first 12 years of his life in Trapani, Sicily, and after many trips back and forth to food shows and exhibitions, he is very tuned in to the effect season and place has on cooking. Spaghetti with squid ink perfectly prepared in a trattoria in Cefalu, Sicily on the north coast will not necessarily be duplicated in a different part of the island or in Pompano, Florida, for that matter. Nor can it be had in July even in Cefalu because it's the wrong time of year for the young mollusks. Using the best of local ingredients, making the dish simple but flavorful, those are the secrets to good Italian food, according to Jim and his recipe for wild mushroom pizza proves it. If you don't have any truffle oil, try this pizza anyway — it's delicious.

Allow the pizza dough to rise and come to room temperature, covered in plastic. Preheat the oven to 425 degrees. Oil a 12 x 16 inch pan. Punch down the risen dough with well-oiled hands and press it into the pan. Allow it to rest, if it is very elastic, and press again until it reaches the desired thickness and goes

1 Basic Pizza Dough or a store-bought dough

5 plum tomatoes (fresh or canned)

6 tablespoons olive oil

4 fresh basil leaves, torn into bits (or 1 teaspoon dried)

Salt and pepper to taste

1 pound mushrooms (oyster, porte-bello, shiitake, porcini)

1 clove garlic, chopped

3 green scallions, chopped finely

1 tablespoon truffle oil mixed with 1 tablespoon olive oil

almost to the edges of the pan. Spread 2 to 3 tablespoons of oil over the top. Set in a warm place for about 20 minutes or until it puffs slightly.

If using fresh tomatoes, chop them coarsely, cook in the microwave or on top of the stove just until soft. Drain off excess water and puree through a food mill. For canned tomatoes, cut in half and remove seeds. Drain well and puree through a food mill. Season with 2 tablespoons olive oil, the torn basil leaves, salt and pepper to taste. Set aside.

Wash and dry the mushrooms and slice finely. In a skillet, heat a little oil, add the mushrooms, in batches, and saute at high heat. Season with salt and pepper. Mushrooms will give off a fair bit of liquid. Continue to cook until the liquid is completely reduced. Add the garlic and cook for about two minutes. Add the chopped scallions, stir a few moments and turn off the heat. Allow the mixture to cool slightly.

To assemble the pizza, make indentations with the fingertips all over the stretched, puffed pizza dough. Spread the tomato mixture over the top. Season with salt and pepper again. Prick the dough all over with a fork. Cover with the sauteed mushrooms.

Bake in the middle of a very hot oven set at 425 for about 15 minutes. When the bottom and edges have formed a lightly golden crust, remove from the oven. Combine 1 tablespoon of regular oil with the truffle oil. Drizzle this over top of the pizza just before serving. Cut into 2-inch squares and serve hot.

Makes one 12 x 16 inch pizza

I have often longed to taste truffles au naturel - that is, not hidden by a multitude of other flavors as has always been my experience. Whenever I have ordered a dish with truffles in a restaurant, the taste has been elusive. They must have all landed in someone else's plate. Or, perhaps the proprietors decided that waving a piece of truffle over each dish was a sufficient way to impart the taste and much more economical.

Years ago, I experienced the thrill of smelling a white truffle up close in a little shop in Cortona, but that was as far as my pocket-book would allow. Once I bought a jar of truffles in Umbria which is famous for the black variety. I put them on some of the local pasta called "strangozzi" with a few mushrooms but, sadly, it was a disappointment. The truffles had been preserved in such a way as to destroy all the flavor. The bottled variety had none of the earthy, complex tones of the fresh fungus - in fact, they had no tones whatsoever. Since I never buy lottery tickets, I gave up on eating truffles until recently.

At an olive oil tasting at the Italian Trade Commission, I sat at a table with an olive oil importer. His oils were not part of the presentation but the description of his truffle-flavored oil from Umbria rekindled my interest. The next day, I rushed out to buy some at the local Italian gourmet shop.

The label describes the oil as a "Condimento" which means it is a dressing. It further explains that this oil is an infusion made from olive oil, truffles and "aromi." This last gives the impression that the flavor could be artificial, but there is a small piece of black truffle sitting in the bottom of the bottle. The 7 ½ ounce bottle sold for an acceptable figure, considering the fresh ones cost up to $2000 a kilo, so, with great hope and a little apprehension, I carried it home.

The first sensation when the bottle was opened was an overpowering, heady scent - much stronger than my recollection of the fresh truffle I had inhaled. It had the heavy, lugubrious effect that smelling gasoline has on the back of one's throat but it also compelled you to sniff again. I have been told by a reliable source that there is a law in Italy about the transportation of truffles. It states that insurance companies are not liable for accidents that may occur when truffles are transported in closed vehicles if the truffles are not enclosed entirely in rice and sealed properly - such is their intoxicating effect.

I couldn't wait to try the oil on some pasta. Cooking truffle oil would cause it to lose its fragrance, so I experimented with a modified carbonara sauce and prepared some mild greens on the side. The first trial was on pasta with just the egg, cheese and oil. It left my taste buds reeling as I had put in too much oil (3 tablespoons for ½ pound of pasta). Once I added the greens, the tornado was harnessed. The explosive subterranean flavors tempered by the steady earthiness of the chard was pure bliss. The urge to eat very slowly, taking small bites, savoring each mouthful overcame me (normally I'm a fast consumer of pasta.) It is an experience that demands to be shared with friends - or better still, lovers.

Not all truffle oils are equal. According to M. DuBois, the North American distributor of the oil I tasted, the quality of this particular product has to do with the low acidity of the basic oil. It is produced using artisanale methods by the Del Sero family who have a modest establishment in the little hamlet of Moriano in Umbria. The southeast exposure of the regions guaranteeing maximum sun plus the lack of polluting industries in the area create optimum conditions for producing great oil. The labor intensive cold pressing contributes to the quality as does the fact that chemical fertilizers and pesticides are not used. You get what you pay for as I discovered when I tried a cheaper, less noteworthy truffle oil that is made with truffle extract and "aromi" while the Del Sero one is made by infusion.

It is important to note that only a small amount of truffle oil is required to impart a desirable flavor - particularly when it is used on its own. If adding greens, do not use strong, bitter types like rapini or dandelion as they would interfere too much with the multi-layered, subtle qualities of the oil. Mushroom being a fungus, as are truffles, the two combine very well. I have started adding truffle oil to mushroom dishes with wonderful results. Try a spoon over the Whole Wheat Spaghetti with Porcini Mushrooms (p. 85) or in Mushroom Risotto. Whatever the chosen method of consuming this addictive concoction, remember that less is definitely better than too much or the consequences can be unsettling.

Sfinciuni

SICILIAN FLUFFY PIZZA

This Sicilian specialty is like a puffy yeast cake with a savory topping and is generally eaten as a snack or a starter. In fact, once you start eating it, it's very hard to stop. The first time I made it, I had a small slice, just to try it, though I was not particularly hungry. Five minutes later, I had to try a little more to experience again the pleasure of biting into the soft, fluffy texture of the bread accented by the sharper crunch of the onion, and the spicy tomato and cheese crust. This bread-cake will disappear in minutes so you might want to make a double batch. To achieve a 3-inch height, Rosalina Genua bakes it in a small 8-inch cake pan. Her version of Sfinciuni, made in the area around Trapani, does not have filling in between 2 layers of dough as it is done in other parts of Sicily - particularly the famous Sfincione of San Vito. The sardines used are salted and packed in oil like anchovies. They should be scraped free of any small bones before using.

To make the dough, dissolve the sugar in warm water in a large bowl and sprinkle in the yeast. Let sit 5 minutes. Combine 2 cups of flour and the salt. Stir the frothy yeast and water, then add the oil. Gradually stir the flour into the liquid, stirring with a fork to form an irregular sticky dough. Continue adding the flour until the dough can be worked by hand. Place on a lightly floured surface and knead for 5 minutes, adding a few tablespoons of flour to make a soft dough which is smooth and elastic. Place in a clean bowl, cover with plastic wrap and let rise for 1 ½ hours.

When the dough has doubled, punch it down and knead it into a ball shape. Flatten the ball to a disc about 1 ½ inches thick. Place in a greased 8-inch springform cake pan.

Blend the pureed tomato with the onion, oil, oregano, salt and pepper.

Preheat the oven to 400 degrees. Dot the top of the dough with the chopped sardine. Spread the tomato mixture over top and

½ teaspoon sugar

1 cup warm water

1 package dry yeast

2 ½ tablespoons oil

2 cups plus 3 tablespoons all-purpose flour

1 teaspoon salt

Oil for greasing the pan

½ cup pureed plum tomatoes

2 heaping tablespoons onion, finely chopped

1 tablespoon oil

1 teaspoon oregano

¼ teaspoon salt

¼ teaspoon pepper

2 sardine fillets, packed in oil, chopped

2 tablespoons grated Parmigiano

1 8-inch springform cake pan

let the dough rise in the pan for 30 minutes. As it rises, a little of the juice may drip down the sides of the springform pan; set the pan on a plate to catch the drips. Just before baking, sprinkle on the grated Parmigiano. Bake in a preheated oven at 400 degrees for 25 to 30 minutes. A tester inserted into the dough should come out quite dry. Allow to cool before cutting. Serve at room temperature, cut into wedges.

Makes one 8 inch pizza

Salsa per Pizza

BASIC TOMATO TOPPING FOR PIZZA

2 cups plum tomatoes, peeled, seeded and chopped

3 tablespoons olive oil

2 cloves garlic, finely minced

1 teaspoon dried oregano, crumbled

½ teaspoon dried basil, crumbled

¼ teaspoon salt

Pepper to taste

The classic Neapolitan tomato topping for pizza, according to Jim Savona, used to be taken from a bunch of slightly desiccated tomatoes that normally hung in the kitchen of the pizza makers. They were hung in a big "grappolo" (bunch) like grapes and in time, the pulp would become more concentrated. When some topping was needed for a pizza, the pizza-maker would take a few tomatoes and squeeze out the dense pulp, scattering it here and there over the pizza crust covering it intermittently so you could still see the crust underneath. Pizza overloaded with a heavy topping loses it character as a bread. The sauce or raw tomato topping should be balanced with the weight and texture of the crust.

When using canned plum tomatoes that are very firm and in a watery juice, it helps to cook the pizza sauce to reduce the liquid and develop the flavor. Canned plum tomatoes that have "Product of Italy" stamped on them generally are denser, darker and sweeter so cooking will not be needed.

Fresh tomatoes, unless they are very ripe, may need to be cooked in a little oil to dry out the excess liquid. Canned, imported plum tomatoes can be used. Drain the canned tomatoes, reserving the thick juice. Cut the tomatoes in half lengthwise to remove seeds and tough stem. Chop the tomatoes finely and drain off excess water. Strain the reserved juice from the can through a fine mesh sieve to remove the bitter seeds. Add enough juice to the tomato pulp to make 2 cups.

Season the tomato pulp and juice with the olive oil, garlic, herbs, salt and pepper.

Makes 2 cups topping - enough for one 12 x 16 inch pizza

Sweets

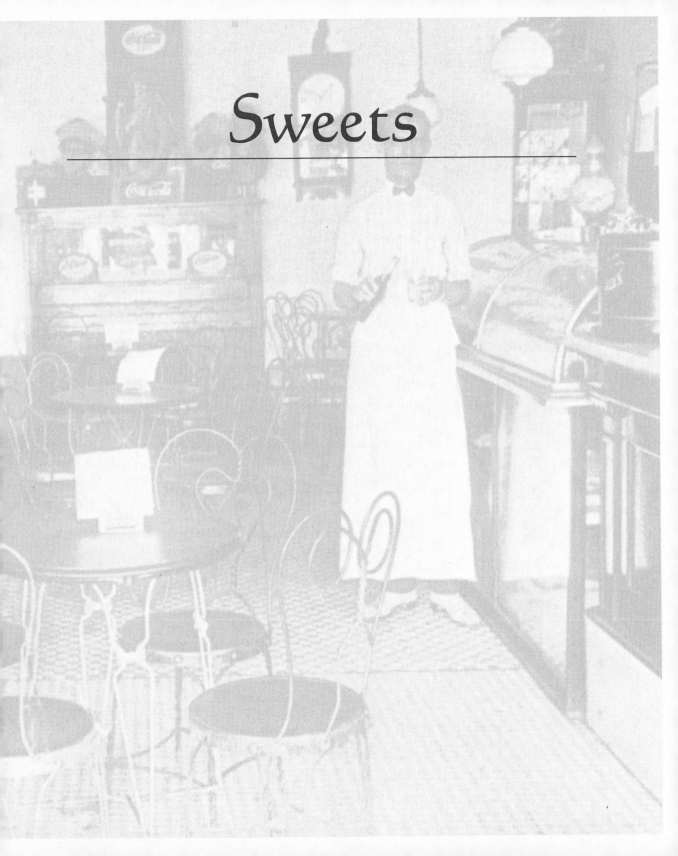

Amaretti

ALMOND COOKIES

¾ pounds raw, unskinned almonds

1 cup sugar

2 eggs

2 teaspoons almond extract

Oil for greasing baking sheet

36 almond slices (slivered or raw, unpeeled) for garnishing

These flourless nut cookies are moist and chewy when fresh from the oven and become crunchier, but still slightly chewy, when cooled. They keep a long time when frozen or in airtight containers. Mrs. Elvira Severino tells us that the trick to making them is to take them out of the oven when the tops only just start to crack. The bottoms will be a little brown but they will still look raw on the top. A slice of raw, unpeeled almond dotting the top looks better, but a single piece of slivered almond makes the cookie easier to eat. This recipe can be doubled and cooked in batches.

Preheat the oven to 300 degrees. Grease a cookie sheet. In a blender or food processor, grind the almonds with ½ cup sugar until very fine but not a paste. Beat together eggs, remaining sugar and almond extract. Stir the egg mixture into the ground almonds. Using either lightly oiled hands or 2 spoons, shape into small balls about the size of large cherries. Place on a greased cookie sheet. Press a thin slice of almond on top of each cookie. Bake in a preheated oven at 300 degrees for about 20 to 25 minutes or until they begin to crack slightly on top. The amaretti will look raw when you take them out. Allow to cool on a rack before storing in an airtight container.

Makes 36 cookies

The two biscotti recipes (Biscotti Calabrese and Sciusciumiel) were provided to me by Mrs. Teresa De Francesco. She keeps all her recipes for "dolci" (sweets) in a 5 x 11 spiral bound book which is as neat and meticulous as her tidy house and very well-organized kitchen. There are tons of recipes for sweets. Each of them has a title and a person's name associated with it to help her keep track. When I looked through the notes, I was not surprised to find there were only quantities listed - no method. The other interesting point is that for many of them, the amount of flour indicated was simply "quan-to vuole" which means as much as is required. She has been making biscotti for a long time - even through the years she worked full-time in a shoe factory and kept house for her husband and 4 children - so she knows exactly when to stop adding the flour. She recommends you try it a few times until you get it just right.

Biscotti Calabrese

CALABRESE COOKIES

All Mrs. De Francesco's cookies are called biscotti but none of them is baked twice. There are fewer nuts in proportion to dough and the nuts are added whole in the nut cookie below. These biscotti are not rock hard like the ones you find in Tuscany. The trick is to make the dough soft and not bake it too long. The recipe can be cut in half but Teresa always makes the full batch and freezes them to have on hand for her 4 children and 12 grandchildren. For convenience, she sometimes freezes the baked whole, or partially cut, logs and slices them as needed.

Beat the eggs well with the sugar, vanilla and baking powder. Stir in the nuts. Add the flour gradually mixing it in until a ball of dough is formed. Knead briefly. Shape into 7 or 8 coils about 2 fingers wide and not much more than ½ inch thick. To help stop the sticking when rolling the coils, dust the surface with some icing sugar to coat the coils lightly all around. The dough will feel very soft and pliable.

Place on a prepared baking sheet and bake for 15 to 20 minutes or

6 eggs

2 cups sugar

1 package vanilla powder or 1 teaspoon extract

1 teaspoon baking powder

1 ½ to 2 cups walnuts

1 ½ to 2 cups hazelnuts

1 ½ to 2 cups almonds

4 to 4 ½ cups flour

until the coils puff and spread and are almost dry. They will have a pale, off-white crust from the icing sugar. Remove from the oven and cut into ½-inch slices. Store in the freezer in plastic bags.

Makes 100 to 120 cookies

Sciusciumiel

GLAZED HONEY-COCOA COOKIES

¾ cup icing sugar

1 egg white

3 eggs

1 cup sugar

½ cup liquid honey

1 teaspoon vanilla extract

4 cups flour

3 teaspoons baking powder

2 teaspoons unsweetened cocoa powder

1 teaspoon cinnamon

Mrs. De Francesco laughed when I asked her to repeat the name of these cookies so I could write it down correctly. It's in Calabrese dialect and has something to do with the fact that honey (miele) goes into the recipe. There are probably many ways to spell it and it may very well be called something entirely different in another town in Calabria.

When Mrs. De Francesco makes these, she usually doubles the recipe as they are very fast and easy to do. She sometimes puts in nuts. "Any kind will do; it's up to you. In this batch I didn't put any in and they are still good." Quite right! The ones I tasted had none, and tasted terrific.

Line 2 baking sheets with foil and brush with some oil. Preheat oven to 350 degrees. Beat together the glaze ingredients. Cover and set aside. Mix the liquid ingredients with the sugar by hand. Combine 3 ½ cups of the flour with the baking powder, cocoa and cinnamon. Add the dry ingredients to the liquid, mixing to form a soft dough. Knead in approximately ½ cup more flour. The dough should be soft but not too sticky and will hold its shape when a small piece is rolled into a coil.

Shape the dough into coils about the width of a finger. Cut the coils diagonally into 2 inch lengths. Place on a prepared baking sheet and brush on the glaze. Bake at 350 degrees for not more than 15 minutes. Check the cookies frequently to make sure they do not overcook. Remove from oven and cool on a rack. Store in plastic bags in the freezer.

Makes 5 to 6 dozen cookies

Biscotti al Anice

ANISE BISCOTTI

While the hard kind of biscotti are wonderful for dipping into wine or coffee, sometimes I am afraid an unsuspecting person might suffer serious damage to their teeth. For years I have enjoyed Nancy Vetere's tender anise biscotti that dissolve easily in your mouth whether or not they are dunked. She very generously passed on her cherished recipe. It has been halved for convenience.

Preheat the oven to 325 degrees. Lightly flour one baking sheet. In a mixer, beat the eggs and almonds until the eggs become frothy. Add the sugar very slowly, beating until the mixture becomes pale and increases in volume. Beat in the oil, anise and vanilla extract.

In a separate bowl, combine 2 ½ cups of flour with the baking powder and salt. Using the mixing attachment, stir the flour mixture gradually into the egg mixture. Mix for about 4 minutes or until well combined. Scrape the sticky dough onto a floured board and knead in the remaining flour. The dough will feel very soft and sticky.

Divide the dough into thirds. Shape into logs about 1 ½ inches in diameter. Place the logs on the prepared baking sheet spaced well apart. Bake for 15 to 20 minutes or until the logs are barely colored. Remove from oven. Turn oven to 425 degrees.

Cut each log diagonally into ½-inch slices. Lay each slice flat on the baking sheet and bake again, for about 10 to 15 minutes, turning once. Remove from the oven when they are lightly colored on both sides and quite dry. Cool on a rack. Store in airtight containers.

Makes 32 to 36 biscotti.

3 extra large eggs

½ cup slivered almonds, toasted and chopped

¾ cup sugar

½ cup corn oil

1 tablespoon anise extract

½ teaspoon vanilla extract

3 cups all-purpose flour

1 tablespoon baking powder

½ teaspoon salt

NOTE

If you double the recipe and bake two pans at the same time, they will need more time in the oven. For both the first and second baking, rotate the pans, moving the top one down and the bottom one up, to avoid uneven results.

Biscotti di Mandorle e Nocciole

ALMOND AND HAZELNUT COOKIES

1 ½ cups raw almonds and hazelnuts, unskinned

3 cups all-purpose flour

1 teaspoon baking powder

Pinch of salt

5 large eggs

1 teaspoon vanilla extract

2 cups sugar

In a family-run trattoria in the perfect medieval town of Pienza in Tuscany, I had ordered a glass of the local sweet red wine called Vin Santo as dessert. The little glass was set on a doily-covered dish with a single biscotti alongside for dipping. It made a perfect winter dessert. These nut cookies are cooked twice and become very hard and dry. They are meant to be dipped into coffee or wine and when they absorb the liquid, they soften sufficiently to be chewed but still hold their shape. Do not try to eat them without softening them first in a liquid. Because there is no added fat in these biscotti, they will keep a long time when stored in airtight containers.

Lightly toast almonds in a medium oven. Cool and chop coarsely. Toast hazelnuts separately and remove skin by rubbing the toasted nuts in a kitchen towel. Chop coarsely and mix with almonds.

Combine 2 ½ cups flour, baking powder and salt. Beat the eggs lightly setting aside 2 tablespoons for glazing. Beat the vanilla into the egg. Mound the flour mixture and make a well in the center. Pour the beaten eggs and the sugar into the well and mix together to form a dough. It will be very sticky. Stir in the chopped nuts, distributing them evenly throughout. Place the sticky dough on a floured board incorporating the remaining ½ cup flour if necessary to help reduce sticking. Knead lightly until the dough is smooth.

Shape the dough into 2 or 3 long rolls about 2 inches wide and 1 inch high. Place on a greased and floured baking sheet. Brush with the reserved lightly beaten egg. Bake in a preheated oven set at 350 degrees for about 30 to 35 minutes. Remove from oven and cut diagonally into slices ¾ inch thick. Set each slice on its side and return to oven at 325 degrees for about 10 minutes, turning once. Cool on racks and allow to sit for a day in an airtight container before serving. Serve with espresso or caffe latte, or alongside a glass of Vin Santo as a dessert.

Makes 36 biscotti

THE FIG COOKIE PHENOMENON

When Louise spoke to the two Sicilian sisters in the butcher shop about getting a recipe for fig cookies, (sometimes known as "Cucidati") both spoke up eagerly and at once, supplying details and ingredients, advice and admonitions. Unfortunately, they could not agree. One said you couldn't make them without zucchini jam, the other said this was not so. The disagreements persisted on a second visit so, to avoid causing a breakdown in family relations, Louise let the subject drop. There are so many ways of making this classic Sicilian cookie, it is difficult to select one definitive recipe.

An interesting phenomenon that emerged in our quest for the ideal fig cookie was how recipes were transformed as they passed from one generation to another and moved from one country to another. Perhaps it was to accommodate personal tastes or to adapt to local ingredients. Two branches of one extended family have provided an example of this process in the two slightly different recipes below.

Around 1890, Mary (Giordano) Como was born in Agrigento, Sicily which is famous for its magnificent ancient Greek temples. Sicily and Calabria were once a part of Magna Graecia and inhabited by emigrating Greeks seeking dominion over more land - hence some of the best preserved Greek temples can be found in Italy. As a young girl, Mary came to America with her parents, arriving in New Orleans where she stayed for a few years and then migrated to Kansas City to raise a large family with her husband Albert Como.

It was an annual tradition for Mary to bake these fig cookies at Christmas and package them as gifts for family and friends who were not familiar with these delicious Italian pastries. Mary became well-known in the community for her wonderful fig cookies and her marvelous Italian cooking.

Mary and Albert had nine children. One daughter, Josephine, married Louie DeAngelis and moved to Toronto, Canada. There, she continued the family tradition, passing on her mother's recipes to her children and grandchildren. With her great passion for cooking and a meticulous attention to good quality food, Josephine's take-out sandwich emporium on Clinton Street became a mecca for Italian immigrants in the 1950's and 60's. People would come from all over and stand in line to get her famous veal on a bun for only 50 cents. Her mother taught her well. And now her grandsons are creating novelty cheeses and so the culinary wheel turns.

Biscotti di Fichi alla Siciliana

SICILIAN FIG COOKIES

1 pound almonds

2 orange peels

4 pounds dried figs

2 pounds white raisins

8 ounces mixed citrus peel

2 ¼ chocolate bars with nuts

1 heaping cup honey

*3 cups pineapple preserves or
24 ounce can crushed pineapple*

½ cup whiskey, brandy or rum

3 teaspoons nutmeg

2 teaspoons cinnamon

12 cups flour

2 ½ cups sugar

3 tablespoons baking powder

1 tablespoon salt

1 pound lard or shortening

1 stick (¼ pound) butter, softened

9 eggs

1 cup milk

2 tablespoons vanilla

Creative cooks usually put their stamp on what they make so Josephine DeAngelis and her sister Minnie made these cookies slightly differently. Their daughters, Mary Borgo and Mary Clossen remember eating their mothers' version of these cookies with pleasure. It is to them we owe this record. Below is Minnie's version.

Toast the almonds and orange peels in the oven. In a meat grinder, grind the almonds and orange peels, figs, raisins, mixed peel and chocolate bars. Stir in the next 5 ingredients and mix until well combined. You may need to double grind it.

Mix together the flour, sugar, baking powder and salt. Blend the lard and butter into the flour mixture until it is a uniform consistency, as for a pie dough. In a separate bowl, beat the eggs milk and vanilla until fluffy. Combine liquid and dry ingredients and knead briefly until the mixture is smooth.

Work with one piece of dough at a time. Roll out the dough to a rectangle (about 3 x 12 inches). Lay a strip of filling along the center, moisten the edges with some egg white and fold the dough over to form a seal. Place the seam side down. Cut slits into the top of the dough using a sharp knife or a razor. Either bake the strips whole, with the edges curved to form a half ring shape or cut into smaller cookies. Set on a greased, floured baking sheet. Bake in a preheated oven set at 350 degrees for 8 to 10 minutes or until lightly golden on top.

Makes 100's of cookies

5 pounds flour

2 ½ pounds

20 teaspoons baking powder

2 ½ to 3 cups sugar

9 eggs

1 tablespoon vanilla

3 cups milk

2 pounds dates

10 pounds figs

3 or 4 pounds raisins

5 to 8 cups sugar (to taste)

1 or 2 pounds nuts (any kind, almonds, walnuts, hazelnuts)

1 pint rum, wine or whiskey

1 pound mixed citron

4 teaspoons cloves

4 teaspoons cinnamon

4 teaspoons nutmeg

4 teaspoons orange peel

Bake for 12 minutes at 400 degrees

Mrs. Bellisario's "Mice" Cookies

¼ cup butter, room temperature

5 tablespoons brown sugar

2 tablespoons water

1 teaspoon vanilla extract

1 teaspoon almond extract

1 cup walnut pieces, finely chopped
(but not to a powder)

1 ¼ cups cake flour

My friend couldn't tell me the original name of this delicious, shortbread-like, beige cookie that her mother, Teresa Bellisario used to make. Ever since she can remember, they have been simply called mice - perhaps because of the slight resemblance.

In a mixer, cream the butter and sugar together until smooth and light. Beat in the water, vanilla and almond extract. Stir in the chopped walnuts.

Using a wooden spoon, add the flour to the mixture, stirring it until everything is well combined. Pick up a small piece of dough, roll it in your palm into a half-moon shape 2 inches long. Place on a very lightly greased cookie sheet. Shape the remaining dough. Bake in a preheated oven at 350 degrees for 13 to 15 minutes.

Makes 30 cookies

Cornetti di Guiseppina

CINNAMON-WALNUT CRESCENT COOKIES

1 pound butter

4 cups flour

2 egg yolks

1 ½ cups sour cream

½ cup walnut pieces, crushed

½ cup sugar

½ to 1 teaspoon cinnamon (to taste)

This is one of the many cookies and pastries Giuseppina hauls out of the freezer when people come to visit (she has two big freezers - one wouldn't be enough). It took two cups of espresso to sample one of each kind and, in the end, I still could not decide which was my favorite. There was a bigger assortment than usual as Easter had just passed. Giuseppina got this particular recipe from a "Ciociara" friend ("ciociara" is someone who comes from Lazio).

Cut the butter into the flour until it forms a crumbly mixture. Beat the egg yolks and sour cream together. Pour this into the flour mixture, working it together to form a ball of dough. Do not overwork the dough. Divide the dough into 6 balls. Wrap each one in plastic and chill in the refrigerator for several hours or overnight.

Just before rolling out the dough, combine the crushed walnuts, sugar and cinnamon. Preheat the oven to 350 degrees.

Roll out a ball of dough to a disc about ¼ inch thick. Brush some melted butter on the dough. Cut the disc into 12 to 15 wedges and sprinkle a small amount of filling over top. Starting at the wide end, roll each wedge into a miniature croissant shape (about 2 inches long). Set on an ungreased baking sheet. Shape the remaining dough to fill the baking sheet. Bake in batches, one tray at a time for 10 to 15 minutes. Set on a rack to cool. Store in the freezer.

Makes 6 dozen cookies

OPTIONAL GLAZE

Line the baking sheets with parchment paper or aluminum foil. Brush the crescents with one egg white lightly beaten with a tablespoon of water. Sprinkle with granulated sugar before baking.

Torta di Noci e Cioccolato

CHOCOLATE NUT CAKE

A young chef who comes from an extended family of restauranteurs recommended we try the flourless nut cake he had just developed for the new menu at the trattoria where he worked. It was light, yet rich - not exactly fluffy but definitely airier than other nut cakes I had tasted. He wouldn't give out his secret recipe at the time but I went home determined to duplicate it or find a reasonable approximation. This is the result.

Preheat oven to 350 degrees. Grease a 9-inch springform pan and line the bottom with parchment or wax paper.

In food processor, grind the nuts in batches until fine but not a paste. Set aside. Cut the chocolate into chunks and grind with half the sugar until it is the same consistency as the nuts.

Separate the eggs. In a mixer, beat the yolks until thick and pale, add the chocolate mixture, lemon and orange zests and beat just until combined. In a clean, dry bowl, beat the egg whites and remaining sugar until soft peaks form.

1 ½ cups hazelnuts, lightly toasted and skinned

1 ½ cups walnuts, freshly shelled

1 cup almonds, raw, unskinned

7 ounces semisweet chocolate

¾ cup sugar

8 large eggs

1 teaspoon lemon zest, grated

1 teaspoon orange zest, grated

Sweets 223

4 ounces semi-sweet chocolate
1 tablespoon corn syrup
1 tablespoon orange blossom water
(orange extract or Cointreau)
3 tablespoons water
4 tablespoons soft butter

Melt chocolate in a double boiler.
Stir in corn syrup and water. Blend
until smooth. Add orange blossom
water and butter. Stir until well
combined. Pour the warm glaze over
the cooled cake.

Stir a quarter of the egg white mixture into the yolk mixture to lighten it. Gently fold the nuts and remaining egg white mixture alternately into the yolk mixture. Pour the batter into the prepared pan. Bake for 55 minutes or until a tester comes out clean.

Allow the cake to cool completely. Remove the sides of pan. Peel off the parchment paper. Place the cake on a platter and spread with warm Chocolate Orange Glaze or decorate the top with sifted icing sugar, cut into serving pieces and garnish individual plates with very thin slices of unpeeled orange.

Makes 8 to 10 slices

Pinsa

CORNMEAL SQUASH CAKE

½ teaspoon sugar

½ cup warm water

1 package dry yeast (2 ½ teaspoons)

1 small acorn or butternut squash, cooked (1 cup mashed)

5 ounces dried figs, finely chopped

5 ounces golden raisins, whole

¾ cup grappa and rum

5 eggs

1 cup sugar

Pinch of salt

½ cup milk

1 cup butter, melted

Pinsa was always made on January 6, to celebrate the end of the the Christmas season. Angela Romano's grandmother from Pessicanna, a small town in Friuli, normally baked the pinsa in a wood-burning oven often over cabbage leaves. She always used lard instead of butter as was the case in many traditional recipes. Pinsa was always served with "brule" - a flambeed, mulled wine (p. 260). The cake is a dark, golden, orange colour and has a slightly granular crunch from the cornmeal. The use of both yeast and chemical leavening (lievito) seems odd but we are warned not to vary from this traditional method!

Preheat oven to 360 degrees. Butter and lightly flour a 9 x 12 inch baking pan. Dissolve sugar in warm water, sprinkle in yeast and let stand for 5 minutes until it bubbles.

Puree the cooked squash through a food mill. Cook 1 cup of puree in a nonstick skillet to dry out excess water.

With an electric mixer, beat the eggs and sugar until smooth. Add the salt, milk, melted butter, pureed squash, lemon and orange zests and fennel. Mix until combined. Using a wooden spoon, stir in the dissolved yeast, figs, raisins and the alcohol. Gradually stir in the cornmeal. It will appear very mushy. Add the flour a little at a time. Sift in the envelopes of vanilla-flavored lievito and vanilla sugar. The mixture should be thick but pourable.

Pour the batter into the prepared pan, smoothing it out to the edges. Set on the middle shelf of the oven and bake for 40 to 45 minutes or until a tester inserted in the center comes out dry. Do not be alarmed that the cake does not rise very much. Allow to cool before cutting into 2-inch squares.

Makes 24 2-inch squares

1 orange, grated zest only

1 lemon, grated zest 1 only

1 tablespoon fennel seeds, crushed to a powder

1 cup coarse cornmeal

2 ¼ cups all-purpose flour

1 envelope vanilla lievito (see Glossary)

1 envelope vanilla sugar

Tiramisu

This layered dessert has become so popular in recent years since it is so easy to make - as long as you can find Mascarpone cream. These days, most Italian delicatessens and many specialty cheese shops sell locally made brands. It is better if the dessert is made the night before as the cookies have a chance to soften. Orazia Di Cesare skips a step when she makes it. She does not bother to separate the eggs and fold in the beaten whites. She also advises that you dampen the cookies briefly with the coffee and rum as this makes them soggy.

In an electric mixer, beat the eggs and sugar until pale and thick. Stir in the Mascarpone.

Combine vermouth and espresso. Moisten some of the ladyfingers with the coffee mixture using a pastry brush. Be careful that they do not become soggy. Cover the bottom of the serving dish with one layer of moistened cookies. Pour a layer of the Mascarpone cream over the ladyfingers and dust with cocoa. Repeat with one more layer of moistened ladyfingers. Top with the remaining Mascarpone and end with a dusting of cocoa. Cover and refrigerate overnight. Serve chilled. If desired, decorate the top with chocolate covered espresso beans or dark chocolate curls.

Makes one 9 x 11 pan.

3 very fresh extra large eggs

3 heaping tablespoons sugar

1 pound Mascarpone cheese (2 cups)

5 tablespoons sweet vermouth or white rum

1 cup espresso coffee, cooled

1 package Italian ladyfingers (40-45 cookies)

½ cup unsweetened cocoa powder

1 rectangular, glass serving dish

ALTERNATE SERVING METHOD

Tiramisu is very attractive when presented in a tall, straight-sided glass bowl. There will be more layers and you will need to break the cookies to make them fit to the edges. To get more air into the cream and give it a fluffier consistency, separate the eggs, beating the yolks with the sugar. Whip the whites until stiff and fold them into the yolk mixture alternately with the Mascarpone.

Torta di Frutta

FRUIT CAKE

4 eggs

1 teaspoon of salt

1 cup of sugar

1 lemon (grated rind)

1 orange (grated rind)

1 ½ ounces of pure vanilla extract

8 ounces of rum or brandy

½ cup butter, melted

2 ½ cups of flour

4 teaspoons of baking powder

1 cup of mixed candied fruit

1 cup of red and green candied cherries

1 cup of walnuts (coarsely chopped)

1 cup of blanched almonds (coarsely chopped)

1 cup of raisins (washed in cold water)

Elizabeth Giacometti provided the recipe for this special, Italian-style Christmas cake with candied fruit. The resulting cake is very dense and rises only about three inches. It should be made several days before serving as the flavors need time to mellow.

Preheat oven to 350 degrees. In a bowl, beat the eggs, salt, sugar, lemon and orange rinds, vanilla, rum, butter. Add the flour and baking powder together and gradually add to the wet mixture and combine with the mixer. Stir in the candied fruit and cherries. Lastly, add the almonds, walnuts and raisins. Let the raisins soak in water for 10 minutes before adding to the mixture. Before baking, decorate with some cherries and walnuts.

Spread the thick mixture into a greased, floured loaf pan (14 x 9 inches). Bake for one hour. Let the cake cool and then remove from pan. Store in an air-tight container for several days before serving.

Makes one 9 x 12 loaf

Torta di Ricotta-Ananas

RICOTTA PINEAPPLE CAKE

Italian immigration brought with it many new imported foods and products to North America. At the same time, many Italian emigres were quick to adopt certain North American processed food when it was convenient. This recipe illustrates this cultural mix well. Lidia Cattapan discovered this fresh, light-tasting dessert at a wedding shower. Originally, the recipe called for graham cracker crumbs but Lidia uses either social tea cookies or the imported biscuits called Pavesini which she gets from her local Italian grocery store. Using Lemon Jello instead of a plain gelatin with lemon zest and sugar is purely for convenience and makes this a very fast, easy summer dessert.

1 ½ cups Pavesini

⅓ cup butter, melted

1 pound ricotta

1 package lemon Jello

1 cup heavy cream, whipped

1 cup icing sugar

1 19-ounce can crushed pineapple

In a food processor, crumble the Pavesini cookies. Mix the Pavesini with the melted butter and place in an oven casserole (12 x 7½ inches). Press the crumbs into the casserole with your fingers and bake at 320 degrees for 8 to 10 minutes. Let cool.

Dissolve the lemon Jello in half of the water suggested on the package. Do not allow to cool completely. Whip the cream. Run the ricotta and icing sugar through the food processor until smooth. Combine the lemon Jello, whipped cream, ricotta, crushed pineapple and its juice. Mix well. Pour this mixture into the casserole. Sprinkle the top with Pavesini crumbs. Leave in the refrigerator for a few hours or overnight. Decorate with fresh fruit, such as strawberries, blueberries and kiwi.

Serves 10

Torta di Formaggio al Cappuccino

CAPPUCCINO CHEESECAKE

2 cups graham cracker crumbs, crumbled

⅓ cup brown sugar

3 tablespoons cinnamon

¼ pound unsalted butter, melted

3 packages Philadelphia cream cheese

4 eggs

½ cup sugar

2 teaspoons pure vanilla extract

½ cup instant espresso powder or mocha-flavored powder

¼ cup Kalhua liqueur

1 cup heavy cream

2 tablespoons sugar

1 tablespoon pure vanilla extract

1 ½ tablespoons cinnamon or cocoa for dusting the cake

Many Italians were quick to pick up on good foods and adopted popular North American-style recipes. Some would adapt them and add a few Italian ingredients or Italianize the name. "La Philadelphia" is one such example. Many Italians mentioned cheesecake when asked about what desserts they like to make. But it turns out not to be the typical Sicilian-style cheesecake (Torta di Formaggio) made with ricotta cheese. Perhaps the great marketing efforts that Kraft has put into Italy has filtered across the ocean.

Connie Esposito Dametto likes to serve this cheesecake with a strong cup of espresso and a shot of Barolo grappa. She often uses instant cappuccino powder as a flavoring. The cake should be prepared the day before so it has a chance to set, but the topping is best prepared an hour before serving. The cake can also be frozen, without the topping.

Preheat oven to 375 degrees. Combine the crackers, brown sugar and cinnamon. Add the butter and mix well with a fork. Press this mixture into the bottom of a 9-inch springform pan with your fingers. Refrigerate for 1 hour.

For the filling, add the cream cheese to a food processor and mix until smooth. Add one egg at a time and continue mixing. Gradually add the sugar, vanilla, powdered coffee and liqueur. Continue mixing. Pour the mixture into the springform pan and bake at 375 degrees for 45 to 50 minutes. Allow to cool and refrigerate overnight in the pan.

An hour before serving prepare the topping. Beat the heavy cream, sugar, and vanilla until it holds its shape. With a spatula, spread this on top of the cake and shape into soft peaks so that it looks like the top of a cappuccino coffee. Dust with cinnamon or cocoa.

Makes 8 to 10 servings

Torta di Riso

RICE PIE

Sharon Dauito's aunt Kay (Catherine Tamagni of New Jersey) makes the best rice pie. She's been making it for over 50 years now and says that every year she thinks she'll stop but, her family is happy that she has continued the tradition. It's a recipe she learned from her mother. She usually makes double the recipe and gives it away to her relatives at Easter time.

Place the first five ingredients in a blender and blend in two batches until smooth. Combine all the filling with the cooked rice. Set aside.

Cut the flour and shortening together until the mixture resembles peameal. Mix in the sugar, salt, the beaten egg and as much cold water as is needed to form a dough. Knead very briefly but do not overhandle.

Divide the dough into 3 pieces. Roll each piece between two sheets of wax paper to make a disk that will fit a 9-inch pie plate. Line the pie plates with the rolled out dough. Make a fluted edge around the top of the dough. Pour one third of the filling into each pie plate. Bake in a preheated oven at 375 degrees for 35 to 45 minutes. The tops will be slightly yellow in color. Allow to cool. Store in the refrigerator until ready to serve.

Makes three 9-inch pies

3 pounds ricotta cheese

9 eggs

3 cups sugar

2 can evaporated milk (12 ounces each)

3 teaspoons vanilla extract

2 cups cooked, cold rice

4 cups flour

1 ¼ cups shortening

2 tablespoons sugar

½ teaspoon salt

2 eggs, lightly beaten

½ cup cold water

Gubana

FRIULI SWEET BREAD

4 ounces fresh cake yeast
(3 envelopes dried)

½ cup warm water

½ teaspoon sugar

1 ½ cups milk

½ pound butter

4 large eggs, plus 2 yolks

2 cups sugar

1 teaspoon salt

½ cup oil (corn or sunflower)

1 package vanilla sugar (8 grams)

2 tablespoons rum (or 1 tablespoon
rum extract)

1 lemon, grated zest only

3 cups all-purpose flour

1 ¼ pounds sultana raisins

10 ounces almonds ground coarsely in
food processor

5 ounces walnuts, broken into small
chunks

This specialty sweet bread is found only in Friuli and is apparently of Slovenian origin, having made its way into Italy via Trieste. Guba, in Slovenian, means fold. The dough is folded around the filling then folded again into a snail shape. It is made usually at Easter and Christmas time. Making a large batch is convenient as it can be frozen. In fact, the strong, heady flavors from the alcohol taste better if the bread is allowed to sit for a day or so and "mature."

Elizabeth Giacometti recommends that the dough for each bread be rolled out, if possible, all at the same time so the filling can be divided evenly among them. She usually crushes the social tea cookies in small batches in a brown paper bag with a heavy rolling pin. That way you get a mix of crumbs and small chunks. (A food processor would grind the cookies too finely.) She always weighs the ingredients for the filling rather than measuring by volume. If time permits, she recommends a longer period of time for the 2 risings and a final, third rising after the dough is filled and shaped.

Dissolve yeast in ½ cup warm water and ½ teaspoon of sugar. Let it sit for about 10 minutes until it foams.

Heat the butter and milk until it melts. Allow to cool. With a mixer, beat the eggs and sugar. Continue beating and add salt, butter/milk mixture, oil, vanilla sugar, rum and lemon peel. Stir in the yeast. Gradually start adding the flour and mix well with a wooden spoon. Once the dough is solid enough to be worked by hand, place on a floured work surface and knead, adding more flour as necessary. Knead for 15 to 20 minutes until a smooth dough is formed. The dough should feel soft but not stick to the board or your fingers.

Shape the dough into a ball, place in a clean, dry bowl, cover with plastic and allow to rise at room temperature for 1 to 2 hours until almost double in size. After the first rise, transfer the dough to a floured board and knead again for about 10 to 15 minutes. Return the dough to the bowl, cover again and let rise for another 1 ½ hours. Prepare the filling.

Wash the raisins in cold water. Drain and dry them. In a large bowl, combine the raisins, nuts, cocoa powder, sugar, and crumbled cookies. Combine the rum and the grappa and gradually stir into the dry filling mixture. Mix thoroughly until all is combined and the filling is totally moistened. It will not be very wet but it should cling together.

Preheat the oven to 350 degrees. After the second rise, punch down the dough and divide into 6 equal pieces. On a lightly floured surface, roll out a piece of dough into an oval about 14 x 12 inches and ¼ inch thick. Roll out the other pieces.

Divide the filling evenly among the 6 ovals. Spread the filling evenly over each oval leaving a small border of ½ inch free around the edges. Use your fingers to break up and re-distribute the pieces of filling that stick together. Starting from the longer side, roll out the dough to make a log. Pinch the ends together and place the seam on the bottom. Shape the log into a snail-like coil with the innermost coil slightly higher than the outer one.

Place two of the coiled doughs on a greased baking sheet. If giving a third rise, cover with plastic and let rise for 30 minutes. Brush the dough with lightly beaten egg whites to get a shiny crust. Bake for 45 to 50 minutes. Do not open the oven door for the first 40 minutes and don't be alarmed that the crust is dark brown - that is the normal colour. Bake more than one at a time.

Remove from the oven and let cool completely. Let the bread sit for a day before serving it to allow the flavors to mellow. The gubana will keep for several days covered in foil. It can also be frozen. To serve, cut the gubana in half then into wedges and dip it into espresso.

Makes 6 breads

6 ounces pinenuts, whole

7 ounces cocoa powder

1 pound sugar

28 ounces (2 packages) social tea cookies, crumbled

1 cup rum

1 cup grappa or brandy

2 eggs, beaten

Pizzelle con Cioccolato

CHOCOLATE PIZZELLE

3 eggs

¾ cup sugar

½ cup melted butter or margarine

2 teaspoons grated orange

2 teaspoons rum (optional)

2 tablespoons semi-sweet chocolate, grated

2 cups flour

2 teaspoons baking powder

My very first close encounter with cooking as a profession was when I helped out one summer at the restaurant run by Sabina Masci and her sisters Anna and Eva. My father's cousin, whom we always called Aunt Sabina, is a very natural, spontaneous cook. Five days a week, they used to prepare homemade soups, sandwiches, main courses, vegetables and desserts for the factory workers. Her clients looked like a very cheerful, contented lot which was no wonder considering the fresh, home cooking that was available to them at a subsidized cost. They were desolate when she retired many years ago and a large, catering concern took over.

Recently, over a cup of tea, she brought out some crisp, marbled pizzelle made in her new, nonstick electric pizzelle maker. They were some of the nicest I have tasted. At first, she followed the recipe that came with the instructions but then varied it, as many expert cooks do, adding a little of this, changing that, transforming them to her liking. The end result with an interesting filling variation is below.

Beat together the eggs and sugar until light and fluffy. Add the melted butter, orange rind and optional rum. Stir in the grated chocolate.

Combine the flour and baking powder. Stir this into the egg mixture, beating it in to make a rather stiff batter that can be dropped from a spoon.

Heat the electric pizzelle maker. Drop a tablespoon of the batter onto the very middle of the hot pizzelle plates. Press down. Cook about 15 seconds, until nicely colored. Serve as is. When they have cooled, store in an air-tight container.

Makes 30 pizzelle

Chocolate Pizzelle with Date Filling

Make the above recipe for Chocolate Pizzelle but add a warm date-orange stuffing. The pizzelle become soft and moist instead of crisp.

1 ¾ cups dates, chopped finely
2 oranges, juiced plus grated zest from one orange
1 tablespoon rum, optional

Combine the chopped dates, orange juice and zest in a saucepan. Cook over very low heat until a soft paste is formed. Stir in the optional rum. Keep the filling warm or reheat when ready to fill the pizzelle.

Prepare the chocolate pizzelle recipe. As soon as the pizzelle comes off the maker, while it is still warm and flexible, spoon some warm date filling on one side, top with another freshly made pizzelle and cut into half. Continue making and filling the pizzelle in this manner. Keep in an airtight container or freeze.

Pizzelle di Papa

DAD'S PIZZELLE

Pizzelle are a decorative, waffle-type pastry offered at every special occasion. There are two basic versions. The very thin, crisp type can be eaten as is or joined together with a filling. Then there is the sturdy, dunk-them-in-your-espresso type that are more like a sweet flatbread. The second is the version I grew up with and my Dad still makes them this way over a gas flame with his monographed waffle iron.

The pizzelle iron used to make this firmer type was a gift from a friend who was grateful to Dad for helping him get a job in construction. It had been specially designed with my father's initials (V.P.) in the centre of each waffle. This tool was built to last a lifetime or longer. It is fabricated of heavy cast iron and

4 eggs

1 tablespoon vanilla extract

¼ cup butter, melted

1 lemon, juice and grated zest

¾ cup granulated sugar

2 teaspoons baking powder

2 ½ cups flour (or as needed)

meant to be used at an open fire. It consists of two long rods joined at one end with a hinge attaching the two flat, waffle making panels. The iron is heated, greased with a small piece of pork fat and a small lump of dough is positioned between the two plates and the handles pressed firmly together.

As a child, it was magical to watch the transformation of a lump of dough into a pretty waffle with the initials in the center. These days, electric waffle makers are more widely available than the old irons, so the crispy variety have become prevalent. Below are the two versions.

Beat together eggs, vanilla, melted butter, lemon juice and rind. Beat sugar into the egg mixture until it is smooth. Mix together baking powder and 2 cups flour. Stir the dry ingredients into the egg mixture to form a slightly sticky dough. Place on a floured board and knead in the remaining flour or as much as is necessary to form a smooth, shiny dough. Let the dough rest, covered, for a few minutes.

Flatten the ball of dough into a disk about ¾ inch thick. Cut into strips 1 ½ inches wide, then cut into logs about 3 inches long.

Heat a pizzelle iron over a gas flame. Brush the molded plates with a little melted fat (oil or butter). When the iron is hot, place a log of dough in the centre of the plate. Clamp down the top iron and cook for 15 seconds on one side and 12 seconds on the other or just until the waffle turns golden.

Makes about 20 pizzelle

Cassatedi

SWEET RICOTTA TURNOVERS

According to Mrs. Rosalia Genua, these particular sweets are made only in her village near Trapani, Sicily. However, fried pastries are popular with many Southern Italians. Other regions have a similar type of fried, filled turnover with a different name and different filling. In Campania they are called "sfogliatelle"; the Abruzzese version is "ceci ripieni"; the Molisani fill them with chestnuts and call them "calciuni." They are shaped much like ravioli or agnolotti but the filling is sweet. In most cases, the dough is worked as you would pasta all'uova and rolled into thin bands with a pasta machine. The dough can also be stretched with a rolling pin as it is a little softer than regular egg pasta. This version tastes good even when cold. Serve them with a glass of sweet Marsala.

Drain the ricotta in a wire mesh sieve for several hours or overnight to remove excess water. Mix in the sugar, vanilla sugar, optional cinnamon and half an egg white to help bind the filling.

Mix together eggs, shortening, sugar, and milk. Mound 3 ½ cups of the flour on a board and make a well. Pour the egg mixture into the well and sprinkle in baking powder. Use a fork to incorporate the liquid into the flour to form a dough just like for pasta all'uovo. Add a little more milk if necessary. Knead briefly until the dough is smooth.

Divide the dough into 4 pieces. Keeping the other pieces covered, flatten one piece, dust with some of the remaining flour and pass it through the rollers of a pasta machine as for making pasta. Do not roll to the thinnest setting, but stop at #5. Each strip should be about 1⁄16 inch thick and about 4 inches wide.

To shape and fill, follow the same procedures for making ravioli except that the dough will be folded over the filling instead of laying one strip over the other. Working with one strip of dough at a time, place 1 rounded teaspoon of filling along one side of the dough at 3 ½ inches intervals. Fold the top half of the

1 pound ricotta, drained

2 to 3 ounces sugar

1 package vanilla sugar

½ teaspoon cinnamon (optional)

½ egg white

4 eggs

¼ cup shortening, melted

2 tablespoons sugar

⅓ cup milk

4 cups all purpose flour

½ teaspoon baking powder

Oil for deep frying (about 2 cups)

Sugar for sprinkling over fried pastries

strip of dough over the filling and press edges together to enclose the filling completely. Cut into squares or half-moons. Lay on a lightly floured sheet. Continue forming the remaining dough and filling in this manner.

Heat plenty of oil in a deep skillet or use a deep fryer. Fry several turnovers at a time until golden. Remove with a slotted spoon and drain on paper towels. Serve warm with sugar sprinkled over top.

Makes 25 to 30 pastries.

Zia Angelina's Crostoli

6 eggs

12 tablespoons sugar

1 teaspoon salt

4 tablespoons butter (melted)

2 ounces rum

2 ounces grappa or white wine

1 orange, zest and juice

½ lemon, zest only

1 package of vanilla lievito (see Glossary)

1 package vanilla sugar

6 cups flour

3 to 4 cups corn oil for frying

¼ pound Crisco shortening for frying

Icing sugar for dusting

When the family first came from Italy, Louise remembers that sweets meant fried pastries. These were always made for "Carnevale" in February. Everyone agreed that Zia Angelina's crostoli were the best so her daughter, Elizabeth Giacometti, provided the recipe. No one ever makes them alone. Usually it's a family affair with a continuous assembly line production from kneading and shaping to frying. The kneading is very important as it makes the pastries crisp and tender. Keep the unshaped dough covered as you work. If the oil gets dark, it should be changed.

Beat the eggs well, and gradually add the sugar, salt, butter, rum, grappa, orange and lemon zests, orange juice, lievito, and vanigliato sugar. Mix well. Gradually add the flour and continue mixing with a wooden spoon until consistency is ready for kneading. The dough should not be sticky. Add more flour if it sticks excessively.

Transfer dough to a floured board and knead for about 15 to 20 minutes, dusting lightly with flour as needed. Cover the dough with plastic wrap and let rest for about 1 hour. Knead again for about 5 minutes.

Working with one piece of dough at a time, run it through the rollers of a pasta machine. Roll long strips of dough through to the thinnest setting of the machine. Lay the rolled dough on a floured tablecloth and cut into about 2 x 4 inch rectangles. Make a single, 2-inch incision in the center of each rectangle. Form all the dough in this fashion. Allow the dough to rest for about 30 minutes before frying.

Heat the oil and the shortening in a large frying pan. Fry the crostoli a few at a time at a medium heat. Make sure not to crowd the frying pan. Fry the crostoli on each side for about half a minute. They should be golden in color. Use tongs to lift the crostoli out of the oil and place on a paper towel to drain fat. When cooled, sprinkle with icing sugar or superfine sugar. Store in plastic bags in a dry place.

Makes 100 to 120 crostoli.

Fragole al Balsamico

STRAWBERRIES WITH BALSAMIC VINEGAR

This unusual way to serve strawberries may seem strange but balsamic vinegar is not like any other. It has the mellowness of an aged port and brings out the flavor of the berries. This preparation is so simple that only the best ingredients should be used. After tasting a 24-year-old balsamic vinegar at a function put on by the Italian Trade Commission, I was forever prejudiced against the balsamic vinegars of lesser stature. Cheaper brands of balsamic that have flooded the market are not as smooth as the ones aged at least 12 years or more. It is worth the investment in a better quality imported brand, carried in most gourmet shops. It may seem expensive but it goes a long way. Choose ripe but not mushy berries and be sure to remove all the sand.

1 quart strawberries

4 to 5 tablespoons sugar

2 tablespoons balsamic vinegar

½ cup heavy cream whipped

1 tablespoon sugar (optional)

Clean strawberries carefully. Cut away the stems and slice in halves or quarters depending on the size of the berry. Sprinkle with the sugar, stir and allow to sit for 30 minutes at room temperature. Add balsamic vinegar and stir again. Allow to sit another 20 minutes. Serve berries in small glass bowls, with the syrup drizzled over top. Garnish with the optional sweetened whipped cream.

Makes 6 servings

ABOUT BALSAMIC VINEGARS

The differences between regular wine vinegars and traditional balsamic are so notable it is like comparing rubbing alcohol with a fine, extra old cognac. Apart from the price, (a small bottle of 25-year-old traditional balsamic retails for well over $100) there are substantial differences in how it is produced and used.

Wine vinegar is made by introducing a "mother" or bacterial culture to a still wine. Balsamic starts with the freshly pressed juice (must) of trebbiano grapes that is not allowed to ferment. The must is heated and condensed to a third of its volume. This reduction is then poured into a series of barrels of different sizes and types of wood: mulberry, ash, cherrywood, chestnut and oak. The barrels are usually housed in high and dry areas like attics. Time and the changing seasons act on the must transforming it through natural fermentation to an elixir of complex aromas and tastes.

There are many vinegars on the market which are being called balsamic but are not made the traditional, time-consuming way. These are made with regular vinegar to which small amounts of balsamic have been added. There is a big difference in taste, and generally, price. Some of the very inexpensive brands are not worth considering but there are others that taste fine that will not scorch your pocketbook. The type labeled "tradizionale," like a rare, aged Cognac, may not be within your budget. But, if money is no object, a bottle of the 25- or 12-year-old traditional balsamic will go a long way. Only small amounts of it are needed to provide the right amount of seasoning to a dish. Remember never to cook balsamic or the flavor will dissipate. Add it just at the end of the cooking process when the food is just about to be served.

Croccante

CANDIED ALMONDS

Nancy Vetere would often bring these candies as a hostess gift when invited to dinner. Handle the syrup carefully, since cooked sugar is extremely hot, and beware of the fact that almonds occasionally pop as they are cooked. Use a nonstick skillet to make the cleanup a lot easier. In case the sugar starts to darken too quickly, to prevent it from burning, immerse the bottom of the skillet in a shallow pan of cold water. Nancy uses slightly more almonds but we found that for novices, using fewer makes it easier to get an even coating of sugar. Do not try to do it in excessively hot and humid conditions. Croccante keep well for many weeks in airtight jars.

1 ½ cup sugar

½ cup water

1 ⅓ cup raw almonds

Oil for greasing pan

Grease a heavy, 12 x 18 inch baking sheet. In a heavy, nonstick skillet, cook the sugar and water, stirring, until dissolved. Boil for about 2 minutes. Add the almonds and cook in the sugar syrup, stirring. Eventually, the syrup will crystallize and the mixture will appear "curdled."

Continue to cook, stirring and watching for the syrup to liquefy again. Adjust the heat to make sure the sugar does not burn. As soon as the bubbles are mostly gone and the mixture is liquid and a clear, golden brown, but not burnt, pour immediately onto the greased cookie sheet, spreading the almonds so they are all in one layer. Allow to cool and harden completely. Use a spatula to lift the hardened almonds off the baking sheet and break into bite sized morsels. Store in an airtight container.

Makes one 12 x 14 inch tray

Torrone

ITALIAN NOUGAT

4 large eggs, whites only

1 pound superfine sugar (also called fruit sugar)

1 pound clover honey (or other light-flavored type)

1 package Vanillia (vanilla sugar)

2 pounds hazelnuts, toasted and skinned

1 pound almonds, blanched, skinned and lightly toasted

2 sheets rice paper (18 x 24 inches)

Torrone is a candy confection that is very similar to French nougat. Imported commercial brands are sold at Christmas and Easter in Italian bakeries, delicatessens and grocery stores. They come in long bars or in small squares enclosed in pretty boxes. There is the hard kind and the soft version, sometimes flavored with chocolate. Below is the recipe is for the soft, white torrone.

Making Torrone is a laborious process but it is a labor of love well worth the trouble. Elizabeth Giacometti uses a mixer with a revolving bowl. To get a smooth texture, it is important to beat the sugar with the whites until it is no longer granular. Use the best quality natural honey. If it is solid, melt it before adding it to the egg whites but do not cook it too long or the flavor changes.

Rice paper (also known as baker's wafer paper or "ostia" in Italian) is available in specialty baking shops and some bulk foods outlets. There are different brands and qualities. Elizabeth prefers the large (18 x 24 inch) imported sheets which are imprinted with a diamond-shaped pattern and have zigzag edges.

According to Elizabeth, an empty glass bottle (wine bottle or tall mineral water bottle) works best to smooth out and flatten the torrone. She says that the smooth glass is less abrasive against the fragile rice paper.

In an electric mixer, beat the egg whites at a high speed, gradually adding the superfine sugar until they thicken and become creamy (7 to 8 minutes). Add the vanillia and continue beating. Lower the speed of the mixer and slowly add the liquid honey. Continue to beat at a low speed for approximately 20 minutes.

Bring water to a boil in the bottom of a large double boiler. Pour the beaten egg white mixture into the top pot of the double boiler and start cooking over a medium heat. Stir continuously with a wooden spoon for about 50 minutes. Stir in a circular motion and try to keep the mixture from sliding up the sides of the pot.

Adjust the temperature of the water so that it boils without causing the egg white mixture to color or stick.

After 50 minutes of cooking and stirring, add the hazelnuts and almonds to the egg white mixture and stir until all the nuts are totally coated. It will be very stiff and require some exertion to mix in the nuts evenly.

On a rectangular baking sheet (12 x 18 inches), place 1 sheet (18 x 24 inches) of rice paper. (It will hang over the edges of the baking sheet.) If using smaller sheets, use three sheets, overlapping each one at least 1 inch. Spread the nougat mixture onto the rice paper-lined cookie sheet as evenly as possible and flatten with a spatula, being careful not to damage the fragile rice paper. Place another sheet of rice paper over the mixture, pressing it down gently with your hands. Use a rolling pin or an empty bottle to flatten and even out the top, pushing the nut mixture into the corners of the pan. It should form a solid, dense mass approximately 1 ½ inches high with no air spaces. It may not reach the corners of the baking sheet and the edges will be uneven. The rice paper sticking out from the edges can be trimmed after it has been chilled.

Set the torrone, still on the baking sheet, in the refrigerator or in a cool cellar for 2 to 3 hours. Remove from the refrigerator and with a long, sharp knife trim away the uneven edges of the nougat along with the excess rice paper. These can be cut into small pieces to snack on right away.

Using a ruler as a guide, cut the torrone into long bars 2 ½ inches wide. Wrap each bar in wax paper then in foil. Keep in the refrigerator for special occasions.

To serve, cut the long bars into slices ranging from ½ to 1 inch thick. Only cut what you will be serving. Store the rest of the torrone wrapped in wax paper and foil in a cool place. Torrone will last for several weeks but will probably get eaten within days unless you hide it. If giving as a gift, wrap the long bars in decorative wrapping paper.

Makes one 12 x 18 inch tray

HOW TO SKIN NUTS

To skin hazelnuts: spread nuts on a baking sheet and toast in the oven at 300 degrees for about 20 minutes. Wrap warm nuts in a towel and rub to loosen the skins. Gather up nuts, leaving behind as much skin as possible. Place in a sieve and roll the nuts around, pushing more skins through the holes.

TO SKIN ALMONDS

Boil almonds for about 2 minutes. Check to see if the skin comes off easily. Drain and squeeze the skin off each almond. Allow almonds to dry overnight before using. To toast almonds, place on a baking sheet in a 300 degree oven for 15 minutes or until they become a very light beige.

Preserves, Condiments and Wine

THE ITALIAN GARDEN

When my father casually announced he wanted to cut down some of the trees at the cottage because their roots were creating havoc with the sewage system, we all cried in alarm, "You can't, it's a beautiful tree!" His reply was to speak in what we thought was disparaging terms about the trouble of those useless trees or "piante pazze" which was his colloquial phrase for trees that don't bear fruit. Piante pazze translates as "crazy plants."

This reflects the values held by many Italian ex-farmers (contadini) who emigrated to the city and moved into tenement buildings or old town houses with tiny front and back yards. Some houses had either no gardens or soil to speak of or tiny patches crowded with shrubs, wild trees and flower beds. Considering the fact that many of the contadini left because they had no land, and most of the small villages where the farmers lived had no gardens space attached to the

dwellings, the value of a little plot of soil is totally understandable. Generally, in farming areas of Italy's cultivated fields were outside the town. Often it meant a very long walk to get to where the crops needed to be worked. Houses were constructed next to or on top of others often in terraced, steep streets with cobblestones. That any arable land should be put to its most productive use is, therefore, the most understandable attitude.

That does not mean to say that pretty flowers and flowering shrubs and shade trees were held in disdain. It was simply a matter of priorities. If there was only a small patch of soil, it was set aside for growing edible things which were, to many people's eyes as beautiful as they were tasty.

For the many Italians living in the old downtown neighborhoods, either above stores or in houses with narrow lots, tiny gardens and small basements, one of the many attractions of moving to the newer developments was the promise of lots of garden space. There was also a big, finished basement which could house a cantina or cold cellar and large garages to hold the cars as well as the tools and paraphernalia of a self-sufficient household.

If you visit the newly developed Italian neighborhoods built in the 1970's for the now prosperous families of the big 50's and 60's wave of immigration, you can't help observing evidence of a commonly shared Italian aesthetic. Well trimmed lawns, tidy flower beds and shrubs in the front and, in the back, a meticulously kept vegetable garden along with the standard cement patio, barbecue, picnic table, and at least one or two fruit trees. Cherry, plum, apricot and occasionally apple or peach trees are the most popular. Since most of the big, old deciduous trees where torn down to facilitate the mass development of the land, the residents quickly domesticated the terrain and created their own private market gardens.

The ability to provide for most of the family's vegetable needs throughout the summer and well into the fall is not just an indication of frugality or good economy. It reflects much more the desire to have the freshest, quality produce, when it is at its peak. There is nothing like the taste of sun-ripened cherries, or salad greens fresh from the garden. The scent of tomatoes when they are just picked and still warm from the sun is a reminder of the pleasant tastes of many summers past. Simple, good ingredients make up the essence of what is great in Italian cooking. The secret is that nothing much has to be done to the food to make it better. A little chilling, some careful washing, a bit of salt and olive oil are all that is required.

To preserve the fruits of the garden is another testament not to economy but to household pride. "Here, try some of our marmelata," the hostess offers. "These beets are from my garden," Papa proudly announces. A store-bought offering does not honor the guest nearly as much as something homemade and homegrown. An invited guest receives the utmost compliment when homegrown or preserved food is offered and should never refuse a small taste, whether one is hungry or not.

Antipasto

MIXED VEGETABLE PRESERVES

2 pounds carrots, cut into ¼ inch circles

2 pounds green beans, cut into 1 inch lengths

2 pounds pickled onions

2 pounds celery, sliced

2 pounds cauliflower, cut into medium pieces

2 pounds peas, frozen

2 pounds red peppers, cut into short slices

3 cans (10 ounces each) mushrooms, whole

3 cans (5.5 ounces each) tomato paste

1 jar (10 ounces) green olives with pimento

3 cans (2.5 ounces each) tuna, packed in oil

2 cups white vinegar

2 cups oil (canola or sunflower)

EQUIPMENT:

One large stainless or enamel stock pot

12 2-cup mason jars

Giuseppina Fini always makes huge batches of preserves whether it's tomatoes or this delicious vegetable mixture below. If you are not up to dealing with such a large quantity, you can reduce the amounts to half. There is no boiling bath needed for canning in this way as a vacuum is created by bottling the mixture while still very hot. So if you like having jars of pickled vegetables on hand to serve at the start of a meal, this is not a difficult recipe to try.

Wash and sterilize mason jars by placing in a 200 degree oven for 15 minutes or until completely dry and too hot to handle.

Prepare all the fresh vegetables. In a very large pot, bring to a boil the vinegar and oil. Cook the vegetables one at a time, leaving each one in the pot as the others are added. Start with the carrots and green beans. Cook for 10 minutes. Add the cauliflower and cook 5 minutes. Add the peppers and peas and cook 10 minutes more. Add the mushrooms and cook another 10 minutes. Add the tomato paste, olives and tuna and simmer for 5 minutes. Taste for salt, but it probably will not need any.

Using tongs to handle the jars and a wide-mouth funnel or small ladle, fill each jar with the boiling hot mixture. Leave ¼ inch of space at the top. Seal and let stand. Wait for the jars to pop, thus forming a vacuum before storing in a cool cellar.

Makes 12 2-cup jars

Funghi Sott' Olio

MUSHROOMS IN OIL

Mushrooms are a standard part of an assorted antipasto plate. They can be preserved as described below or prepared in smaller quantity to be eaten immediately. Adriana Dametto, who learned how to do this from a Pugliese friend, always adds a pinch of flour to the boiling liquid to keep the mushrooms from discoloring.

Wash the mushrooms thoroughly and trim ends. In a large pan, combine water, vinegar, salt and pinch of flour. Bring to a boil, add the whole mushrooms and cook for about 5 minutes. Drain but do not rinse. Place mushrooms on a paper towel and let cool.

In a large bowl, season the mushrooms with half cup of the oil, garlic and oregano. Taste and add salt and pepper if needed.

Pack the jars with mushrooms and cover with the remaining oil leaving ¼ inch free at the top. Wipe the rims, seal and process in a boiling water bath for 20 to 25 minutes.

Makes four 16-ounce jars

4 pounds button mushrooms, whole

4 cups water

4 cups white vinegar

1 ½ tablespoons salt

Pinch of flour

3 to 4 cups olive oil

3 cloves garlic, finely chopped

Oregano to taste

Salt and pepper to taste

Melanzane Sotto Olio

MARINATED EGGPLANT

5 large eggplants

2 to 3 tablespoons salt

Equal parts white vinegar and water to cover

3 cloves garlic, peeled and sliced

1 small bunch fresh mint leaves, torn into small bits

Salt to taste

3 small, dried, red chili peppers (optional)

Oil for topping up jars

TIP
When making a large batch, Mrs. Severino finds it easier to drain the salted eggplant overnight in a colander. She covers it and puts a heavy weight over top then leaves it to drain until the following day.

Mrs. Elvira Severino's eggplant in oil is some of the best I've tasted. It has none of the sharpness or acidity of the commercial brands. This is due to a fairly short stay in the vinegar solution. You can use either the dark purple type, or the round, fat, pale purple ones known as Sicilian eggplant. The former has more seeds and darker flesh while the later is paler and more delicately flavored.

Mrs. Severino does not bother to use the boiling bath method to preserve these. She says they keep well due to the salt and vinegar, but, more to the point, they get eaten up very quickly. The following is a small batch adaptation of her recipe

Wash and peel the eggplant. Cut into ½ inch slices then cut into small strips, 2 x ½ inch. Layer the pieces in a bowl, salting generously between the layers. Cover with a towel and leave for 24 hours. The next day, drain off the liquid that comes out, squeezing it out with your hands.

To get a measure of how much liquid will be needed, place the drained eggplant in a large pot, cover with a mixture of half vinegar and half water. Remove the eggplant from the vinegar solution. Bring the vinegar and water to a boil. Add the eggplant pieces and cook for 1 to 2 minutes, or just long enough for the eggplant to soften and lose its rubbery texture. Do not overcook or it will become mushy. Drain and let cool. Squeeze out most of the liquid with your hands or with dish towels.

Place the drained, squeezed dry eggplant in a bowl. Season with sliced garlic, fresh mint and salt to taste. Mix well. Taste and adjust seasoning, if necessary. Pack seasoned eggplant pieces in dry, sterilized 1-cup jars, pressing down firmly until they fill the jar. Add one dried chili to each jar if you like. Pour any remaining marinade into each jar, dividing it evenly among them. Top up with vegetable oil to cover. Seal and store in the refrigerator.

Makes about 3 cups

Olive Verde Sotto Sale

PRESERVED GREEN OLIVES

When olives are abundant in a given climate, it makes sense to preserve them. In the little town near Agrigento, Sicily where Mrs. Paola Terrano is from, many varieties of olives are plentiful. She considers them an essential staple in her cellar along with her bottled tomatoes.

Since the price of fresh olives fluctuates from year to year, you may want to preserve them only when there is a good harvest. If you can find jumbo green olives at a good price, it is worthwhile to bottle them. It is easy though a bit time consuming. Don't be alarmed by the quantity of salt that is necessary. Mrs. Terrano uses re-cycled jars of various sizes as long as they have a fairly wide mouth and the lids have a good, rubberized seal. Mason jars are, of course, acceptable.

Crush the olives slightly to crack open the flesh but do not remove the stone. Wash them well. Put them in a pail, cover with water and place a wet tea towel directly over the olives to keep them immersed. Soak for 2 days, changing the water 2 times a day. Discard the soaking water.

Prepare the canning liquid. Measure water into the canning jars. Put this quantity of water in a deep pot, add the salt and heat until the salt is completely dissolved. Allow to cool.

Place the drained, crushed olives in sterilized canning jars. Add the cooled salt-water. Fill the jar so the olives are completely immersed. Place a slice of lemon on top to help keep the olives covered. Seal the jars. Process in a hot water bath for 20 minutes.

Makes 12 one-quart jars

1 case jumbo green olives

1 ¼ pounds salt

8 quarts water (to fill canning jars)

8 slices lemon

Peperoncini Sott'Olio

CHILI PEPPERS IN OIL

16 long red chili peppers or yellow hot peppers

4 to 15 dried red chili peppers

Olive oil for topping

Every September, Mr. Bellisario used go to a farm to buy the hot peppers known as "corne di capra" or hot banana peppers. He threaded them with string and hung them on the patio to dry in the full sun. At night, he would bring them into the garage so the dew wouldn't harm them. By October, if the peppers still were not dry, he'd take them down to the furnace room. Being a lover of hot spice, he started the practice of bringing a small jar of his famous chili oil to weddings so that the immediate family could put some on their pasta. He carried it in a small, baby food jar, wrapped in plastic and a paper bag causing a certain amount of embarrassment to the kids. There was no need for ceremony, he thought, and everyone should be pleased to have the extra spice that had taken him many weeks to make.

If you don't have time to dry your own peppers, you can buy dried red chili peppers instead and follow the same procedure. This oil is not for those with timid stomachs. It is fiery hot so drizzle just a little bit of the oil over pasta. Those who enjoy lots of heat can spoon on the pulp and seeds as well as the oil. It really wakes up the sinuses!

Buy fresh, unbruised, long, red hot peppers. If these are not available, use the pale yellow peppers which will eventually turn red as they ripen and dry. Secure a single strand of strong thread through a large darning needle. Thread one pepper at a time, passing the needle crosswise through the core at the very top. Attach 3 peppers in the same way to make a ring. Continue to thread the peppers to form a long chain of 16 peppers which is approximately 18 inches long. Stagger the peppers in such a way that they do not crowd each other too much to allow the maximum exposure to air and sun.

Hang the peppers in the sun, making sure to bring them in at night to avoid condensation forming, and of course, in case of rain. A cement or stone patio is a good place. Otherwise, the peppers can be hung in a cool, dry area like the furnace room. They eventually turn quite red and blacken in parts when completely dry. They also shrivel to less than half their size. This could take up to 4 or 6 weeks depending on the environment.

The chili peppers must be completely dry before they are crushed. The best way to crush them is to wear rubber gloves and use your hands. Spread newspaper over a table. The seeds will fly everywhere so give yourself plenty of space. Detach the dried chilis from the string, break off the stem and discard it along with the core. Keep the seeds as they give the peppers their hotness. Break from 4 to 15 dried peppers up into small pieces depending on how hot you want the condiment.

When all the peppers are crushed, heat 1 ½ inches of oil in a large skillet. Keep the temperature quite low as the peppers burn quickly. Add half the crushed peppers, or as much as will fit comfortably in the pan. Cook at a very gentle heat for about 4 to 5 minutes, stirring constantly and watching to see that they don't burn. If this happens, and it does from time to time, the peppers must be thrown out.

After the peppers have been cooked in the oil, take them from the skillet and place in sterilized glass jars. Top up the jars with more oil. Store in a cool place. As the chili peppers get used up, you can keep adding some oil to top up the jars.

Makes 1 quart

Putting up tomatoes when they are plentiful is part of the natural rhythm of the seasons for many Italian families. Also why pay for the tinned, imported ones if you can get bushels at half the cost and double the flavor when the tomato crops come in.

Those who like to produce big batches have made the process less labor - intensive by buying big, electric pureeing machines, huge vats and outdoor, portable gas cookers. They share the equipment with their extended family and friends. Since it is used only once a year it makes sense to share this expense. As a result, one can easily produce two hundred jars of bottled tomatoes - enough to last until fresh tomatoes come around again.

There are several ways to bottle tomatoes depending on how you intend to use them. Some like a very thick, raw, smooth puree of plum tomatoes. Others like the tomatoes to be more juicy so they use beefsteak tomatoes that have a higher water content. Still others preserve whole, peeled tomatoes for recipes requiring chunks of tomato. Some cook the tomatoes with some herbs and puree them before bottling. You can also dispense with the whole canning process by just stuffing quartered, ripe tomatoes in plastic bags and freezing them.

If you have storage space and access to some basic equipment, it is worth making a day of it. Invite friends to help and share the results. It will get done in no time and you'll be thrilled with your stock of home preserved tomatoes in the dead of winter.

Below are some methods for preserving tomatoes "al modo mio" (my way or the way I like them). One is for large quantities, the other two are for small batches. The large batch involves the additional step of processing the filled bottles in a "boiling bath" which kills any bacteria and create a vacuum. The "open kettle" method, which does not require processing in a boiling bath, is best for smaller batches. Choose the one that most suits your circumstances.

Pomodori Conservati

PRESERVED TOMATOES

LARGE BATCH METHOD

Mrs. Elvira Severino makes about 200 jars at a time and has the special equipment to do it all in one batch. This includes a huge aluminum pot called in Calabrese dialect "lu fustu." It's about the size of a small old-fashioned bathtub. She puts this over a propane-fired gas ring on a sturdy stand. An industrial size electric food mill is used to puree the huge quantity of tomatoes. The bottles she uses are irregular sized jars which have a rubberized lining inside the lid that forms a good seal. She saves pickle jars, big jam jars, olive jars - any kind of wide-mouthed jar where the white rubberized seal is still in good shape is kept for canning. Mason jars are good too, she says, but the lids rust so she prefers to reuse her bottles.

She buys 6 bushels of plum tomatoes to fill approximately 200 jars. The most common variety is the Roma tomato. The San Marzano variety usually has to be ordered specially and are not always easy to find but they make a superior sauce. She buys the tomatoes one week ahead and lays them out on a board and allows them to ripen. Once ripened, the tomatoes are washed and sorted, in case there are rotten ones. Then they are split and put into a large pot with a little water and cooked for about 20 to 30 minutes - just until some foam rises to the top and a lot of liquid has been released.

The tomatoes are then strained. She lines a bushel with clean towels and strains them through this to remove the excess water. She likes a very thick, dense puree. The drained tomatoes are spread out on trays and allowed to cool before being ground in the electric food mill. She puts them through the machine twice and lets even more of the water drain away.

The tomato puree is then salted, (2 teaspoons per quart), funneled into sterilized, dry jars, filled to about ¼ inch of the top. Usually, she adds a big sprig of fresh basil to each jar, but it's not absolutely necessary. The lid is put on and tightened well.

The huge cauldron, "lu fustu," which comes lined with a trivet at the bottom, is then filled with all the bottles. They are laid on their sides, one on top of the other, then covered completely with cold water. This is brought to a boil over the propane cooker and the jars are kept in the boiling water for 30 minutes. Since they can't easily be removed when hot, Mrs. Severino leaves them all in the cauldron overnight, or until the water has cooled completely. She says that occasionally a bottle will break but that it is not a significant enough quantity to be a problem.

The bottled tomatoes are kept in a cool cellar. When tomatoes are needed for a sauce, 2 or 3 jars get opened and the jars and lids are washed and kept for next year. Before adding salt to a tomato based recipe, it is best to taste first. With a very dense puree like this one, it will be necessary to add some water to the sauce particularly if it is going to be cooked with a large amount of meat.

SMALL BATCH METHOD

12 pounds plum tomatoes

2 tablespoons salt (or to taste)

If it feels daunting to contemplate preserving 200 bottles of tomatoes, there are easier ways to capture the taste of fresh tomatoes in the winter. The simplest, though least space efficient, is simply freezing whole or chopped tomatoes in freezer bags. When thawed, the skins slide off easily. The tomatoes can be pureed as they become soft and wilted from having been frozen.

If freezing is not a practical solution, making small batches of tomatoes using the open kettle method works very well. This alternate procedure is one I have used for years and find it a great way to use up that basket of fresh tomatoes purchased on impulse. Particularly when they start to ripen before you can organize the dinner party you were planning to have when you though about buying them in the first place.

Many people like to add a sprig of fresh basil to each jar, though this is not necessary and fresh or dried basil can be added once the tomatoes are made into sauce. One or two-cup jars of tomato puree are convenient for putting on one batch of pizza dough or in soups and some vegetable dishes. A one-quart jar will make enough sauce for about 1 ½ pounds of pasta.

Wash the mason jars and rinse thoroughly. Place the cleaned jars in an oven set at 250 for 20 minutes or until they are too hot to touch. Sterilize the rims and lids in boiling water. Use tongs to handle the jars and the lids. Do not set hot jars on cold surfaces or the glass will crack.

Wash and quarter the tomatoes removing the green stem. Place the cut tomatoes in a large pot but do not fill more than two-thirds. Crush some of the tomatoes to form enough liquid in the bottom so that the tomatoes will not scorch. Cover and simmer, stirring occasionally, until the tomatoes are soft enough to puree through a food mill. The longer you cook the tomatoes the denser the puree; however, the fresh tomato flavor is diminished with prolonged cooking. Puree the tomatoes and return to the pot. Add salt to taste. Keep the pureed tomatoes hot over a low burner until ready to bottle.

Fill the sterilized, hot jars with the hot tomato puree to within $3/16$ inch from the top. A sterilized ladle or funnel helps. Wipe the rim with a clean, damp cloth. Seal immediately: lay the flat lid down and screw on the metal ring tightly. Handle the jars carefully. Avoid sudden changes in temperature. Do not set hot jars on a cold surface. As the steam evaporates a vacuum will form and the lids will pop down. When all the lids have popped and the jars are cool, store in a cool cellar.

Makes 5 quarts

Microwave Method

Wash and sterilize five 1-cup mason jars. Wash the tomatoes, slice in half or quarters lengthwise and remove the tough stem. Place half the tomatoes in a lidded 2 quart microwave pot. Cook at high for 4 minutes. When the tomatoes are soft, puree them through a food process. Keep the puree hot, on a very low burner, until ready to fill the jars. Do the remaining tomatoes in the same way. Combine all the tomato puree in a pot. Season with salt to taste. Use about 1 teaspoon per 4 quart. Remove hot jars from oven using tongs.

3 pounds fresh plum tomatoes

1 teaspoon salt (or to taste)

Makes 5 cups

Rape Rosse Conservate Sotto Aceto

PRESERVED BEETS

2 ½ pounds beets

16 ounces water

8 ounces white vinegar

1 small onion, cut in half

1 celery stalk, cut in half

10 peppercorns

1 teaspoon salt

1 32-ounce sterilized jar

T**IP**

Select the same-size beets. If making a large quantity, boil the beets in small batches.

Every year in late summer, Daniela Pavero, who now lives in Liguria, would come to visit just when the beets were plentiful and help make jarred beets to last for the winter. Once they are preserved, the beets can be served as they are, or you can add some olive oil, parsley, and green onions. It's hard to judge the right cooking time of the beets - the first time they might turn out mushy. They should be cooked so that they remain very slightly crunchy. The quantity can, of course, be increased.

Bring the water and vinegar to a boil. Add the onion, celery and peppercorns and boil for about 10 minutes. Let cool totally.

Wash the beets and boil them in plenty of plain water until they are partially cooked. They should be quite firm but not raw. Test with a fork. Drain and allow to cool. Peel the beets and cut in half or quarters.

Put the salt into a 32-ounce, sterilized jar and add the beet pieces. Cover with about 16 ounces of the water and vinegar mixture leaving ¼ inch free at the top. Wipe the rims, seal and process in a boiling water bath for 10 minutes. If a jar shows evidence of leakage or a poor seal, use the contents immediately.

Makes one 32-ounce jar

Prugne Sotto Grappa

PRUNES PRESERVED IN GRAPPA

A common way of preserving fruits it to soak them in alcohol "sotto spirito" - often with the addition of sugar. This is done with cherries, grapes, various berries, apricots, mandarins or combinations of any or all the above. You start the big jar when strawberries are in season, then keep adding seasonal fruits as they are harvested. The method below is a simpler way of lacing your fruits and is ready within a few weeks. It's a good choice for the winter when fresh fruits are not at their best. Use a good quality Grappa.

Pack the prunes in a 32-ounce, sterilized jar. Add the Grappa leaving about ¼ inch at the top of the jar. Seal tightly and place in a cool place. Allow the prunes to stand for about 3 to 4 weeks before serving.

Makes 8 servings

2 cups dried prunes, pitted

2 cups Grappa

1 32-ounce jar, sterilized

SERVING SUGGESTION

Arrange 2 scoops of vanilla ice cream in each serving dish. Spoon the prunes over the ice cream adding some of the syrup.

ABOUT GRAPPA

My father tells of how the only interaction he had with northern Italians before emigrating to Canada was in the army and during the "vendemmia" (grape harvest) in his village. People from the north with their unfamiliar, clipped dialects, would venture far south in pursuit of "le vinacce" - the remains from pressed grapes. The stems, skins and seeds left over from pressed grapes were eagerly purchased at bargain prices by the northerners to be distilled into grappa. It is similar to the French "marc" and has a high alcohol content (usually 40 %) with a faint taste of straw. Serve it as an after dinner drink instead of brandy. It is not to everyone's taste, but when served below or at freezing point, it creates a sensation best described as imbibing fire and ice.

Encase the grappa bottle in ice the following way. Cut the top off an empty 2 quart, waxed cardboard milk container. Rinse well and fill with water. Set it in the sink and place the full bottle of grappa into the container. Put into a deep freezer, in an upright position. When the water around the bottle has frozen completely, remove the cardboard. Keep in the freezer until ready to serve. It makes a stunning display.

Puree di Carciofi

ARTICHOKE PUREE

1 can (12 ounces) artichokes, packed in water

1 clove garlic, sliced

1 tablespoon Dijon mustard

1 tablespoon grated fresh or bottled horseradish

1 tablespoon mayonnaise

2 teaspoons chopped, fresh parsley, chopped

Salt and pepper to taste

If unexpected guests arrive and you want to serve something quick and easy, this can be a lifesaver. Serve it with sliced fresh fennel as a dip. It also goes well with Carpaccio (p. 11) and Grilled Flank Steak (p. 194).

Drain the artichokes. Place in a food processor, along with sliced garlic, and grind until fairly smooth. Stir in the Dijon mustard, horseradish, mayonnaise and parsley. Taste and season with salt and pepper.

Makes 1 ½ cups puree

Spicy Rosemary-Garlic Oil

1 large clove garlic, minced (1 heaping teaspoon)

2 teaspoons fresh, whole rosemary leaves

2 big pinches (¼ teaspoon) dried marjoram, crumbled

¾ teaspoon salt

1 dried red chili pepper, cut in half

1 cup extra virgin olive oil

Wash and completely dry a 10-ounce fancy oil bottle or a 1 ½-cup jar. In a measuring cup, combine the following: the minced garlic, the whole rosemary leaves (with no trace of blemish and with the tough stem end pinched off), the crumbled, dried marjoram and the salt. Pour in ½ cup of the olive oil and stir to dissolve the salt. Taste on a small piece of bread and adjust the seasoning. Pour this into the fancy bottle or jar. Use a funnel and wooden skewer to push the leaves through if the bottle has a narrow neck. Add the dried red chili pepper, broken in half. Pour the remaining olive oil over and seal. Let stand for several hours in a cool, dark place. Keep refrigerated and use within 2 or 3 days. If the oil becomes thick and cloudy in the refrigerator, let it stand for a short time at room temperature before using.

NOTE

Flavored olive oil is susceptible to botulism if kept a long time in unsuitable conditions. Commercial flavored oils have antibacterial agents like phosphoric or citric acid added to prevent bacteria from forming. Once opened they should be kept refrigerated. To be safe, homemade flavored oils should be made in small quantities that can be used up within several days.

Salsa Piccante alla Mostarda

PIQUANT MUSTARD MAYONNAISE

Mash the yolks of 2 hard-boiled eggs with vinegar till smooth. Add the raw egg yolk. Season with salt and pepper to taste and mix well. Using a wire whisk, slowly add oil, a drop at a time at first, whisking constantly. Keep adding the oil gradually but as the sauce thickens, the oil may be added more quickly. Add only as much oil as the egg can hold. When it is very thick and creamy, mix in the parsley and mustard to taste. Stir in the minced, pickled onions. Keep refrigerated.

Makes 1 ½ cups

2 hard boiled eggs, yolks only

2 raw egg yolks

1 tablespoon vinegar

Salt and pepper to taste

1 cup olive oil

2 tablespoons fresh parsley, chopped

1 to 2 tablespoons strong mustard (Dijon or peppercorn)

5 to 6 pickled onion, minced

Salsa Piccante di Raffano con Panna

HORSERADISH CREAM SAUCE

1 slice dry Italian bread, crusts removed

¼ cup milk

½ teaspoon mustard powder

1 tablespoon white wine vinegar

2 to 3 tablespoons fresh horseradish root, grated

1 tablespoon sugar

Pinch of salt

¼ cup whipping cream

Soak the dry bread in some milk until it softens. Squeeze out excess liquid and crumble so it resembles grated horseradish. (You will need about ⅓ cup, densely packed.) Dissolve the mustard in the vinegar. Add the remaining ingredients and beat well. Taste and adjust the amount of horseradish, adding a little more if you prefer it to have more punch. Keep well-chilled. Serve with bollito or grilled flank steak.

SUBSTITUTIONS

A fast variation of this sauce can be made with 2 teaspoons bottled horseradish, 2 teaspoons Dijon mustard and 3 tablespoons mayonnaise.

Makes ⅔ cup sauce

TIP

When grating fresh horseradish, use the side of the grater that has the small, rough holes. Try not to breath directly over the grating process as this irritates the sinuses and causes your eyes to water fiercely. Cover your nose and mouth or wear a mask. Working outside helps. Horseradish can be grated in a food processor. The consistency is a little coarser and the taste is sharper.

Salsa Verde per Bollito

GREEN SAUCE FOR BOILED MEAT

Giuseppina related details of her mother Benizia Battitori's impeccable cooking in the service of La Contessa Mafalda and explained some of the culinary rules followed when dining with aristocracy. Roasted or boiled meat and fish always came with its own special sauce, served, in an elegant sauce boat. Any herbs or vegetables in the sauce had to be chopped very, very finely - using a mezzaluna - to make a smooth consistency. A food processor will not do as good a job and alters the taste according to Giuseppina who has adopted her mother's scrupulous attention to details. Cognac was used frequently in many of her sauces. This one goes well with white fish as well as boiled meats.

1 small bunch Italian parsley

¼ cup pine nuts, lightly toasted

¼ cup grated Parmigiano cheese

¼ teaspoon hot pepper flakes or 2-3 dashes cayenne

2 to 3 tablespoons Cognac

⅔ cup olive oil

Salt and pepper to taste

Wash and dry the parsley. Remove the stems and discard or save for soup. Chop the parsley leaves very finely together with the pine nuts. Stir in the grated cheese, hot pepper flakes, Cognac and salt and pepper to taste. Start adding oil slowly, beating it in to form a smooth sauce. Taste and adjust seasoning. Serve with thinly sliced boiled meats or with fish.

Makes 1 ½ cups

Burro di Scalogna all' Aceto Balsamico

SHALLOT AND BALSAMIC VINEGAR SPREAD

Shallots are not commonly used in Italian cooking. I acquired a taste for them while I was living in Paris and attending cooking school. Every green grocer carried them and they were as inexpensive as onions. It used to be that one had to go to specialty produce markets to find them on this side of the ocean. However, these days, more and more North American supermarkets carry shallots at a reasonable price. This savory butter goes into little pots for guests to spread on grilled or

¼ cup shallots, finely chopped

1 tablespoon oil

¼ pound butter, room temperature

Salt and pepper to taste

¼ cup dry red wine

1 heaping tablespoon fresh parsley, chopped finely

1 tablespoon balsamic vinegar

toasted bread. Heat brings out the flavor and aroma of the balsamic. Only a little of this very rich spread is needed. It is especially good with raw, marinated beef slices or just on its own as a topping for crostini.

SERVING SUGGESTIONS:

Spread the butter very sparingly on thin slices of grilled or toasted bread. Serve while warm. Or, serve pots of this spread as an accompaniment to Carpaccio (p. 11) or Grilled Marinated Flank Steak (p. 194).

Slowly cook the shallots in the oil and 1 tablespoon of butter. Do not allow the shallots to blacken. Season with salt and pepper. Add the wine and cook until it has almost evaporated. After the shallots have softened completely, place in a hand chopper or blender and puree. Blend in the remaining softened butter and the chopped parsley. Allow to cool before mixing in the balsamic vinegar. Taste and add salt if needed (especially if using unsalted butter). Transfer to two small ramekins and chill until ready to serve. Bring to room temperature before using.

Makes ¾ cup

Brule

MULLED WINE

6 cups red wine

⅓ cup sugar

1 small apple, cored, quartered

1 small pear, cored, quartered

1 stick cinnamon

3 cloves

Brule is a cooked red wine and is normally consumed during the winter season. It is especially good on ski trips or served with pinsa according to Arrigo Rossi who provided us with the recipe.

Boil the red wine, add the sugar, apple, pear, cinnamon and cloves. Cook for about 25 to 30 minutes or until the apple and pear are tender. Strain the wine and serve immediately.

Makes 4 servings

Making Wine

Walking to school in September and October had a few pleasant moments. Like when we would pass houses with crushed grapes boxes at the front. The sweet, sticky smell was like a heady hit of sugar. It filled the air at this time of year in certain neighborhoods. Because there was wine on the table every night with dinner, making it was an absolute necessity.

Having a cantina where we could make wine and store it was a priority so, at the first opportunity, (there was a big strike in construction), Papa got his buddies at work to help him dig out a basement to our house. Being an expert at cement work, he made a crushing vat out of concrete. It drained into a small, deeper well. He put on rubber boots that had been sterilized and stomped on the grapes, crushing them first before they were put into the press. The whole process was fascinating and, of course, I begged to help. Balancing yourself on slippery grapes in oversize boots is not an easy feat, as I soon found out. Drinking the juice that gushed into the well was much more fun.

For instructions on how to make wine at home, I sought the expert advice of Oliver and Lorraine Pace - two dedicated wine aficionados. They have made wine for many years using various methods. I learned how to do it from them so it is only fitting that their explanation of the process be presented. Their detailed and very thorough explanation is presented just as they wrote it. They are abroad so it came by fax - thank heaven for modern telecommunications.

WINE-MAKING IN TORONTO'S LITTLE ITALY
FROM OLIVER PACE

Toronto is a city of immigrants. In the 1950's, the great majority of them (me included) hailed from Italy. With them they brought their centuries-old traditions, those steeped in food and wine being an integral part of their daily rhythm of life. The quasi-religious belief that good food and wine are inseparable components of a satisfying meal resulted in the development of a thriving business of the importation of grapes from California. Their arrival at the rail terminals of Caledonia Road by early October each year brought throngs of Italians intent on acquiring as few as five and as many as 150 cases of "innocent and legitimate" fruit, in this instance, the wine-producing "vinifera" grapes. There was no talk in those days of making wine from concentrates or from unfermented grape juice (must) because the quality of vinifera grapes imported from California produced a much better wine.

The most popular varieties were the red Zinfandel and Alicante and the white Moscato; however, as the demand for grapes increased over the years, the quality of these grapes, and the wine they would render, became unreliable. This is not to say that one could not find good vinifera grapes today, but one has to know how to look for them as the retailers of this fruit can even be found in such unlikely locales as plaza, mall or super-market parking lots.

We have found that an acceptable wine, although never as good as the wines we made by crushing grapes up until the early 80's, can be had by buying "must" (the juice from crushed grapes) and fermenting it. Sadly, the camaraderie and joy which was a part of the annual expedition to get the cases of grapes, the crushing of them, the waiting with delightful anticipation for the first signs of fermentation, the periodic but essential breaking of the "cap," the pressing of the skins to extract more wine and yeasts, the first racking - all celebrated in the company of dear friends, great food and house wine (last year's vintage, if there was any left!) have been sacrificed on the altar of expediency, ruefully indicative of the times in which we live. The advantage of juice over grapes is that the quality is pretty-well ensured (if certain simple steps are followed) and the process of fermentation and bottling is certainly less labor-intensive and significantly cleaner.

Take yourself to an importer/distributor of "must." Some possess a creditable enological knowledge. There you can get just about any varietal vinifera juice from California, Italy, Chile etc., for example, Cabernet Sauvignon (some aging required), Pinot Noir (Burgundy), Montepulciano D'Abruzzo (San Giovese grapes which make Chiantis), Merlot (mellow wine, pleasant bouquet), Red Zinfandel and Alicante as well as several whites including Moscato, Pinot Blanc (Chardonnay, Semillon, Malvasia etc. you can make your wine from one varietal or combine them too your taste. (Chianti, for instance, is a mixture of several reds and a white.) We have come to like the following:

RED
1. 100% Montepulciano D'Abruzzo from Italy
2. 50% Montepulciano, 25% Cabernet Sauvignon, 25% Merlot

WHITE
1. 100% Chardonnay, fermented entirely dry
2. 100% Moscato, fermented entirely dry

The "must" comes in 18- to 20- liter buckets. Yeast has been introduced and the sugar/acid equilibrium has already been established by the distributor using the latest of winemaking methods so that there will be a good consistent degree of quality in the end product.

METHOD FOR JUICE FERMENTATION:

Step 1. In a relatively warm place (70 degrees F, 21 degrees C) set the buckets on the floor. Remove the lids.

2. Replace, loosely, the lids on the pails to keep fruit flies and dirt from getting into the juice.

3. Fermentation will begin within 1 to 24 hours.

4. Check periodically. After 5 to 8 days primary fermentation should end.

5. Pour the wine to within an inch of the top of a large glass vessel with a narrow neck. (Five gallon water bottles are good).

6. In lieu of a cork or fermenting lock, we use a piece of commercial see-through plastic wrap tautly secured with a sturdy elastic band to cover the opening to keep the air from getting to the wine. Too much air will make the wine taste like caramel due to oxidation.

7. With a needle or pin, prick a hole in the center of the plastic wrap. (This ensures escape of carbon dioxide during the secondary fermentation phase while preventing foreign substances from entering the wine.)

8. Wait three weeks and rack to a clean glass container. Siphon

the wine from the first container taking care not to allow the settled sediment to enter the new vessel.

9. This time, two layers of plastic wrap secured by elastic bands should be placed over the top of the containers. The wine is now ready to drink, albeit very immature. It will be much better 2 or 3 months down the road, and better still in 5 months.

When you wish to begin drinking your wine, place your containers at waist level and siphon off the wine as needed. Bear in mind that leaving an air space for more than a few days will ruin your wine; to avoid this, you must keep siphoning your wine into smaller containers filled up to the top and covered tightly with plastic. Remember, air is the enemy of wine! You can also, at this point, bottle, cork and label your wine. We always seem to deplete our reserves too quickly to be involved in this laudable enterprise. Knowing that it is a quaffing wine, we simply pour it into gallon bottles, then subsequently into ½ gallon bottles and from them into liter or quart bottles as the necessity for leaving no air space dictates.

It would be a good idea to pour a sulfite solution (available where you bought your must) into each washed container (swill around and pour out) in order to sterilize the inner surfaces before siphoning your wine into it.

This procedure for making wine has worked splendidly for us over the past 15 years. It is simple, fun and rewarding. It gives us immeasurable pleasure to go down to our cellar and come back up with the liquid fruits of our labors so that we can add to the bonhomie of evenings at the dining table surrounded by friends and family.

A note of encouragement - the wine you make will not be a Brunello or a Chateau Latour but neither will it embarrass you! It will be a palatable quaffing wine, comparable to any table wine we have savored in Southern Europe.

Glossary

CHEESES AND CHEESE TERMS

Asiago - hard, aged cow's milk cheese with a pale, creamy color; a popular table cheese; also used for cooking.

Bel Paese - soft, creamy, yellow cheese with a delicate texture and flavor.

Bocconcini - "little mouthfuls" - semi-soft, unripened cheese shaped into small balls; made from stretched curd "pasta filata" like mozzarella; stored in water.

Caciocavallo - firm, cow's milk cheese with a characteristic shape of gourd; usually a table cheese; when aged it becomes sharp and can be used in cooking.

Crotonese - hard, aged sheep's milk cheese from either Calabria or Sardegna; used for grating over pasta; not as salty as Pecorino Romano.

fior di latte - semi-soft, unripened cow's milk cheese; made from stretched curd "pasta filata" like mozzarella; can be used instead of bocconcini.

Fontina - creamy, light-yellow, semi-soft cheese; nutty flavor; light brown rind; melts well.

Friulano - also called "Furlano" - firm, young, table cheese, resembling Montasio but from partly skimmed milk; mild flavor good for sandwiches; flavor develops if it is aged.

Gorgonzola - a soft, pale yellow, veined cheese; pungent scent and spicy flavor; beige or reddish crust and also wrapped in aluminum foil; adds zip to sauces.

grana - general term for hard, aged cheeses with a granular texture; refers to Parmesan cheeses like Grana Padano and Parmigiano Reggiano

Grana Padano - (Parmesan) a hard, granular cheese (hence the name); strictly regulated production controlled by a consortium, limited to certain areas in northern

Italy near the area where Parmigiano is made. Use it in the same way as Parmigiano.

Mascarpone - a fresh, double cream cheese with a buttery flavor; used in desserts and sauces.

Mozzarella - semi-soft, unripened cow's milk cheese from stretched curd "pasta filata;" used in making pizza.

Mozzarella di buffala - mozzarella made from the milk of buffaloes; packed in its own whey in parchment paper; very delicate, fresh flavor, used in caprese salad and on pizza.

Pasta filata - term referring to types of cheese that are made by pulling and stretching the curd until it becomes like threads (fila); used in unripened cheeses like mozzarella, scamorza and bocconcini.

Pecorino Romano - a hard, sheep's milk cheese, aged 5 - 8 months (the older one is for grating). Pale, off-white color. Sharp, salty taste. It is suitable grated over pasta dressed with a strong, rich sauce; younger cheese is eaten as a table cheese.

Parmigiano Reggiano - (Parmesan) a hard, cow's milk cheese, pale yellow, with a fine, granular consistency. Aged 2 years. It is usually grated and sometimes broken into flakes and served as a table cheese. Strong but not sharp. The best type of Parmesan for pasta.

Provolone - firm, compact textured cheese, pale yellow with a smooth, shiny crust; bound with a cord and hung, often in pairs; gets sharper in taste as it ages.

Ricotta - a soft, white, unripened cheese made from cooking the whey, a by-product of the cheese making process; used in desserts and savory fillings; in Italy, may be made from sheep's milk.

Sardo (il fiore Sardo) - hard, aged, sheep's milk cheese, produced in Sardegna; has a strong, salty taste, like Pecorino Romano; fairly oily.

Scamorza - a mild, unripened cheese made from stretched curd ("pasta filata"); has a pear shaped, with a knob on top; slightly firmer than mozzarella.

Siro - whey

Torta (Torta di Gorgonzola) - creamy cheese shaped into a loaf; made from alternating slices of gorgonzola and mascarpone; popular table cheese; less intense than gorgonzola.

OTHER TERMS

al dente - having some bite; referring to the consistency of cooked pasta or rice.

Amaro - alcoholic beverage made from a base of herbs, nuts or other food; served after a meal as aid to digestion. Each region of Italy makes their own particular variety using local ingredients. Varies from slightly to very bitter.

antipasto - course served before the meal, i.e., before the first course of soup, rice or pasta.

caponata - vegetable dish consisting mostly of eggplant in a slightly vinegared and sweet sauce.

conservati - preserved or canned foods.

crostini - toasts made from rustic country breads, usually served with a topping as a starter.

finocchio - fennel

frico - Friulano dialect word for a flat, melted cheese dish

grappa - alcoholic drink, like the French "marc" made from distilling the lees (crushed grape skins, seeds and stems of wine-making grapes)

gubana - specialty sweet bread from the Friuli region

involtini - small roll, usually referring to meat but also to sliced, rolled vegetables.

lievito (or lievito vanigliato) - leavening agent with vanilla powder. It is imported from Italy and comes in small 16 gram packets (the most common brand is Bertolini). In areas with a large concentration of Italians, it can be found in Italian grocery stores and delicatessens. Substitute 1 teaspoon baking powder and 1 teaspoon vanilla extract (or use vanilla sugar)

Marsala - fortified wine (like sherry) from Sicily; it ranges from dry to very sweet; used in some desserts.

mezzaluna - half-moon shape instrument for chopping finely.

mortadella - a popular cold cut made from cooked pork meat spiced with pistachios, salt, pepper and other closely guarded secret ingredients; usually sliced thinly. Fine consistency larded with pieces of fat.

ostia - rice paper used in the making of candy confections like torrone.

pancetta - cured pork belly; very salty, like bacon but not smoked. It is sometimes sold in slabs or rolled into a cylinder and sliced. It comes spicy or sweet.

pane casereccio - rustic, home-style bread

panna - whipping cream (35 % butterfat)

piccante - spicy, piquant

pinsa - cornmeal cake; specialty of Friuli

pizzelle - small waffle-like pastry; either very thin and crisp, or thicker and bready.

porcini - (*boletus edulis;* also called cepes) variety of wild mushroom, usually imported from Italy; sold dried in small packets of 10 grams (.35 ounce) or 30 grams (1 ounce).

prosciutto - cold cut made from cured, pork leg, aged 10 - 12 months. Usually served cut very thinly.

prosciutto cotto - cooked ham

salume - the general term for any cured meats, especially from pork, that are served as cold cuts.

semolina - coarse, granular flour from durum wheat used in the making of dried pasta.

sopressata - type of salami that is pressed giving it a flattened, oval shape sotto sale - preserved in salt; usually refers to canned or bottled vegetables.

stoccafisso - air-dried cod fish

stracciatella - literally "little rags," referring to a soup made with broth and beaten eggs and cheese.

sugo - sauce, generally referring to a rich, tomato-based sauce for pasta.

torrone - Italian nougat candy.

torta - cake

tubettini - small, dried pasta like cut tubes; generally used in soups

vanillina - vanilla sugar, generally sold in little packets (some are 5 grams, some 8 grams), imported from Italy. Available in Italian grocery stores and delicatessens. Substitute approximately 1 teaspoon vanilla extract or use home-made vanilla sugar by placing a whole vanilla bean in a container of extra fine sugar.

USEFUL MEAT TERMS

bollito - boiled; generally refers to boiled meat, e.g., beef, tongue, chicken, etc. that is served with piquant sauces.

braciole - thin slice of meat, filled and rolled, beef, veal pork or chicken

brassato - braised; generally a cut of meat suitable for being braised, e.g., rump

fegatini - small livers, refers usually to chicken livers.

fettine - cutlets (usually refers to veal).

girello - eye of the round.

muscolo - shank, usually meaning boneless

osso buco - dish made from veal shanks with bone

porchetta - roast suckling pig; also used for roasted pork.

scaloppine - veal cutlet, cut from part of the leg.

spalla - shoulder.

spezzatino - literally "little cuts," referring to chunks of meat from almost any cut of veal, beef, lamb etc.; sometimes with bones; usually braised.

spiedini - little skewers; any lean, tender meat used especially for grilling or broiling on skewers.

stinco - whole veal shank

sulle brace - over coals

in umido - in a sauce

Pasta Terms

bucatini - long, dried pasta like spaghetti but thicker with a hole inside like a straw.

capellini - long, dried, very thin pasta; sometimes called "angel hair."

cavatelli - home-made or dried pasta shape from eggless dough, shaped into elongated nuggets with a cavity along one length.

chitarra - guitar; referring to an instrument used to cut pasta; specialty of the Abruzzi region.

Cjalcons - type of ravioli, specialty from Friuli.

conchiglie - shell-shaped dried pasta; usually ridged.

ditali - dried, short pasta resembling a thimble; suitable for minestrone, occasionally as a pasta course (as long as the thicker, ridged variety is used).

farfalle - dried pasta shaped like a butterfly, or bow-tie.

fettuccine - another name for tagliatelle used especially in region around Rome; also a name of a dried, flat, ribbon-like pasta shape.

fusilli - short, dried curly pasta spirals.

gemelle - literally, twins; refers to dried, short, pasta shape, resembling intertwinning sticks.

linguine - dried, long, thin pasta like flattened spaghetti.

lisce - smooth

orecchiette - "little ears" specialty pasta from Apulia; made from eggless dough; home-made or dried

pappardelle - wide, flat noodle either dried or home-made

past' asciutta - literally, "dry pasta," meaning pasta served with a sauce or dressing as opposed to pasta in broth.

pasta all' uovo - home-made pasta made with regular flour and eggs

penne - short, dried pasta resembling quills; either smooth (lisce) or ridged (rigate)

perciatelli - long, dried "pierced" pasta, slighty thicker than bucatini.

rigate - ridged

rigatoni - short, dried, tubular pasta with ridges; thick consistency; good for baked pasta dishes.

tagliatelle - home-made egg pasta cut into long, flat ribbons.

tagliolini - home-made egg pasta cut into very narrow, long noodles; often used in soup.

trenette - dried, long, wavy, ribbon-like pasta; also the name for long, flat home-made pasta typically served with pesto in Liguria.

vermicelli - long, very thin, dried pasta, like capellini.

Metric Conversion

All quantities used in the recipes in this book are in imperial measures. For convenience the conversion from imperial to metric measures has been rounded off into units of 25 grams. See table below for recommended equivalents. Never mix metric and imperial measures in one recipe. Always use level measures.

DRY MEASURES

Imperial	Recommended Metric Conversion
1 oz.	25 g.
2 oz.	50 g.
3 oz.	75 g.
4 oz.	100 g.
8 oz.	225 g.
12 oz.	350 g.
16 oz. (1 lb.)	450 g.
20 oz. (1 ¼ lb.)	575 g.
2 lb. 3 oz.	1,000 g. (1 kg.)

LIQUID OR VOLUME MEASURES

Imperial	Recommended Metric Conversion
½ tsp.	2 ml.
1 tsp.	5 ml.
1 tbsp.	15 ml.
1 fl. oz. (2 tbsp.)	30 ml.
2 fl. oz.	50 ml.
5 fl. oz. (¼ pt.)	150 ml.
½ pt.	300 ml.
1 pt.	600 ml
1 ¾ pt.	1,000 ml. (1 liter)

Index

ABOUT THE AUTHORS

Maria Pace has taught Italian cooking for over 14 years and operates The Cooking Workshop, a program of full-participation cooking classes. She has demonstrated Italian cooking on TV at the Royal Ontario Museum, the Ontario Science Centre and at various food shows and exhibitions. She has consulted on Italian food for feature films and organized culinary trips to France and Italy. She attended La Varenne, Ecole de Cuisine in Paris and took classes with Marcella Hazen in Bologna. When not working on food-related projects, she teaches English to immigrants and travels regularly to Italy and France.

Louise Scaini-Jojic has extensive connections to a broad network of Italian friends, relatives and business associates. She works as the assistant to an Italian chef and caterer. She also organizes cooking classes at the Famee Furlane, a Friuliano/Italian community center and banquet facility. She has helped cater events at the Italian Trade Commission and for Italian weddings and parties.

PRINTED IN CANADA